D1577567

The Universal Heart

This book seeks to honour the work of poet, peace activist and teacher the Venerable Thich Nhat Hanh.

My longest-standing relationship is with my sister, Geraldine Killalea. I would like to dedicate this book about relationships to her with love, and with the greatest respect for all that we have shared.

The Universal Heart

Golden Rules for Golden Relationships

STEPHANIE DOWRICK

MICHAEL JOSEPH
an imprint of
PENGUIN BOOKS

MICHAEL JOSEPH

Published by the Penguin Group
Penguin Books Ltd, 80 Strand, London WC2R ORL, England
Penguin Putnam Inc., 375 Hudson Street, New York, New York 10014, USA
Penguin Books Australia Ltd, 250 Camberwell Road, Camberwell, Victoria 3124, Australia
Penguin Books Canada Ltd, 10 Alcorn Avenue, Toronto, Ontario, Canada M4V 3B2
Penguin Books India (P) Ltd, 11 Community Centre,
Panchsheel Park, New Delhi - 110 017, India
Penguin Books (NZ) Ltd, Cnr Rosedale and Airborne Roads,
Albany, Auckland, New Zealand
Penguin Books (South Africa) (Pty) Ltd, 24 Sturdee Avenue,
Rosebank 2196, South Africa

Penguin Books Ltd, Registered Offices: 80 Strand, London WC2R ORL, England

www.penguin.com

First published in Australia by Viking 2000
Published in Great Britain by Michael Joseph 2002

1

Set in Centaur
Printed in Great Britain by Clays Ltd, St Ives plc

A CIP catalogue record for this book is available from the British Library

ISBN 0-718-14508-9

Contents

ACKNOWLEDGEMENTS

This is a book that shares many stories. Among those generous people whose stories or interest brought this book to life are Eurydice Aroney, Wendy Ashton, Margaret Blow, Josephine Brouard, Dean Brown, Nikki Brown, Noel Carpenter, Mary Cunnane, Klaus Endler, Linda Epsie, Anne French, Janet Gibson, Katherine Gollan, Christine Goold, Helen Greenacre, Eric Hansen, Barbara Hicks, Kim Hopson, Megan Simpson Huberman, Caroline Josephs, Susan Kalota, Michelle Kermode, Barbara Lepani, Amanda Lohrey, Taylor Love-Taylor, Pamela Margoshes, Christine Moginie, Tom Morton, Marcia Murray, Margaret Perrin, Suzan Piper, Yvonne Savage, Niels Schonbeck, Julia Sideris, James Sierra, Lu Sierra, Michele Sierra, Michael Spence, Elizabeth Stead, Joy Storey, Susan Street, Elizabeth Strickland, Cyndi Tebbel, Margie Thomas, Andrea Ulbrick and Margaret White. I thank you all, and am no less grateful to the people who cannot be named here. The contribution made to this book by poet Lauris Edmond is particularly meaningful. We talked at length about its themes and Lauris made a direct contribution that was typically thoughtful. Only months later, she died. I will miss her for the rest of my life. My dear Quaker friend Shelagh Garland also died during the writing of this book. What a blaze of loving inspiration she left behind. For several fruitful years I was regularly 'On the Couch' for *Life Matters* on ABC Radio National. I want to thank Geraldine Doogue, Jo Upham and Katherine Gollan. I also contributed to *New Woman* for some years. The stories of Victoria and Carey and of Bethany and David appeared there in different forms.

For permission to quote from their inspirational work, I want to thank most sincerely Naim Attallah, Robert Bly, Anne Deveson and Piero Ferrucci; Faber and Faber Ltd regarding T. S. Eliot, *Collected Poems 1909–1962*, Random House Australia on behalf of Dean Ornish and the Syda Foundation on behalf of Swami Chidvilasananda. Very special thanks too to my agent Carole Blake of Blake Friedmann in London; Sally Gillespie, patient friend and colleague; and Wendy Weiser for her travel plans and kindness.

During the last stages of writing I have again been truly supported by Penguin Australia. I want to lavish abundant praise and thanks on publisher Julie Gibbs, designers Ellie Exarchos and Sandy Cull, artist Rosanna Vecchio and sales supremo Lyn Amy. Particularly, I want to thank editor Lesley Dunt for her deeply encouraging belief in this book.

In thanking my family, I want to acknowledge how inevitably writing books also makes demands on the people nearest to you. So for all their love, good humour and honesty – for the life they unfailingly give me – I want to thank my children, Gabriel and Kezia Dowrick, as well as Mary Helen Dowrick, Geraldine Killalea, Melissa Shannon, Jocelyn Krygier and, in countless ways, Jane Moore, a shining exemplar of wit, constancy and goodness. I hope my appreciation of what they give me sings through these pages.

Introduction

This above all:

love one another.

GOSPEL OF JOHN 15:12

*T*his is a book about relationships. Anything new in that? I hope so.

For a long time now I have felt restless about the intense focus that people are encouraged to place on a single sexually intimate relationship. This one relationship is in prospect highly idealised: 'the stuff that dreams are made of'. In real life it is often confusing and disappointing. And no wonder. That particular version of love is supposed, somehow, to make up for lingering hurts from child-hood and previous relationships. It is also supposed to reassure us that we are lovable (even when we doubt this), comfort us in the face of working in a ruthless world, compensate us for the loss of community and extended family, and subdue our fears about whether life has any meaning.

That's quite an ask.

The Universal Heart began for me with thinking about how we could approach the idea of love much more generously – if we could regard love as a way of living rather than as a prize to be given (and withdrawn) a few times only.

What would it take, I wondered, to open to a life that's drenched in love? In a world ruled by notions of scarcity, how could we discover that the more freely we give love the more we have to give? Would peace of mind follow if we could think more about how to be loving than about our hungry dreams of how love might save us?

It's clear that at the beginning of a human life and again at the end, love – expressed through delight, gratitude, constancy, interest, good humour, kindness – is what matters most to us. In between, however, except in short bursts of high romance or at times of crisis, love tends to get squeezed out by more urgent demands: work, money, power, *getting on.*

We take seriously almost everything but love. We improve our skills in almost everything except how to give and receive more freely within our relationships. We ask each other constantly what we 'do' for a living, not how well we live. We move our attention away from the people we love for years at a time. And we wonder why the relationships we intended to value and honour break down or disappear.

An absence of love is something that countless people experience on a daily basis. They may call it loneliness, isolation, dissatisfaction or emptiness. Often what it adds up to is that they have become strangers to love – and in significant ways strangers to themselves.

Love joins us to others. And we need that. The longing to care for others and to be cared for is fundamental to our shared human nature. We are social beings, using our relationships throughout our lives to find out not only what we are capable of giving, but also to discover who we are: what makes sense to us; what insight we can achieve; what kind of life we are in the process of creating. Love connects us and inspires us. For the sake of love we can transcend selfishness, burst through the mundane. And this need not be personal love only. The fire fighter who enters a burning house to rescue a confused elderly person; the stranger who holds the head of a young man dying on the street; the foster mother who offers a home to abandoned children: in all such moments, and there are millions like them, love is alive.

The wellbeing of our towns, cities and countries depends absolutely on whether we, as individuals, are willing to care about how life is for other people. A safe society is one where trust exists and concern for others is readily expressed. If we are cut off from our capacity to give and receive love, we go beyond loneliness; we become dangerous to others as well as to ourselves.

A life worth living *is* a life of love. And anything worth discovering about love will deepen not just one but every one of our relationships. Just as crucially, though, love joins us to the deepest parts of ourselves. It allows us to know that our own life has legitimacy; that from our own inner world we can reach out to give willingly to other people. And receive what they can give to us.

In *The Universal Heart* I certainly do pay close attention to the sexually intimate relationships that most of us have or want. Those are the relationships where we most openly experience our longings to give love and to be accepted and loved for ourselves. But I do that within a much broader and more inclusive context than is usual.

This book is about the many faces and phases of love, the universality of love. It's about loving with fewer demands and conditions. It's about living well whoever you are with and whatever you are doing. There is exhilarating freedom in that. It lets you off the hook of waiting for the perfect relationship or person to give you permission to be loving. It makes everything possible, right now.

Love and freedom are the great themes of this book. One allows the other; one leads to the other. Looking around my own life and listening in to the lives of many other people, I am intensely aware of how we can tangle ourselves into knots or disrupt our best intentions. We want love. We may even want love desperately. Yet sometimes love – or our need for it – seems to cause us our worst agonies and problems.

In this book, discussion of those everyday problems and difficulties leads not so much to 'solutions' – for those can be mechanical or facile – but to a way of thinking about relationships that will positively affect every aspect of your life.

Through stories and discussion, and by returning to key themes in a number of different ways, I lay open some of the most common psychological and emotional traps that we unconsciously set for ourselves and other people. I show how we can see them anew and avoid them – how we can go way beyond them.

The Universal Heart is alive with a sense of what's possible.

In an age of unprecedented individualism, it is exhilarating to recognise that bringing together the insights of contemporary psychotherapy and the universal truths of the great spiritual traditions of East and West gives us more possibility than ever of understanding and delighting in each other. And caring enough to keep each other safe.

The shift in attitude begins with you. *Love starts where you are.* This statement may be clichéd, but it's also true. You have the capacity to live lovingly, however overlooked or unlovable you may sometimes feel. You have the capacity to receive the love that others can give you, however defensive you have become.

To love confidently in a world where love is trivialised and traded, we need support and inspiration. We need to know how other people have met some of the challenges that we are facing. We need to know how to lose our loneliness. We need reminding that we can afford to make mistakes and how possible it is, to borrow the Zen promise, to be 'knocked down seven times and rise up eight'.

This book offers exactly that help. And it does so not through stories and ideas only, but through simple yet profoundly effective 'rules' for loving well. These are not rules to bind you. On the contrary, just as love does, they set you free. Loving generously; observing how much power you have to affect other people positively; knowing that you can make changes as they are needed; responding intelligently to what each situation demands of you; trusting you can let hurts go and love soar; allowing yourself to be enchanted: none of that is beyond your reach.

Learning from each other, we remember what we share.
What is well planted cannot be uprooted, the *Tao* teaches.
What is well embraced cannot slip away . . .
How do I know about the world?
By what is within me.

Love

Generously

O love, O pure love, be here, be now . . .

Make me your servant, your breath, your core.

JELALUDDIN RUMI

*T*here is no other way to love but generously.

Love treasures who you are. Love brings depth, balance, integrity to the life that you are creating.

Love opens you up to all that you are capable of. Love makes it possible for you to receive what others can give you. Love honours and expresses freedom. Love demonstrates itself through acts of kindness, respect, delight, trust and patience.

Love finds what is good and speaks of that. Or sings of it, paints it, acts it, writes it, lives it out. Love laughs loudly and often. Love is daring, bold, colourful. Love seeks and offers beauty. Love is subtle too, and discerning.

Love knows what to overlook. And the value of silence.

Love is willing to surrender control and the false, confining need always to be right. Love can listen with an open mind. Love is willing to tolerate imperfection; to be bored or restless without blaming; to be fired up and exhilarated; to be delighted for someone else's sake; to see things through and to stand alongside, even in times of discomfort or difference.

Love lets someone go when they need to.

Love mends wounds and dissolves hurts. Love is forgiving. Love gives and seeks mercy, even in the face of injustice. In love, there are no opponents.

Love is courageous. Love wishes the best for the other, always, and even when it is afraid of the answer, love asks what that best might be.

Love gets out of bed night after night to look after a sick child or friend. Love has the same reassuring conversation many times with an elderly partner or parent. Love makes envy manageable when someone else has what you most want. Love seeks to understand choices that you would not make. Love affirms diversity and difference. Love delights in it.

Love takes you to sports you had no interest in; into books you had no idea you could enjoy; into cultures, up mountains or deep under oceans you hardly knew existed. Love teaches you new languages: not least, the language of love.

Love dissolves prejudice and challenges preconceptions.

Love makes you vulnerable. Love mends broken hearts.

Love allows bad times to be survived and good times to be treasured. Love brings you into the present moment. Love teaches you to see things as they are.

Love that is not love is also powerful.

It can be lust, desirousness, delusion (although they can be part of love too). It can be interest, adoration. It can be neediness, control, possessiveness, sentimentality. It can be a longing for approval, masquerading as love.

LIVE AS A LOVING PERSON

We learn what love is through all our varied interactions and connections – friendships, family, love affairs, partnerships, work, community and neighbourhood relationships – and not through our sexual partnerships only. In or out of a physically intimate relationship, we are inevitably 'in relationship' all the time. Those varied outer connections, as well as our own inner reflections, dreaming and longings, let us know what we want love to give us and how good love feels. We also find out what the absence or withdrawal of love feels like (pretty chilly). And we learn, sometimes with shame or disappointment, how conditional and limited our own and other people's declarations of love often are ('How can I possibly love you when you . . . ', 'No son of mine could ever . . . ', 'If you can't . . . then I won't . . . ').

We are helped in our efforts to love if we have been loved and know what love feels like, yet one of the marvels of the human story is that nothing is neatly predictable. Many great-hearted people grew up in horribly unpromising circumstances. Many people who have been loved devotedly and selflessly remain marooned on a tiny island of self-concern.

To move off that island, we must wake up to other people's reality – and care about it. We must see other people not as opportunities for us to exploit or as monsters who could exploit us, but as fellow travellers, wanting what we want: to suffer less and to know comfort and connection at first-hand. This is not so hard. And the rewards totally outdistance the dangers.

No great change is needed either. You don't have to become a different person in order to express love, respect, interest and concern more generously. You need only look with new interest at what drives your familiar hesitancies and defences, question whether you still need those defences – and ask those questions in a self-loving, respectful frame of mind. *Power over your own life shifts back to where it belongs.* What other people do or fail to do becomes far less important than *seeing yourself as a loving person* who is free to express respect and concern in all your encounters.

True self-assurance follows from this simple but profound shift in attitude: 'I am creating a life that expresses the very best of who I am.' Even then it will be your own experience of how balanced and at ease you can feel that will show you, more powerfully than anything I could say, that loving generously is a sustaining and entirely possible way for you to live.

Love is your 'original blessing', your original nature, however distanced from this awareness you may sometimes feel. Bitterness, a loss of trust, a galloping case of perfectionism or self-criticism may cause you to retreat from love. But these obstacles are not greater than love is. Love is available to you always. It's expressed through acts of forgiveness, tolerance and selflessness. Just as powerfully it comes to life through those precious everyday moments of human connection: the chat you look forward to in the morning with the man who sells you your newspapers; your own willingness to drive out of your way to help someone get home earlier; the hilarity that erupts when colleagues burst through a moment of pompous solemnity; the excitement a whole street feels when a neighbour comes home with a new baby.

There are countless times when we can open up to other people in a heartfelt way. And can unselfconsciously discover: *This makes me feel good too.*

Creating harmony, benefitting others: that's not outside our range. We limit that capacity only through undervaluing ourselves and what we can give: belittling our own efforts before they can take off; telling ourselves that we have so little, we can't afford to give. Or telling ourselves that many things are not our business. We are scared of intruding. We are distracted by our own concerns.

Yet our instincts and our own lives show us that when people come together to meet a crisis or emergency, or just to enjoy a few minutes' good talk and laughter or a moment of sympathy, the feeling of connection that they receive far outweighs the inconvenience of putting their own agenda temporarily aside.

Loving generously, no one is left out. The vast inner wealth of love belongs equally to us all. It's what we share. Where we differ is only in our confidence to tap into it, to trust it, to draw from it and, drawing from it, to discover how it defies the rules of the external material world.

The rules of scarcity do not apply to love. Love is like water: that's in everything. And like air: that's everywhere. Only our fears about how other people see us – or how they might interpret our motivation or behaviour – are limiting.

It's true that misanthropy is rife in the great Western village. It thrives wherever personal success is narrowly defined and worshipped, and wherever people are driven by competitiveness, envy, hostility, fear – rather than mutuality, support, respect. From that world view, it makes sense to hoard our capacities to love until we meet one single, special person: then, and only then, can we experience ourselves as a loving person.

But the crazy – or tragic – thing about this view of love is that it ignores a great truth: that we grow skilled and confident at what we practise. If we hoard love (or love as we conceive it) we don't allow ourselves to know it truthfully. When finally we give ourselves an opportunity to love, it becomes too easy for us to confuse love with possessiveness, neediness and social approval.

Lately I have been reminded of this when I listen to very young women talking. I'm fortunate enough to hear quite a few teenage conversations at this point in my life. And I notice that, although it is a long time since I was 15, young women and men continue to be intensely interested in how their friends see the objects of their affection. 'He's so hot. *Everyone* thinks he's hot' seems the greatest accolade one girl can give another about her love interest. The approval, or better yet the envy of her friends, may mean as much to the 15-year-old love novice as the affection and interest that the boy himself shows her and whatever she herself feels.

Love can be as simple as breathing: you take it in; you give it out.

When you draw on love and *express love lavishly*, your sense of what you have continually increases. That's why the happiest people are also the most altruistic. And why the most altruistic people experience the highest levels of satisfaction in all areas of their lives; why they recover from setbacks quickly; are the most accepting and tolerant; expect to be liked and *are* liked.

Nothing will influence the quality of your life more profoundly than your willingness to accept responsibility for the attitudes and behaviour you bring to other people. This is not true for special people only. It is true for all.

RECEIVE WHAT OTHERS HAVE TO OFFER

Love comes fully to life when we can also receive with grace what others are willing to give us. Openness of spirit is again called for and often a yielding of certainties. To receive love, we must accept other people as they are. That's already quite a challenge. And we must accept their way of loving us, at least when their intentions are well meaning.

Our irritations can so easily get in the way here, as well as our fixed ideas about what love should look like or how it should be expressed. Someone makes us a meal when actually we long to talk. Someone gives up something for our sake and we feel frustrated, not grateful. Someone asks us tenderly how we are just at the moment when we are about to solve an internal problem or our favourite show is starting on TV.

These failures of good intention crisscross our daily lives. We may rail against them. We may call them failures to love. But meeting our needs, immediately and in the ways we want it to, is not all that love's about. That's an infant's experience of love: that the 'good mother' instantly supplies what's needed. The same mother becomes 'bad' when she occasionally requires the baby to wait a few minutes or to tolerate a discomfort that she can't fix.

Growing out of babyhood, with a far greater range of experience available than an infant has, we can loosen that tight equation of love with need.

We will always have difficulty seeing love in what we are being offered if our minds tune in only to what's wrong or absent. If love is to smooth out those irritations, a larger vision is called for. Goodwill needs to be assumed, and complaints must be curtailed, so that in love's presence we can recognise what's on offer – however odd its disguise. Love opens our eyes. It opens our hearts also.

RELEASE LOVE FROM THE LIMITS OF THE PAST

It's love too that can change your views entirely about your 'rights', your disappointments, your convictions about what you are 'owed' and your certainty that in a difficult situation only the other person is wrong. You are perfectly free to cultivate those self-justifying and resentful thoughts indefinitely, but this will cost you dearly. Switching your attention from the wrongs that have been done to you, to an awareness of how you can make a complex situation tolerable, is strengthening as well as healing. That loving, self-respecting attitude can make an impossible situation possible. It can also transform your view of what a difficult situation is.

And as it does that, *it will enhance how you experience yourself.*

Cultivating a sense of injury is deeply unsustaining. It keeps your mind fixed on what's wrong; it falsely strips you of your power to see what's right. Moving on from that sense of injury, or at least seeing it in the context of a range of different experiences, does not mean condoning what has been wrong or pretending that what has happened did not happen. On the contrary: it simply acknowledges the dynamic life force that moves through us and brings us inevitably forward.

First, though, we must allow that.

Here is a wonderful example of the profound change that an apparently small shift in attitude and insight can achieve. The story is told by Nikki Brown, who is a publicist and arts coordinator and the mother of an adolescent daughter. She is talking about a relationship with her own mother, Moya, that had been conflicted and disappointing for much of Nikki's life.

'Our history together had been so checkered, so fraught with misunderstandings, irritations and unpredictable behaviours, that I determined to try and tackle it head on,' Nikki explains. 'At the age of 52, I had a strong sense of this being the right time. That as the oldest child I should face my demons and confront my mother.'

This was by no means easy for Nikki even to contemplate. 'I am scared of confrontation. And my mother, even after all these years, still had the capacity to give me a look that would set my heart thumping, my pulse racing and my face to suffuse with heat. I've always been scared of her, which is probably why so many of our arguments ended with me yelling, "That's it! I'm going", and exiting in a riot of slammed doors and instant regret.

'Both of us, I'm sure now, harboured very deep-seated anger about our relationship. I was a disappointment to her, with a succession of failed relationships, jobs and marriages. She was not the mother I longed for – which was for a spontaneous person, able to down tools in the kitchen and hand over to me, or someone to whom I could open my heart without her being judgemental.

'Over the years we had confrontations that were bitter and we never really got to the root of our mutual difficulties. I longed for her approval and I think that she longed for my understanding of her own sense of failure and inadequacy.'

After a particularly difficult Christmas, and with no real confidence in a positive outcome, Nikki nevertheless had an internal shift in the way she saw her relationship with her mother. Put plainly, she wanted things to be better than they were and was willing to set aside those inner whisperings that told her it was a waste of time . . . that she could only get hurt . . . that it was hopeless even to make the effort . . .

Instead she asked Moya to join her for lunch in the city where she lives, so that they could 'really talk'.

Nikki: 'I knew what I wanted to say. That it was time to acknowledge our differences, to agree that our time together might be limited and that, at the end of the day, she was my mum and I was the oldest daughter.

'I was scared that the meal would not please her. I felt all the usual terrors of saying how I felt. But I gritted my teeth and opened with my hope that we could do things differently from now on. Please.

'For the first time, I sensed her own nervousness and discomfort at what I might be about to say. And I relaxed, allowed our eyes to meet and reached for her hand. We spent the whole day talking. She talked of her sense of failure as a mother. Of the feeling that she had abandoned my sister and me as teenagers when she and my stepfather went to live overseas. She cried, but I made no move towards her as I was determined we should face it all, without the complications of an embrace.

'We sat together later in the warmth of my house, eating sandwiches, drinking coffee and edging towards each other in a way that had never before seemed available.'

And that's not the end of the story. Nikki goes on: 'My mother died six months later of a sudden, totally unexpected brain haemorrhage. I looked at her in the hospital before they withdrew life support – my heart so full of longing for her survival – incredulous and overwhelmed. I wrote her a letter, which I placed in her coffin, and told her of my joy that we had really communicated that day. The six months that we had after that conversation had been a time of healing, closeness and understanding. That time changed our relationship. But my regret is profound – that I lacked the courage to say those things and open up to her earlier. I wish so much that we had had more time to build on that. And to enjoy each other's differences – rather than railing against them as we did for so many years of our relationship.'

Nikki's courageous action shows brilliantly how an increase in generosity in our way of loving can profoundly enhance our sense of what's possible in our relationships. And it can certainly dramatically change our sense of what *we ourselves are capable of creating*.

It's clear that Nikki could have nursed a sense of righteous indignation and disappointment about who and what her mother was, what had passed between them, and especially about Moya's failure to be the person Nikki wanted her to be, to the day of Moya's death. And maybe to the day of her own death also. She would have found plenty of people to agree with a negative view of her mother. After all, she had been hurt; she could have nursed such a hurt. But what a loss of opportunity that would have been.

It's a willingness to allow love to move along our thoughts and guide our actions that shifts the connections between people most effectively. Love frees us from the self-defeating need to defend a shaky ego by being 'right', even when this makes us feel horribly 'wrong'. It also shows us that some things are worth doing for their own sake – whatever the outcome.

For myriad reasons it might not have been possible for Moya to respond to what Nikki was offering. Would that have made Nikki's effort any less worthwhile? I don't think so. Recognising our capacity to affect other people positively, we become far less dependent upon a specific outcome. *Acting freely, we become free.*

Perhaps as you read Nikki's story your thoughts were already flying to the relationships in your life where you could show greater concern, be more open or spontaneous, or perhaps offer or accept forgiveness. Or where you could see someone else's differences and shortcomings with greater understanding or look past those to the real person and the love you share.

Any shift of consciousness that allows you to think about other people more generously is highly significant. It can heal wounds. It can certainly save you from agonies of regret. It can restore your capacity to give and receive love in all your relationships.

ACCEPTANCE EXPRESSES LOVE

Most of us long for acceptance. An absence of self-acceptance, or the fear that we could never be wholeheartedly accepted by other people or even the people claiming to love us, underscores feelings of isolation and despair. Whoever we are, however brilliant or acclaimed or ruthless we may be in the outer world, we usually want more than anything to be loved for who we are and accepted for all that we are.

Loving generously gives us our best chance for this to happen. It lets us cease believing that our primary expression of love should be an attempt to mould, trim or change the people we care about, even (or especially) where we have convinced ourselves that those changes are entirely for their good. It allows us to keep those essential lines of communication open – even through clenched teeth. It helps us to keep in realistic proportion the things that irritate us or drive us to despair.

We can allow our knowledge of what we share with other people to soften our rush to judge, convict and condemn. And doing this for others, we will find that quite inevitably we are also able to be more genuinely accepting and kinder to ourselves.

This is already remarkably beneficial (for us and other people). Loving generously, though, takes us further.

LOVE CAN BE GIVEN FREELY

We are used to thinking about love in trading terms. Consciously or unconsciously, for our love investment we expect a good return. In fact, we may quite carelessly assume that the more we love someone the more right we have to comment on or even intrude upon and determine their life. We may also assume that other people should win our love (or that we should win theirs). And, what's more, that to keep our love they should continue to show themselves worthy of it by behaving in certain kinds of ways or being a certain kind of person.

Some people deserve love, this mind-set quite clearly tells us. Others don't.

When love is a prize to be given or withdrawn, it makes no

sense to love someone or even act civilly towards them if they don't 'deserve' it. This is shown perhaps most starkly when we get furious if someone we have tried to help is not grateful. Or furious when a lover turns out not to be the person we had in mind. Or when we end a friendship with someone or cut off contact with a family member because they have made choices that reflect their values and not our own.

But what's love worth if it is not given freely?

It is exceptionally liberating to discover through your own experiences that it is possible to be open, respectful, kind, *whoever you are with*. That you can feel and show concern for people whether or not they 'deserve' it.

Inevitably, of course, you will find it a great deal easier to be gracious in some situations than in others. You may find yourself feeling gratitude towards those precious people who 'bring out the best in you'. But that doesn't change the essential freedom of loving generously – which is that *you can be loving for its own sake*. No one else has to make it worth your while, or give you permission. No one else has to convince you that behaving with at least some consideration for others feels good. Awareness of this freedom is the true cornerstone of personal power.

For many people, even the idea of behaving most of the time with concern for other people feels restrictive. How refreshing, then, to discover that you can make these changes not to become a living saint, but *for your sake only*.

You can be friendly, respectful, open – because this is a much less stressful way to live. You can curb your outbursts of anger or self-pity – because this will help you to feel more in control of your own life. You can be tolerant – because this will open your eyes to a more interesting universe. You can be forgiving – because this frees you. You can express gratitude – because this lifts your sense of what is positive and enhancing. You can be courageous –

because this allows you to live your life fully. You can assume goodwill and be generous – because when you don't see other people as opponents, you have less to lose. You can practise empathy – because it deepens all of your connections. You can risk intimacy – because this has measurable benefits for your health.

Making those changes to benefit yourself is a fine place to start. We do best what we enjoy and can feel passionate about. And why not?

Nevertheless, love does not stop where we are. Because we are constantly affecting other people – most of all through our attitudes – it is just not possible to wake up to a greater sense of love and generosity without also positively affecting and influencing other people and the world that lives outside ourselves.

'Love by the way you walk, the way you sit, the way you eat,' says the great contemporary teacher of love, Vietnamese Zen master Thich Nhat Hanh. And, he says, not for your own sake only: 'We need to support each other to build a community where love is something tangible. This may be the most important thing we can do for the survival of the Earth. We have everything except love. We have to renew our way of loving. We have to really learn to love. The wellbeing of the world depends on us, on the way we live our daily lives, on the way we take care of the world, and on the way we love.'

The revolutionary idea that we could love generously even when no one has given us the green light or guaranteed us that it's worth our effort might seem startling, not just at first but for a long time. Yet thinking about the people who have everything but happiness, or the devastation caused by intolerance, disrespect and cruelty, I believe that what Thich Nhat Hanh says is true: *The wellbeing of the world depends on us . . . on the way we love.*

It has taken me half a lifetime to discover that we are free to love generously, no matter what our personal circumstances may be.

That it is possible to set resentment aside and feel much better for that. And that our attitude to love makes even more difference to our lives than whether we have that special 'someone'. Even now there are many times when I hold this as an ideal but resist practising it. And why wouldn't that be the case? We have been trained to respond like Pavlov's dogs to the stimuli in front of us. We have been trained and have trained ourselves to love conditionally, and even then to dish out scraps of love only. We lend love far more often than we give it. Confusing love with approval, we will hastily withdraw even those scraps when something doesn't please us.

Does this mean that we should or could go on loving if someone is behaving unethically or cruelly? Is it reasonable to think generously of people who disappoint us, frighten us, harm us, steal from our homes or exploit for profit people less powerful than themselves?

Maybe not. In any situation where we or someone else is at risk, we need to act decisively to save ourselves or that other person. But having done so, should we then think kindly of those who wanted to harm us?

Again, maybe not.

But we can save them – and ourselves – from a matching outpouring of frustration, violence or contempt. We can save them – and ourselves – from constantly returning to those events as though nothing else that has happened to us has any meaning. As difficult as it may be to do, we can continue to think well of people in general and look for or pray for expressions of kindness, thoughtfulness and harmony. We may also choose to spare them our moralising, especially when their behaviour demonstrates a lack of self-love and inner peace.

Without in any way condoning wrongdoing, or denying what was hurtful, we can leave those painful events behind. We can move on. We can fall in love again with what this present moment offers.

In conflict situations between and within nations we see writ

large grudges and hatreds and injustices sustained over generations. And we see a tragic unwillingness to let go of confining
certainties. It doesn't take much imagination to know that the
people on both sides of any conflict will have much the same
needs as we helpless bystanders do: clean water to drink and pure
air to breathe, food to cook and share, work that has some meaning, a home where they can feel safe, people to love them and with
whom they can love, laugh and share stories, a sense of life well
lived that will accompany them when they die.

In loving even a little more generously – resenting less, giving
the benefit of the doubt where you reasonably can – it becomes
possible to embrace the outer world more realistically and to act
with insight and compassion.

OPEN TO SELF-LOVE

No one is more deserving of love than you are; no one is less
deserving either. Selfishness and self-absorption reflect too little
self-love rather than too much. Cultivating an attitude towards
yourself that is affectionate, respectful, hopeful and encouraging
leads you away from self-absorption. It gives you the courage and
confidence to believe that your presence is positive. And to find
that you can connect with other people through ways of behaving that will feel good to them – and to you also.

The greatest impediment to love may not be the inexplicable or
even the hurtful things that other people do. It may be our own
unwillingness to accept and embrace our contradictions. We often
swing between seeing ourselves as all good or all bad, as hopeless
or marvellous. Or we take directions from what we interpret as
other people's reactions to us. Our moods swing with those opinions. Accepting our own complexity, and the contradictions that
express it; accepting how shifting and various our own feelings and
reactions are, it becomes possible to see how that complexity is also
reflected in other people. And, inevitably, in social relations too.

We become safe from the inside out only when we dare know ourselves in our entirety. Limiting self-knowledge and self-acceptance, making it conditional upon a tight range of 'correct' responses or behaviours, keeps us small and separate. It does not reflect truthfully who we are or how, within each of us, fire and water live side by side. We *are* our contradictions. We *are* our longings for connection.

This dazzling goddess verse survives from ancient Egypt to remind us there is no need to fear that.

I am knowledge I am ignorance
I am shame I am boldness
I am shameless and am ashamed
I am strength I am fear
Give heed to me
I am the one who is disgraced and the great one . . .

Reflecting on how hard won a little self-love is, or a few realistic moments of self-forgiveness, it is good to remember the universality and inclusiveness of love: that love itself is profoundly generous. We may live out pinched versions of it. We may cheapen it. Trade it. Make it ugly. We may betray it and ourselves. But love does much better than survive.

Love is not a prize for winners only. Nor is it a wrathful judge that we must placate. Love is an attitude of mind that is expressed as powerfully through what and how we think as it is through our emotions. *Thinking about love can take us back home again to the experience of love.* There are many times when we will behave unlovingly, however noble our intentions are. We can accept the reality of that without being crushed by it. To return to the ease of thinking the best of other people and accepting ourselves we have only to wake ourselves up, discover again how instantly available love is to us and how unfailingly we can trust it.

'I say to myself, "Be honest", when I start getting into routines of blaming other people or mouthing off about them,' says Stella. She is a 25-year-old marketing assistant, A-grade netball player and active in local politics. She was raised by two sight-disabled parents and learned early on that she could rise above other people's curiosity, pity and even rudeness.

'"Be honest" has become a kind of mantra to me,' Stella continues. 'It's shorthand for all sorts of things, like "Look at the big picture" and "You'll get over this" and even "Aren't you feeling rather sorry for yourself?" You are going to find it hard to believe but all through my childhood, if anything was wrong, both my parents would say, "Look on the bright side, Stella." There was a period when I was about 14 when I wanted to puke if they said that. They were blind! They couldn't see at all! Then once when one of them said that and I started to yell and go on I saw a look of such grief on my mother's face. It was only there for a moment but it absolutely shook me to my core. In an instant I heard that phrase differently. I heard it as a kind of brave statement. Not stupid at all. My mother is very brave. So is Dad. They are wonderful people. But it was that flash of vulnerability that Mum couldn't hide that actually showed me up to myself. Talking to you now, I could say that was the first moment of raw honesty I ever experienced. And I remember it with the same kind of hit of heat that I remember my first kiss or the first time I had sex. It was that intense. I don't know if that's where my mantra came from. But anyway I do value honesty and so do my parents and the mantra itself stands me in great stead.'

With several more decades of life experience, Neil says something quite similar to Stella about how his concern for other people also led him to greater insight, and the self-love and respect that accompany that.

'I wanted to see myself as a good provider,' Neil says. 'That was what mattered most to my own father and I knew how I'd benefitted from it. In my eighteenth year of marriage, with three

great boys still at high school, I lost my job. It didn't only happen
to me. I was definitely part of that odious trend called "slash and
burn". Each person "slashed" and "burned" was a human being.
We forget that.

'I went right down. I applied for jobs. Didn't get them. Hated
myself. Hated the world. My wife's a psychiatric nurse and she did
more and more shifts but the pay stinks even if you go in sixty
hours a week. To cut a long story short, I had a kind of breakdown.
For several months I'd only leave the house if I had to do something with the kids. Otherwise, I was stuck inside the house with
my own thoughts.

'In the end Tracey [Neil's wife] forced me to see our doctor and
get onto some antidepressant medication. Then, still with some
pressure from her, I started volunteering. Through that I met up
with a bloke in a similar position to mine and after a few months
we bought a small business together. We deliver milk to small
outlets, corner shops and the like. It's totally different from the
executive life and a lot freer! But as well as that, I had to get down
to absolute basics. Could the kids still experience how much I love
them? Was I willing to be best friend and husband to Tracey?
Could I let the employers who had probably forgotten my name
by now rule my future? How did I want to see myself?

'For sure I didn't want to see myself as a has-been. I wanted
to see myself as a survivor and as a good husband and father.
Those are far more inclusive terms than "good provider" was. I
had to make the leap. I am not a deep thinker. I would never
have gone beyond "good provider" if I hadn't had to. This doesn't
mean that I'm glad about what happened because I'm not. The
whole thing was handled extremely badly. I'm still angry about
that. It took its toll on all of us. But at least I myself eventually
turned the tide.

'You know, that's nothing I could put on my CV. It's nothing
that will get me back to the money and prestige I had before. It's

made a bloody great difference to our lives though. And some-times when I think about it, I feel invulnerable!'

EXTEND YOUR CAPACITY TO LOVE

Fear can stand powerfully in the way of trusting and experienc-ing love. Fear may tell us that we are not worthy of love. Or that the risks of reaching towards love are far too great. Fear may also tell us that wanting love makes us dangerously vulnerable, partic-ularly if we believe that sexual love is our primary source of comfort and yet are confused about whether that is what we really want.

Agonies of self-doubt – and confusion about what love is – are felt by people of all ages. This has nothing to do with intelligence, awareness or life experience. The paradox remains: love can strengthen us – and also show us how vulnerable we are.

I know that for many years I wasn't comforted by my own ideas about love. On the contrary, my concerns with love aroused some of my most uncomfortable internal struggles. Love was something I was confident I'd had as a young child. And I recognised that love was something I wanted to give as well as receive. But my mother had died at 38 when I was eight. That was confusing as well as shattering. It entangled love with loss and made love seem dan-gerous. Alongside that, though, my mother lived in my memory as someone who was loving. I wanted to be like her. I wanted to see myself as a loving person. Yet I wasn't sure what that was.

Love was certainly confused in my mind with being admired and validated. And the meeting of those needs was certainly con-fused with sex and my own sexual attractiveness. With good reason, I was nervous and uncertain about what other people were asking for in the name of love. What made things worse was that I was mistrustful of my own rights to draw boundaries. Defining my needs, and treating myself well as a matter of course, were the most mysterious parts of this uncomfortable equation. (Friendship was the easiest part.) Some of my worst misjudgements occurred because I was afraid of hurting someone's feelings or being seen to be unkind or 'selfish'.

Now I know that such loss of self, and such potential loss of safety, is not what love asks. In thinking about love, you don't abandon yourself or leave yourself out. *Love excludes no one.* Love comes to life only when you are able to consider other people alongside yourself, and yourself alongside other people.

My sense of myself as a consistently loving person did not come fully to life until I was in my mid-thirties, almost the age at which my own mother had died. Within the space of a little more than a year, I gave birth to my two children. Their existence brought me many things: among the most precious, this essential reassurance that I could embrace the risks of loving unreservedly. This doesn't mean that I hadn't loved before that. I had, but I'd thought about love principally in relation to adult partners and specific relationships and generally in highly circumscribed ways.

The precious experience of surrendering to love that came with the children, and was deepened through the work I was doing, as well as my spiritual practice, gradually changed my experience of love itself.

From those early years of motherhood, I slowly realised that what I had feared most was that despite several significant and sustaining love affairs I was not capable of truly loving. Only when that danger was behind me could I slowly uncover how love had, in my perception of it, become a guarded, individual experience, and a seasonal one at that. You had it, or you didn't have it. It came. It went. Like a child randomly pinning the tail on the donkey, I assigned and limited my capacity to love.

Focusing my longing for love on specific individuals who were probably as confused about love as I was, I had not understood how freely love could be given. And how essential it is that love *is* given freely. Even the God of my childhood kept track of misde-meanours, threatened, bullied and sorted sheep from goats.

What a tragedy exists right there, that human beings could have turned the source and essence of love into a petty, judgemental tyrant! And that for many people this perception of the Divine remains stuck, replaying that same tale of fear, punishment and imminent abandonment.

Recognising how this image of God has been sustained for thousands of years, and how it's mirrored in our own human dra-mas, it becomes much less surprising that we would learn to see our faults in technicolour. And live in fear of other people's judge-ments (of being 'found out') rather than easily opening to the infinite delight, acceptance, humour and goodwill that flow in the presence of love.

How exhilarating it is, then, to discover that whatever difficul-ties and impediments have been put in the way of your becoming a generously loving person, it doesn't take much more to come back to love than a willingness to *remember what really matters.*

Here's an example.

You arrive home tired at the end of a long and frustrating day. Three school backpacks are dumped by the door along with shoes, a hockey stick and a pile of sweatshirts. The dogs have not been fed. Your daughters are playing different music loudly in their rooms. Your son is on the phone. Your head is throbbing. You begin to unpack the mountain of groceries you have lugged in alone from the car, slamming things into the cupboards and the fridge. Suddenly your son is standing beside you. Through some miracle of unrequested grace, you look at him before you com-plain. Looking into his eyes, you see someone who is infinitely precious. You recognise him freshly. Your anger goes. Love takes its place. Quite unexpectedly you feel tremendous gratitude that you have food for your children; that you are all home and safe; that you have a house to live in; that these fine young people, who a moment ago were yet another irritation, are in fact people you know intimately. What connects you, most deeply, is love. With a single intake of breath, everything looks and feels different.

You are living love.

Another example.

It may be your adult brother you resent. He has been rude and selfish for years. Your elderly parents are in despair about him also. The man's a pig. None of you like his wife. She's Mrs Pig. Then suddenly your brother has three weeks to live. You might hear this news with complete indifference. Far more likely, though, you are flooded with desire to make the best of the time that remains; to set your busy life to one side; to do what you can for his comfort; to come to some kind of peace with him; to mend bridges with his wife; to give him the feeling that however difficult your relationship has been, he will leave this life as a man loved by the family of his birth as well as by his wife.

This chain of events doesn't mean that harsh things didn't happen. It may not even mean you are able fully to forgive him. But those divisive hurts take their place alongside a renewed feeling of connection. Aware of how brief your brother's life is and how brief all our lives are, you set aside enough of the old anger and resentment to allow love or concern or mercy to be present.

You too are living love.

EXPRESS CARE AND RESPECT IN *ALL* YOUR RELATIONSHIPS

Your efforts to express love, live it, understand it, or even to describe it, may always be partial, evolving and clumsy. That's how we are. But there's no mistaking the energy and expansiveness you get when love moves through you, brings you into closer contact with other people. *And returns you to yourself.*

Loving generously, we slowly disentangle love from need. We slowly shift our focus from whether we are loved, or loved well enough, to *how we love*. In an age where increasing numbers of people spend part or all of their adult lives without a sexual partner, we find that it is entirely possible to experience ourselves as a loving person whether or not we have a conventionally intimate relationship. There's freedom in this too.

No need exists for us to leave our feeling selves lying around on a metaphorical stone slab until a frog prince or princess happens by to awaken our dormant capacities for love. No need exists either to put sexual love on such a pedestal that we overlook all other opportunities to be known, cherished, laughed with, appreciated, comforted.

Please know that I am not denying the preciousness of a committed sexual relationship. Or the wild forgetfulness of self that sexual love can bring. But there is something precious about other versions of love also: friendships that survive the passing of time; people who inspire each other for an honourable cause; people who create works of art together; people in an extended family who come to know each other as independent adults; people of different generations who share common values or interests; celibate people who live alongside each other in situations of companionship and devotion.

The value of those stories of love can easily be overlooked.

Preparing to write this book, talking to all kinds of people about all kinds of relationships, time and again I would come up against the remark, 'But I'm not in a relationship.' By that the person meant, invariably, that they were not in a sexually intimate relationship. Just as invariably, though, they were in relationships with family members, friends, work colleagues, old school mates, past lovers. And once they began to think seriously about those relationships *as relationships* and to value them *as places for self-discovery as well as comfort, insight, warmth and loyalty*, they inevitably had every bit as much to say about relationships as anyone else.

I particularly remember Harry, a highly charged, inspirational man in his mid-thirties who has spent most of his adult life in remote areas of Thailand. Our first hour together was spent with him attempting to sell me the idea that he had nothing to say of use because so far his love affairs had been as fleeting as they were intense.

The more Harry talked about why he had no experiences worth sharing, the more convinced I was that, far from him 'wasting my time', hearing his vivid stories of involvement in village people's lives was itself a stimulating experience of connection.

Harry's ideas about love were far more restricted than his actual experiences. 'I loved those couple of hundred people I mainly lived with,' he said towards the end of our time together. 'I was a little weird to them, I've no doubt, but I think they saw me as someone who was close to their hopes and dreams. They trusted me. That was a big thing.

'And friends here too, who kept me in touch with home. Sent me books. Called me back at great expense when I rang them and said I needed to speak English for a bit. Reminded me who I am. There was a lot of care in that too.'

Then as he was about to leave, Harry sat down again. 'There is also something else that happens when people are far from home. Maybe it's even why people leave home! The places where I worked were way off the tourist beat but of course some people would show up where I was for various odd reasons. And I discovered what amazingly deep talks you could have when time was finite or fleeing. Friends who are medicos and who work with the terminally ill speak about this too. There's an absence of normal constraints. I sat up late many times hearing men as well as women talk about the most personal things, reliving it as they were talking and letting me feel that I had come close to that person in a real way. I used to think they were telling me things because they would probably never see me again. Or I was telling them things for the same reason. That's only partly it. It's also that in situations of extremity, when people could most justifiably see themselves as strangers to one another, they're actually far more likely to let down their guard and bare their souls.'

DEEPEN YOUR SELF-ASSURANCE

Benefits from living lovingly flow in all directions. Self-assurance and self-respect develop as your stance in the world becomes more open and stable. And as you more securely trust your capacity to take good care of yourself. This arises quite inevitably from valuing your own life and your own journey – and recognising in a real way how inclusive love is: that it includes all of who you are; that it includes a lively awareness of the world around you.

And that's no small thing. Such an attitude involves and develops trust, resilience, flexibility, self-awareness, the capacity to reflect on mistakes and learn from them. *Those are the essential skills of empathy*, needed as vitally in your work life as at home, with friends or out in your community.

Those are also skills that can't be learned theoretically only. They arise from experience, from engaging with life, identifying positive values, putting them into practice – and always, always taking responsibility for yourself and watching out for others.

It may be that no one has ever built a secure foundation for their life except through an active concern for others. Our social needs are paramount. When we can experience them positively, and not as a distraction or intrusion, and when we can trust ourselves to respond positively to other people, then our longings for self-acceptance, respect and love will inevitably be met.

Pamela Margoshes is in her early forties. She is a freelance writer, a wife and a daughter. As a young woman, Pamela felt tremendous anger towards her parents. But the story Pamela tells is less about her parents than about how making a significant change in the relationship with her mother powerfully influenced her attitude towards her husband also.

'My parents were both critical and demanding,' she explains, 'but also very loving – which was confusing for a child. But then seven years ago my mother got a very small cancer in one of her breasts and my whole life and perspective changed. Virtually overnight I forgave her. I understood why she was the way she was. Her parents were killed in concentration camps; she was sent to live with a family at age 8 in England; she had been essentially an orphan since that time.

'I was then able to focus on the many, many wonderful things about her; her regard for intellect, books, music – over materialism.'

As Pamela saw her mother differently, and released herself from the resentments she had carried forward from childhood, their relationship improved dramatically. 'We no longer hold back from each other as we did in the past. She even asks me for advice now – the ultimate compliment from a formerly critical parent! I understand how her past drove her to do what she did. How fear- and abandonment-driven she was.

'After my mother got sick, I had a kind of rock-bottom, transcendent sense of how vital it is just to live life and not get mired down in the bullshit, the bathos, the stupidity. That is the core value I share with my parents – the one that got wonderfully, gorgeously illuminated and rushed to front-of-centre in our new relationship.'

This huge shift in Pamela's relationship with her mother was a great gift for both women. But that time of change had other benefits. When Pamela was in college she had a nervous breakdown. The person who nursed her through this ordeal is the man who became, and has remained, her husband. 'He saw me stripped down to my raw filament, my foundation,' Pamela says. 'And saw through it all to me and fell in love with me, as needy and hurt as I was. I'm forever spoiled by such sympathy as he showed me, such intelligence.'

In the years since, Pamela's husband has, in her words, 'proven himself over and over to be just as sensitive and trustworthy as he was in college'.

Pamela's gratitude for her husband's consistent care and love is clear. What is most striking about this story, however, is that it was only in the upheaval of change following her mother's illness that Pamela also recognised how she could express this gratitude not in words only, but in a change of emotional habits that would benefit her and very specifically benefit her husband.

Pamela says, 'Because of all the stress in my life (guilt over being high-strung plus the accumulated annoyances of being a writer!), I used to have a very bad temper. I'd blow up several times a week. It took a toll on my husband which I didn't realise until my mother got sick and I had to examine my every behaviour, my every feeling, my every rigid thought process, my every emotional block in order to break through it all to have a vastly improved relationship with my mother.

'Doing so – really thinking through my "fixed" responses to life, to stimuli – made me realise how toxic and destabilising my anger had been in the "emotional ecosystem" of my marriage.'

It's easy to imagine how good it must have felt for Pamela to discover that her fixed responses were not so fixed after all.

Our powers of self-persuasion are impossible to overestimate. We are not simply affecting but *creating our relationships through our attitudes* – that web of beliefs about who we are, who others are, what we and they are capable of; about where our limits are; about what we can or cannot do. Few of us take the time to develop the self-awareness that Pamela did. Yet the practical as well as psychological benefits of her willingness to be self-responsible, to take control of her own attitudes and behaviour, are tremendous. 'I'm proud to say that I no longer blow up as often,' she reports. 'I finally learned that this is the best way to "repay", if you will, my husband for so many years of emotional support and empathy.'

CLEAR THE AIR WITH POSITIVE CHANGE

One of the themes that emerged most clearly for me in the writing of this book is how positive the results are when one person in any relationship 'ecosystem' goes beyond the worn routines that keep both people stuck and increase their frustration. (You blame. I blame. You accuse. I accuse. You get angry. I get angrier. You get righteous. I get more righteous.) Those dances of accusation and counteraccusation, of attack and counterattack, can seem utterly compelling. But they are built on habits only, not on rock. When one person can imaginatively take a step backwards, look at a difficult situation more broadly, and *act consciously to bring in a more considered initiative or response*, a vital breath of cleansing air enters the situation and benefits everyone.

The function of psychotherapy and of couple counselling is often to bring in that shift of perspective and the hope that comes with it. Yet such a reviving shift can happen just as effectively outside the formal therapeutic encounter. It can arise because someone is willing to push beyond an impasse and move the situation on.

That was true for Nikki and for Pamela. In a different way, and in the face of different challenges, Michelle's story also shows this.

Michelle is 35 and a self-described 'serial monogamist'. She has had two long relationships, and recently broke up reluctantly and painfully from a shorter significant relationship.

She grew up in a family where she perceived the rule as being 'Never make a wave.' This meant, as Michelle describes it, 'You existed in relationships regardless of how miserable, inappropriate or unfulfilling they may have seemed. Expressing needs or wants or feelings was unacceptable and, if we managed to, expectations were always unmet and we were left feeling unvalidated.'

The change Michelle created was with a man she had loved

some years earlier. She says, 'I chose to forgive my ex, and equally myself, for the mess we'd created in a five-year, on-off, shitty, sexually obsessive relationship.

'At the time, I was participating in a personal development course. One night our topic was forgiveness. We had to choose two separate people and situations where we felt we'd been really wronged and were now going to forgive. For one of them I chose my ex-boyfriend. They took us into a meditation where during the meditation, we forgave them, and ourselves. It was quite powerful during the meditation and felt really cleansing. At the end of the evening, they told us our homework was to contact those people and tell them we had forgiven them. I was *totally* resistant, but because I was serious about the course and actively wanted to dump my baggage I didn't see that I had a choice.

'I actually called him up out of the blue. My heart was in my throat as I made the call and told him I forgave him, and owned my part in it and told him I also forgave me too. He was totally stunned, though pleasantly surprised. He's now a really valuable, dear close friend, something I never in a million years would have expected with him. Interestingly too, since then he often spontaneously in conversation will acknowledge and apologise for how badly he treated me way back when we were in a relationship, and constantly tells me how beautiful I am. Both things I longed for so much when we were together – he often reaffirms now.'

This wonderful outcome – that an opponent would vanish and a 'really valuable, dear close friend' would occupy his place – could occur only because Michelle was prepared to give up the familiar comfort of blaming her former boyfriend for their shared miseries. And because she also ceased to blame herself. Blame is a huge obstacle to love – one of the greatest. It denies your complexity and that of the other person. It shuts out generosity. It keeps you locked in the past. It gives other people the power to spoil or diminish your life. And it creates self-pity and helplessness on a massive scale.

DISCOVER HOW EFFECTIVELY YOU CAN HELP YOURSELF

We can't move through life without becoming aware that there are impulses in all of us that are ugly, self-defeating, even sadistic. We have countless opportunities to encourage other people, to ease their difficulties or to make their lives more comfortable. But often we miss those chances. Self-absorption, self-importance or self-pity can cause us not only to pass those moments by, but to feel justified in doing so.

Resentment frequently blocks the path of love. It can turn our minds into calculating machines, working out constantly what we are owed and who has failed us, rather than looking at the opportunities we have to enjoy life, and relieve ourselves and other people of what can turn into a continual flow of complaints. Resentment can set us up in a childish relationship to the universe ('Why should I . . . ?'). What's more, resentment is highly contagious.

And what we fail to do is only part of the picture.

Words can fly from our mouths that not only demean us, but also injure others. As I was working on this chapter, my friend Manny rang to tell me how dismayed his 15-year-old son had been when he heard older boys at his privileged single-sex school speak with breathtaking contempt about girls they (and he) had danced with at a combined schools function the previous weekend. These boys did not know the girls and their judgement had no value. But what shocked Manny was that such ugly impulses were so available to the boys. Who knows what the trigger was for these remarks, but the sexist venom that emerged was horribly familiar. And even if we interpret it as a defence against the boys' own insecure feelings about girls, it is still possible to see how sad it is that these impulses were so readily available to them.

To live and love generously we need to monitor the tone and content of our most routine remarks. We need to avoid falling into the trap of making lazy assumptions about people whose choices would not be ours. We need to stay clear of the delusional belief that in cutting other people down we can build ourselves up.

We are all capable of behaving badly with other people and of blaming them for our wrongdoing. Sometimes we pretend not to know what we are doing. Sometimes we are totally aware of what we are doing. Either way it's tempting to find reasons why our damaging behaviours not only should but must continue. Yet swallowing that myth, we give up our most vital freedom.

Whatever we tell ourselves, *no one can make us behave badly*. No past harmful experiences can force us to replay those behaviours. No provocations in the present can force us to abandon our values. The moment that we recognise our behaviour is hurting someone, damaging our relationships, or is putting us in danger – *we need to stop*.

Even as your mouth opens to criticise, undermine or yell, *close your mouth*. Even as tears of self-pity well up in your eyes, *wipe them away*. Even as you feel flooded with the negativity you long to express, *silence yourself*.

Doing this, you save yourself as well as others.

Sometimes you may need to leave wherever you are and walk or run. You may need to sit in a quiet space and observe your strong feelings *without judgement* until you experience that they have been transformed or have subsided. Or that time has moved you on.

Esther gave me a valuable description of this process. She is an energetic, passionate woman in her early fifties, whose rapid access to feeling is a great part of her charm. The dark side of this is a quickness of temper that can lead to judgement and injury.

Esther reminded me most usefully that one of the good things about just being with your anger – neither expressing nor repressing it – is that you come to see much more clearly how routine the triggers for it usually are.

'Holding my anger and observing it,' Esther explains, 'is one of the best things I have learned. Seeing it softening and changing as I look at it with my mind's eye and stay with it as it changes. Not denying the anger, not expressing the anger. Just holding it tenderly and observing from where it comes.'

This sounds inviting. But challenging too. Esther agrees. 'This has been a long and difficult practice for me. I used to often feel resentful. Which is just another version of blaming. Seeing the same triggers for that anger has been valuable. Similar patterns emerging. Holding the anger when I feel the hot flush that threatens to explode me into "out of control" blindness. It still happens but with less frequency and a lot less intensity. Sometimes I even get through it without damage.'

And if the tides of fury are coming towards you and not from you?

Then it is also crucial to remove yourself as well as others in your care who could be affected and harmed. *And to know that you are entitled to do so.* To remove yourself from harm – harm from outside yourself and also harm arising from your own self-punishing thoughts or impulses to hurt others – is an essential act of self-love.

RISK LOVE!

Love can grow as you grow. Trusting in your own capacity to love, practising being open, accepting, slow to blame, quickly forgiving – you quite inevitably get better at it. You are good to be around. *It feels good to be you.*

This does not mean that you then love everyone in the same way. However far you get along the path of love, you will be closer to some people than to others. Love asks only that you stretch the boundaries of your attention, move out of your comfort zone, value other people more honestly and less exclusively, *create chances to be encouraging.* And recognise that you need no one else's permission to live lovingly.

Loving generously, you can like and trust all kinds of people. You can include them in your capacity to care. Trusting the value of living lovingly, you find your horizons expand. The wellbeing of the world you live in becomes your business. And where does the world start, except from where you are?

You are the future, Rainer Maria Rilke promises:

You are the future, the immense morning sky
turning red over the prairies of eternity.

Your future extends beyond this moment through the most exquisite expressions of your personal power: to choose to treat other people well; to be willing to be kind to yourself.

And how you look depends on where we are:
from a boat you are shore, from the shore a boat.

HOW TO

Love Generously

Loving generously is the finest expression of belief in yourself: that you are open to giving to others and receiving from them. Your own body can be your greatest teacher here. You have only to remember how tense your body feels when you knowingly withhold something that might help another person. Or when you feel angry, self-pitying or bitter. Contrast that with the expansiveness you feel when what you have done delights someone else, meets their need or conveys to them the love, respect or concern you feel or are teaching yourself to feel.

Loving generously allows you to be a loving person always. (And to benefit from the ease this brings to your daily life.) You don't need to wait for someone else to 'bring you love', give you permission to love or guarantee that your loving efforts will be worthwhile. Loving generously, you discover how it can be your choice to take positive initiatives, express tenderness, practise tolerance and respect – and value *all* your connections.

Loving generously, you grow in strength. And your relationships benefit profoundly.

Cultivating good humour, you become easy to be with.

Behaving with consideration, you develop self-respect.

Behaving thoughtfully, your world grows bigger and more interesting.

Allowing other people their contradictions, you more easily accept your own.

Letting go of past hurts, you move into a livelier experience of this moment.

Looking out for what's pleasing, you find more and more that pleases you.

Taking positive action for love's sake only, you free yourself from second guessing and making judgements.

Living love, your whole life feels alive and precious.

- Remember: *do no harm. Do good.* Keep it simple.
- Use love as the guiding value in *all* your connections. If you are unsure, ask yourself, 'Is this the *best* that I can do?'
- Let unimportant dissatisfactions go. Speak up about what's pleasing. Making this change only would transform many relationships.
- Be *pleased* for other people. Cope with your mixed feelings privately. Don't impose them.
- Release others from your hidden agendas: that they must behave in certain kinds of ways or make specific decisions so you can feel all right about them (or yourself). *Accept them as they are.* Watch them flourish as you cease to be their judge.
- If you want something changed, be direct about it.
- Harbour gratitudes, not grudges.
- Take the pressure off your 'most important' relationships by seeing *all* your connections as an opportunity to be open, caring, trustworthy, generous.
- Notice how your whole life benefits when you don't depend on just a few people to reflect back to you that you are a worthwhile person.
- Don't ask yourself whether someone 'deserves' your respect or concern. Doing that, *you give them the power to determine how you will behave.*
- Don't wait to be 'in the mood' before showing love or respect. Positive behaviours *transform your mood.*
- Recognise how variously love can be expressed. Kindness, delight, empathy, encouragement, openness are all

expressions of love. Practise them unconditionally.

- In your business or casual encounters, translate love into respect, courtesy and honesty. Practise it unconditionally.
- Recognise that self-love matters. It shows in the way you behave with other people. Loving others generously, you will inevitably feel better about yourself.
- See yourself as a loving person. Use the immense power of your imagination to walk yourself through situations, influencing them positively. Then live out this ideal.
- Be aware how you speak *to* people. Know what this conveys.
- Be aware of how you speak *about* other people – even in their absence.
- Practise kindness also to those who seem to have *more* power than you do. (It's easy to be kind to those we are unconsciously patronising.)
- Use empathy as your first response ('You seem upset. Is this a bad day?').
- Create opportunities to be with loving, positive people. Learn from them.
- Know that living as a loving person is the greatest tonic known to humankind, guaranteeing peace of mind, rewarding relationships, satisfaction, optimum good health, delight.
- Let yourself recognise how empowered you feel when you set the tone of your encounters with other people.
- Put reminder stickers wherever you know you might fall into an attitude that seems offhand or abrupt. Short-tempered on the phone? Put a 'Love Generously' sticker there. Grim when you first get home? Take five minutes on the way home to let your body move into a relaxed, open state. *Find a way to remind yourself to do this* (put a sticker in your car, on your briefcase, in your wallet).
- Find a 'Love Generously' hero. Put a picture of that person up

on your fridge, computer screen, bathroom mirror. Tune in regularly for inspiration. (I have a Martin Luther King Jnr flag, with those sublime words 'I have a dream' on it, and beautiful verses from Dame Julian of Norwich on my computer screen, to remind me of what matters.)

- Monitor constantly how your *attitude* affects other people.
- Give the benefit of the doubt routinely. (It relieves stress!)
- Don't walk past opportunities to be generous. Take them all.
- Wean yourself from the need to be rewarded for 'good behaviour'. Know it has its own rewards.
- *Create* opportunities to be generous: go out of your way for others; *look* at a situation from someone else's point of view; *express* your feelings of tenderness, joy and care. Don't leave yourself out: take time for what you most enjoy.
- Practise being generous *when it won't be noticed.*
- Love life itself. See how variously life is expressed in every human being. *Love those differences.*
- Make no demands 'in the name of love'. They are invariably manipulative.
- Respect other people's boundaries scrupulously. People love most easily when they also feel safe.
- Never take for granted the people you know best. Train yourself to see them every day through new eyes ('This is someone I truly value'). Bring yourself into line by reminding yourself, 'This could be my last chance to show concern or love to this person.'
- Other people want to be valued – just as you do. In a difficult situation *bring that to mind.* Your 'enemy' may disappear. In their place may be a friend.
- Be aware of what a different world we would live in if people *routinely* behaved generously. Play your part in creating that world. Believe in the value of what you are doing.

Know What's Going On

In order to have new ideas, we have to open ourselves

to life as it is, not as habit would have it.

We need to surrender to reality.

PIERO FERRUCCI

*K*now what's going on.

Look at those words, lying harmlessly on the page. Gazing at them, I am reminded of a child's wooden train, its brightly painted carriages lying on a floor where they can be stepped over, tripped over, crushed, avoided or ignored.

In the intricate, contradictory but fascinating world of human relationships, even to attempt to know what's going on is rarely easy. I'm not thinking of when life seems to move along almost of its own accord, events flow into each other and a feeling of well-being can be relied upon. In those times we can almost forget ourselves, and certainly take life's goodness for granted.

What's more complicated are the periods when our relationships feel somewhat empty, boring, unreal or unsatisfying. We hear ourselves saying what we didn't intend to say. Our minds fill with dire warnings and mutterings. We witness ourselves backing away from a situation that would usually feel comfortable. We find ourselves picking fault and getting irritable with the people we are working with or profess to love.

We may have a whole range of strategies to use at these times and some of those strategies may work well for us. We can feel proud of what we have learned and confident about what we can handle. Relationships, though, are dynamic, mercurial, ever changing. They don't stand still, any more than we do. Even in the most trusting and committed relationships, familiar strategies are not always enough. Problems can arise that may feel like stumbling blocks or worse. Sometimes a shift of awareness is needed, rather than a remedy.

IN SEARCH OF NEW INSIGHTS

Sensing something in your life is out of harmony or balance, it's always tempting to rush in and talk it over with someone else. Or to fall back on the familiar relationship mantra: that because a situation is difficult it should be put out there, 'processed' or worked at. But I am not so sure about the wisdom of that.

Talking something through with another person can be marvellous. In healthy relationships of all kinds there is usually a good deal of wide-ranging, lively talking. And real confidence that pretty much anything can be said. Sometimes talking can even work miracles as one person truly opens up to the other person's separate inner experience, and the two shift to a different level of understanding. Yet the rush to find out what someone else thinks, or to let them know what you think, can also be a barrier to discovery.

When any version of a close relationship is stuck or feels as though there is a heavy sense of repetition, talking is often *not* the best place to start. Apart from anything else, there is usually one person in almost any relationship who values talking more highly than the other. It is not always the woman in a heterosexual relationship, or the adult child of an ageing parent, or the female parent of the silent adolescent, or the more extroverted of two friends or colleagues. But it is more likely to be. Any entrenchment of roles is a hurdle here. So is talking too soon, or with too much invested in a speedy outcome. That can also limit us, paralyse us in stubborn positions, drain us or keep our attention fixed on justifying ourselves, without learning much that's new or helpful.

What helps most is to start with an honest exploratory conversation with *yourself*, preferably writing out your questions and then your answers, rather than continuing the disembodied conversations you are already having in your own mind. Simple questions can be exceptionally useful: what's familiar here? What seems most confusing? Am *I* feeling out of sorts? Am I being straightforward? What outcome do I want? What would achieve it? Those are questions that can *take you beyond what you already know*. And can give you exquisite relief from the tedium of moving in increasingly smaller circles, growing frustrated and impatient, or searching the landscape for someone to blame.

Even those of you who are most laid-back or the least introspective will have patches when you feel uneasy or unsettled, often without knowing why. Or you know something is being asked of you but don't have a clue how to respond. This can come up at work as often as it does at home. Something in your life is pushing you to a new level of insight – even maturity – and you are floundering, getting irritable, finding it hard to make small decisions. Maybe you are drinking too much, or burying yourself in even more work than usual, or you have begun dreaming of African safaris or retirement to Provence.

Rushing to talk is tempting. But that rush itself tells you that the insight you need is always some place else: not within you.

Talking can also be much more about expressing or relieving our anxieties than it is about communication. We need to get something off our chest. Or to make an attempt to break a circuit of uncertainty. And we make our move outwards too early or too insistently. As one person talks, the other may inwardly turn away, feeling overwhelmed, inadequate or lost because so much is being asked of them and often in ways that are indirect and hard to follow.

In terms of the energy that flows between people, when unproductive talking happens, one person often becomes more and more wound up, energetic, 'over the top', while the other person often literally loses energy, collapses inside and on the outside shrinks into a posture of helplessness.

This kind of talking is obviously frustrating. The point and pleasure of talking is to communicate, but when the communication goes awry at least one person is invariably left feeling frustrated. And the other person may well feel defeated. Or perhaps both become defensively over-emphatic, stating their point of view too vehemently, or withdrawing too rapidly, and stripping the conversation of its appropriate ambiguity and complexity ('If that's all you have to say, clearly there's no point talking about this'). Either way, no one has much more sense of what's really going on.

KNOW YOUR OWN MIND

In psychotherapy there is usually a great deal of talking. Ideally most of it's done by the client and not the psychotherapist! What's interesting, though, is how differently people use this talking time. Over the years I have discovered with real pleasure and fascination that the people I work with unconsciously require me to be a somewhat different psychotherapist for each of them. The relationship between a psychotherapist and an adult client is not the same as a parent–child relationship – unless you grew up spending only an hour or two a week with parents who were always on their best behaviour – but parents will recognise this dynamic, knowing that each of their children experiences each parent quite individually (and each parent experiences each of their children differently also).

Some people want to use their psychotherapy more than anything as a place to get things said. The burden of holding onto something, of not understanding something or of repeating patterns they know are limiting or harmful has become painful for them. Their need is to express this and the feelings that go with it. But even for those people – wanting to know that someone else can tolerate hearing what they need to say – the silences of psychotherapy are vital. In fact, those silences, and *the inward conversation that they allow*, are at least as healing as talk can ever be.

During our fairly constant inner conversations we rehearse all kinds of things that have a profound effect on how we think about life and on what we bring to our connections with other people.

On the bus, in the gym, driving our car, wheeling our trolley around the supermarket, lying awake in the middle of the night, we rehearse who we are and what we want to become. We practise being brave. We practise being defeated. We initiate dialogue. We make ourselves right and others wrong. We own up to some things. We deny other things. We answer back. We strengthen our relationships with some people. We weaken our connections to others.

In the privacy of our own minds, we create our individuality.

Meditation teachers call the place where your thoughts race from one thing to another your 'monkey mind': much movement and chatter; not much sense or stillness. That chatter may be what you think mind is. Yet experience shows that this is a small part of your mind only.

Your mind-beyond-mind is vast. Think of owning a palace and living only on the front porch, and you begin to get it. Think of the infinite basin of sky that can be seen from a boat or ship far out at sea, unhindered by any shore. Or the horizon where sky and ocean meet. Think of that – and you begin to get it.

Moving from the porch to the palace, you can experience peace and comfort at any time. You can *give yourself* peace and comfort at any time. First, though, you must be prepared for just a few moments to do nothing: nothing, that is, but breathe and sense the breath moving through you, returning you to yourself.

Sit and do nothing but breathe, and sense your slow breath. See for yourself how the horizon of your mind extends. And with what relief your scattered sense of yourself gathers and comes back home.

From this place comes a new sense of *what's going on*.

The most simple meditation practice creates trust in yourself. It's that trust that relieves the frustrations of your conscious mind.

Sometimes whatever it is we have been struggling to discover or work out simply becomes less urgent. Or we realise that our instincts are pushing to let us know what's moving forward in our lives and that all we need to do is pay attention.

That realm of tranquillity within us can be our greatest resource. It doesn't distract us from the rational mind; it supports it. But lack of familiarity works against us. Like a tongue returning again and again to a hole in a tooth, so our monkey minds return us to what we often regard as the real or only business of life: to situations that are unresolved and raw. And to the same habits of thought that continue to frustrate us.

These patterns of repetition are not hard to find. The person who talks at you rather than to you, or who insists on telling you far more about a complex situation than you might want to know, may also be doing nothing worse than attempting to relieve their mental aching tooth.

They may feel quite unconsciously caught in a spell, virtually compelled to tell and retell their story and to re-experience at least traces of the feelings that go with it. Often the story that's retold compulsively is explicitly one of injury or powerlessness ('She wouldn't . . . ', 'He never . . . ', 'And you won't believe . . . ').

The feelings being recalled may be quite uncomfortable, but they are familiar and compelling. The person is drawn to repeat them over and over again, even when they bring only the most momentary relief, because that expression of feeling *is not followed by insight and healing.*

This compulsion to repeat his tragic story to everyone he met, yet get no relief, was the curse of the unforgettable central figure in Samuel Taylor Coleridge's chilling epic poem *The Rime of the Ancient Mariner,* who shot an albatross while at sea and in doing that brought death to his fellow sailors. The sailors' death was agonising. Surrounded by 'water, water everywhere but not a drop to drink', they died from a physical thirst that could not be relieved.

Almost worse, though, was the Mariner's own lifelong experience of restlessness and incompletion: talking and talking, expressing an emotional thirst that would never be relieved.

FACE DIFFICULTIES WITH GOOD HEART

We don't need to be compulsive talkers, or restless circular thinkers, to recognise a trace of this dynamic in our own lives and how much this searching restlessly for answers outside ourselves asks of other people. And how easily it might drain our relationships. Even if we lead an untroubled life, we must face the challenge of occasionally looking directly into the heart of a difficult or uneasy situation and trying to make sense of it – not least so that, unlike the poor Mariner, we can leave it behind and move on.

It's not easy to do this. Circling and not landing, denying what you don't want to see, talking around the topic but not about it, or collecting different viewpoints from all kinds of people are strategies that can be much more tempting than sitting alone in a quiet room and asking yourself, 'What's going on here?'

What helps most is a straightforward recognition that some-thing that's oblique or that carries a potentially confronting emotional content does actually need your attention. That's a great start. It brings you back to where your attention needs to be. And then? It's always useful to view your own life more broadly: 'What does this remind me of? Have I felt this way in any other situa-tion? How old do I feel when I start to think about these things? How would this problem seem a year from now?'

It also helps to look more intensely at the particular situation, circling *and* landing – making it the sole focus for a short period of reflection and writing: 'What's going on in my thoughts, feelings, body? Which relationships or area of my life is this affecting most? What would help me most to move through this with insight? What can I do to help myself most effectively and lovingly?'

Writing out your questions and then spending time writing

down the answers is far more fruitful than reviewing questions and speculations only in your mind. It activates your conscious and unconscious processes quite differently from the way that rumination does. You may be willing to put your imagination to even greater use, looking inwardly for a particular symbol that you then describe on paper or draw, which may give you a hint about what's going on or may even let you know quite directly.

Our unconscious minds respond well to the indirect approach we usually associate with playfulness. This is true even with serious matters. You could try imaginatively rolling aside a heavy stone, for instance, so that beneath it you find a 'note' from your own unconscious to guide you to the next step you should take.

A burst of realism – assessing clearly what you can affect or influence; where your influence will be less direct or negligible; how you are talking up or down your own inner sense of possibility – can quite comfortably coexist with this imaginative work and also be empowering.

Katherine is a current affairs journalist, raised in a socially aware, academic household, who has two children of her own. She offers a clear example of how a shift in awareness can change an unhelpful pattern of thought and the miserable feelings that go with it. I like her story because it shows that even if what we worry at most is a high-minded concern, we are still doing ourselves a disservice when we let a pattern of obsessive, reductive thinking take us over.

Katherine says that she used to find herself 'obsessing' about how unjust things were: 'Both the world in general and what was happening to me. I have particular activities during which, through habit, I do most of my worrying and feeling angry – in the shower, walking from the train station to work, or train to home. I used to finish those activities feeling angry and tired because I hadn't solved the injustice I was worrying about. I know I have a good brain, and I used to think that if only I concentrated hard enough I would be able to solve the problem, work out the solution. But I couldn't. So I still felt angry and a failure as well.'

Do aspects of Katherine's story already sound familiar?

Much of what we might regard as thinking is, in fact, not much more than repetitive commentaries on our own or other people's shortcomings and perceived failures. None of that moves us along. Nor does it bring the insights that can relieve our situation. So how did Katherine extract herself from this loop?

She explains: 'Now I get past it through telling myself and understanding and accepting the saying "The world is not a just place." It sounds a negative thing to say but it gives me freedom to move on and add the extra sentence: "But I'm alive, that is a beautiful sunset, I am walking along." I now understand that part of the privilege of being alive is that things are not completely right and they never will be. And that gives me relief.'

MOVE INTO MINDFULNESS

Peter is a research chemist in his forties who has been married three times and is now living with his teenage son. He values intimacy with women highly, but quoting Robin Williams he quips, 'God gave man a penis and a brain and enough blood to run one at a time.'

Looking back to his years of growing up, Peter says, 'Instead of being direct, my parents presented themselves to each other obliquely through their complaints about each other. Especially my father. And his dependence on my mother's acceptance was so outsized that he never stood as an emotionally autonomous man in relation to her.'

Autonomy is not an unrealistic idea that you can somehow get by without other people. It is quite possible to be aware of how interdependent you are while also knowing that you are the principal actor in your own life. You *are* affected by others. But the quality and stability of your life depend primarily on the moral and ethical choices that you make and only secondarily on how others treat you.

For Peter, his father's lack of personal autonomy was highly significant. 'It took me years – decades – to shed his modelling and to abide by the simple words of Emerson and stand on my own authority, to take the risky position of "This is who I am" without first asking permission to be.

'For much of my adult life intimacy has meant that my partner understood me, and she needed to provide evidence of this understanding with requisite words of praise and admiration. Nice, but limiting. What is now important is for me to understand myself and to communicate who I am through both being and doing. And to do so without needing to ask for prior approval. This requires a desire for a real relationship that is stronger than the desire for security.'

Peter has become a man with good friendships and high ideals, not least about sexual intimacy. The ending of his three marriages has clearly been a personal blow to the vision he has of himself as a loving and accommodating person. So I was curious to know if he believes any of his marriages might have survived if he, or the women involved, could have 'walked the extra mile' – gone forward to meet each other on common ground, rather than retreating and fighting for greater autonomy from an increasing distance.

Peter's response may surprise you. But it echoes the experience of many other people I have talked to who believe that they did not take action *on their own behalf* soon enough.

'My mistakes took the contrary form,' Peter explains. 'I walked too many miles and stayed way too long. Two of my marriages were doomed from the beginning and looking back I can see no way I could have ended them gracefully.'

Issues around self-love, as well as quite tough questions about how to value and care for yourself, spring up here and demand attention.

Without trying I can think of many people I have known who were well into adulthood, in some cases approaching the end of their lives, before they could begin to feel that they were entitled to act on their own behalf and had the right to say, 'I have some sense at least of what's going on and my instincts tell me that it's wrong for me.'

It seems incredibly hard for many of us to grasp that we can learn to think of others as well as ourselves *and* ourselves as well as others. The changing circumstances of any life may require us to emphasise one side of the equation more than the other, but this does not mean that we should totally abandon ourselves when we are deeply involved in the care of others, or that we should fear abandoning others when we must focus on ourselves.

Many women who have been raised to think of everyone's happiness except their own may find even the idea of acting on their own behalf difficult, although as Peter's story clearly shows this is not a single-gender issue only. Women and men alike need to step back a little and release themselves from the idea that this is an either/or situation. For love to be meaningful, it must also be inclusive.

Shared values are an invaluable support when it comes to sustaining long-term relationships in a way that protects and nourishes everyone involved. In his three marriages Peter valued talking and open communication, but for him there were 'significant failures' in each of his attempts to live in a way that was mutually revealing, confiding and respectful.

'One of the most astounding discoveries I made with my [third] wife was that she was not truly interested in what I had to say (and therefore in me). My function in her world was that of audience. In the beginning of our relationship I had been mesmerised by the energy of her stories and the brilliance of her humour. I mistook my accommodating, brief responses and her long dissertations as communication.'

Peter's response to this perceived failure is interesting. 'When talking fails,' he says, 'my only recourse is my practice of mindfulness, such as it is. Over the years of training and reading, I have adopted the exercises of sensing, seeing and listening. The purpose is to bring myself into the present moment. It is especially easy to do this when I walk to work.

'I put sensation in my body: I notice how my feet and legs and arms and hands are sensing the environment. I notice the habitual tension in my forehead and relax the muscles of my face. I notice the feel of the pavement or dirt road under my feet through my shoes; I listen to the sounds around me without assigning images or meaning (I say to myself only, "That's a car; that's the wind"). I pay attention to what my eyes are seeing, shifting my glance often so as not to sink into some fantasy or internal dialogue.

'I have walked the same ten blocks in my home city for twenty years. I realised that I am such an introvert and have my attention so inwardly focused as a matter of course that I could not tell you the details of those ten blocks. I was shocked to realise I could probably not have drawn an accurate map with the correct street names. So I added another element to my practice: to notice at least one "new" physical feature along my route each day.'

In that beguilingly simple shift from talking to *walking with awareness*, Peter is describing a dynamic that can be lifesaving. When talking fails us, when we still don't have a clue what's going on, where we are headed, how we are to get there, or even if it's where we want to go, what do we usually do? We talk some more! We talk about the talking. We talk with other talkers. We grow frustrated. We weep or shout. We continue to talk.

And meantime, what's happening to our bodies? And to each of our senses? How can we possibly draw answers out of another person, or find satisfying answers in our own minds, when we have forgotten where we are in the physical universe? When we barely know who we are in relation to other living beings? When we barely know who we are?

EXPERIENCE THE WORLD THROUGH YOUR BODY

Being aware of our physical environment is something that as adults we frequently need to relearn almost from scratch. From middle childhood onwards almost everything we learn is through our minds only. Gradually we detach ourselves from the natural world that enchanted us as children and gave us so much physical release. Many of us move through our lives in a kind of trance so intent are we on the dramas running inside our own minds.

Like Peter, we might be unable to describe in detail the walk we take each day to work; or what flowers are blooming in the garden at home; or what it is like to lie on the surface of the ocean looking down to an entire world of tiny, rainbow-coloured fish below; or how our feet feel on wet sand, new-mown grass, pebbles, earth.

Those simple processes of awareness that Peter practises as he walks daily through the streets of his city have widespread implications for our personal and social good health. How could we feel anything but adrift when we barely remember that there is earth beneath the built environment that creates the world for many of us? How could we feel anything but lonely when we regard our own body as something to tame, reshape or complain about? How could we not feel adrift when we move so fast we don't notice how we are breathing? How could we care about other people when we are cut off from large chunks of ourselves?

Many of us have little idea whether we are tired or hungry, what emotions we are feeling, what causes us to feel sad or empty. We may not know how our voice sounds to other people; whether our touch is gentle; how readily we laugh or smile; whether people feel good when we come into a room.

Regaining an awareness of each of our senses, living more fully in the present moment, we can find the inner balance and focus that allow us a more realistic sense of what's going on. This is always dramatically demonstrated for me when, in psychotherapy, someone tunes in to the language of their body and discovers how powerfully and accurately their physical state is 'describing' their inner world of feelings.

I experienced this recently when I was working with Francesca, a pharmacist in her early forties. Her twenty-year marriage has hit an impasse. She has been depressed for months. Her husband doesn't know how to help her. He feels gloomy too; he cannot help himself. Therapy is out of the question for him. He won't even discuss it. Talk of divorce is suddenly and shockingly in the air. What should she do?

We talked for some time together, and as she talked I noticed how dramatically Francesca's body collapsed into itself. Her shoulders rolled in, her chest sank, her stomach tightened – just as yours or mine might if we were contemplating the involuntary end of a long marriage. Everything in her body spoke of a lack of hope and resolution.

When the appropriate moment came, I asked Francesca to take some time to become more consciously aware of her body: to feel from within how it was expressing her hopelessness and despair. Then I asked her to guess what messages this body posture was giving to her husband. Doing this, I was well aware that Francesca wants her marriage to continue, and that any marriage therapy that was going to get done would be with Francesca only.

We wondered together how Francesca's husband might interpret her body language both consciously and unconsciously; how he might feel in the face of her despair; how they might both be 'reinfecting' each other with a sense of mutual hopelessness conveyed less through words than through tears, a retreating behind piles of washing or opened newspapers, and occasional futile outbursts that left them both weary and frustrated.

Continuing to draw Francesca's attention to her body, I asked her to stand shoeless on a thick rug to find how good that wool felt beneath her feet, and then to imagine that beneath the rug, the floor and my building is earth on which she can steadily rely.

She did this, immediately relaxing as her awareness shifted from her exhausted mind. Then for fifteen minutes or so as I stood close by, she kept her eyes closed and felt from within how differently she literally stood in relation to her problems and anxieties when she could allow herself to experience something as uncomplicated as her feet being on the floor, her body held by the power of her feet and legs and thighs, her spine elongating and growing stronger, her sense of ease increasing, her chest expanding and opening, her face opening up, her breath moving slowly and deeply; and then, with hands held flat just beneath her belly, reminding herself that there was her centre, and *that she has a centre.*

It would be foolish to pretend that this brief increased inner awareness of her body and where it 'stands' in the world is the end of Francesca's difficulties. It won't be. But it would be just as foolish to overlook how powerfully we orchestrate all kinds of situations through the language of our bodies.

Whether we are conscious of this or not, our bodies continually 'speak' to each other. We send potent messages through our posture, our facial expressions and bodily gestures; our sighs and worry lines; our tone of voice; our shortness of breath or temper. And always, always, through our thoughts.

British biologist Rupert Sheldrake takes this idea further: 'Even our thoughts affect other people, and we in turn are affected by others' thoughts . . . The idea of the mind being inside our head, a small portable entity isolated in the privacy of our skulls, is peculiar.' This idea is not only peculiar, it also very specifically expresses the limited obsessions of the last few hundred years. Sheldrake goes on: 'No culture in the past has had this idea, and it's amazing that the most educated and sophisticated culture that has ever existed (as we'd like to think of ourselves) could have such an extraordinary view.'

The language of the body is supremely rich. But the messages it sends are not going one way only. Our bodies express our feelings. What's also true is that a shift in posture can shift our feelings *and* also cause a shift in other people's perceptions of us.

It's safe to guess that Francesca's husband is well meaning. They have been contented enough for many years. Nevertheless, the world of feelings is not where he is most comfortable.

Francesca desperately wants him to reassure her that she's loved and that their marriage will continue. Yet the collapsed 'self' she is presenting to him, and asking him to love, may be the aspect of her that arouses most confusion in him, or even distaste or feelings of hopelessness. When that's pretty much all he is seeing and recognising, and when he himself has no idea how to remedy the situation – and finds *that* almost unbearable – it's no big surprise that he would begin to talk of ending the marriage.

Does this mean that Francesca should present a falsely cheery self to make him feel better?

I don't believe so. But her situation had worsened because Francesca was herself unaware of the messages her own body was conveying. Her mind was saying, 'Show me that you love me.' Her body was saying, 'You can't help me.'

Even now that she understands how unmistakable that message was – and has felt and experienced the different messages in the rise and fall of her body's energy – it is unlikely that Francesca will change her physical posture permanently. We are, above everything, creatures of physical as well as emotional habit. When Francesca feels frightened, she will have to make a conscious effort not to collapse into the posture that shouts 'Hopeless!' Yet if Francesca can make even an occasional shift in her awareness, and a mirroring shift in her body's language, she will be helped. And her husband – and their marriage – will be relieved.

KNOW YOU ARE MAKING CHOICES

Knowing what's going on in the constantly shifting interactions between you and the people and world around you has a significance that goes way beyond your physical and emotional wellbeing. Your awareness of choice, and the sense of personal power that comes with that, inevitably increases as you come to understand any complex emotional situation more realistically. What's interesting is that this is usually true *even when what you discover doesn't lead you to a cheerful conclusion.*

Seeing something clearly may mean that you must take action that's disruptive or hurtful. It may take you to a level of resignation that's not in your picture of an ideal life. It may demand that you give up some negative attitudes for your own sake or for someone else's. It may even lead you to think about your own defensive habits and decide, as Gemma has, that you cannot afford to abandon them.

Gemma lives on an isolated farm with her husband. Reflecting on raising a family of five children, now adults, with a husband she experiences as critical and discouraging but whom she would not consider leaving, Gemma says that she has had to find some serviceable ways of protecting herself. What she has learned after more than three decades of marriage is that her defensive habits limit her – but also protect her.

'I don't think I could give them up,' Gemma explains. 'They help me survive and give a certain amount of security and protection. I withdraw from confrontation. *I can become invisible.* I can disappear into a lovely dark hole and come out when everything has settled down. When I was younger at home with my brothers and sisters, and then when my own children were small, I did stand up for myself, but usually came off second best, since Bill [her husband] always took the children's part, right or wrong. Generally it was me against the world and I found it best not to engage. I knew that trying to win just wouldn't work. I found that out very early, with three older brothers. It's always better just to let it go. I try to handle the upset in myself and not engage with the enemy. It doesn't resolve much, but neither does trying to have it out.'

The crucial factor that relieves tension and allows someone the freedom to get on with the rest of their life is clearly not whether the choice is 'ideal'. It is, more simply, the recognition of choice. And a willingness to make that choice.

This is a complex issue. We are making choices all the time – but often passively. We let things happen. We force other people to choose for us (and then sometimes blame them!). We put things off for so long that we don't (apparently) any longer have a choice.

That particular expression of passivity is no less undermining than any other. Our lives do best when we feel 'in charge' of our choices and can recognise that we really are responsible for our own actions and attitudes. This doesn't mean that we will always make wise choices. Sometimes they may seem disastrous. But at least they will be our own. And we will be saved from falling into the awful trap of blaming others for our very existence.

RESPECT BOUNDARIES AND AUTONOMY

A relationship has its best chance of succeeding when everyone involved is willing to own their part in things and take responsibility for the effect of their attitudes and behaviour. This requires a fairly constant level of awareness, or even vigilance. So it is refreshing to recognise that the moments of raw self-discovery within any relationship are endearingly human and not possible to predict. Two people can sit down to have an earnest, well-meaning talk and get up with nothing changed. A week later, as they sit together chewing toffees and laughing their way through a video, a casual remark from one of them takes them effortlessly to a new level of appreciation and understanding.

As marvellous as that is, however, the very idea of understanding needs to be treated with a certain caution in all of your relationships. And the closer the relationship, the more caution is needed.

Assuming that you understand someone, or that you can read their emotions or predict their attitudes accurately, is not a guarantee of high levels of empathy and affection. On the contrary, it can be a powerful threat to the sense of autonomy and personal integrity that each person is entitled to bring to their interactions with other people. It can also be plain wrong.

The assumption that you inevitably know what's going on for someone else or, worse yet, that because you love each other you will *and should* think and feel alike, is a form of trespass that can cause horrible problems, especially in tight-knit families as adult children try to stake out ground that's authentically their own, or as two adults come to different stages of maturity and insight within a previously fairly equal relationship.

Careless assumptions can be an obstacle to freshness in any long-term relationship. It is courteous and wise always to check out what someone else feels or thinks about any significant situation that affects them.

Asking someone how they see a familiar situation not only avoids misunderstandings, it also provides an essential reminder that as close as any two lives may be, two minds do not (in a healthy relationship) inevitably think as one.

Parents especially can be so caught up in a group mind-set that they become grossly insensitive to any responses or desires expressed by their children that are different from their own. They can quite unconsciously denigrate those differences or try to persuade a child (even an adult child) that their different view makes no real sense and should therefore be abandoned ('How could you possibly think that? No one in this family has ever . . . ').

Speaking *for* someone else is part of this picture also ('We always . . . '). And that trap may be set wide open for a highly intertwined couple as much as it is for a family.

I remember vividly how angry I was as a child when I felt I was being described by someone else or having a version of myself offered up for public consumption: 'Stephanie never likes . . . ', 'Stephanie will always . . . ' I felt impaled by those remarks, as well meaning as they might have been (and they were not always well meaning). I wasn't then and am not now someone you could know through and through. *And nor is anyone else.*

We are dynamic creatures, interacting with a changing inner and outer environment all of the time. This means that we cannot fully know another person. We cannot even know how we ourselves might react in a moment of extreme trial. Assuming that you know someone else totally, or that a person's motivations and attitudes are transparent to you, is disrespectful at best. It is also a sure way to keep yourself stuck, having a relationship with some-one you *used* to know – way back when you were still open, curious and interested.

Adolescents are especially likely to react sensitively or even aggres-sively to any effort to speak for them or sometimes to understand them. Many of the disruptions between adolescents and their fam-ilies or other authority figures arise directly from the disrespect shown when someone assumes they know their way around inside their minds. But this is not an obstacle to intimacy between ado-lescents and their parents only. Emotional trespass can be a major problem in any close relationship. In all kinds of family relation-ships as well as sexually intimate relationships, people often believe that intimacy gives them the right to ask anything, demand any-thing and assume everything. It does not.

Pulling back from making too-rapid or careless assumptions about someone else; curbing the temptation to speak habitually of 'we' and 'us'; limiting your need to require other people to think and act as you do: all of this brings fresh air into a relationship and limits the grief caused by emotional claustrophobia.

Acknowledging this means that you can take new heart when people 'just like us' turn out to be bankers rather than bushwalkers; athletes rather than scholars; extroverts rather than stay-at-homes; celibate rather than married.

Those differences are not in themselves threatening. They become threatening only in a life built on sameness. But sameness is not a foundation for living. It is an illusion, easily blown apart.

I was struck by this recently when I was talking with Constance, a friend of my own age, about reading. She and I both grew up as passionate readers. We have both worked at different times as writers and editors. And reading continues to be the leisure activity we enjoy most. But the children in our families are very different. Each of our children is not just different from us (and we are also different), but within each family different from one another.

Those differences have their echoes in every aspect of our lives.

Reflecting on this Constance said, 'It's important to me to remember that I mustn't want my children to do what I've done, think what I've thought. My daughters are 20 and 22 and their life has to be their own. I'm always amazed by how different their interests and aspirations are from mine. They probably won't be the painters or writers or intellectuals I assumed I'd produce. They're practical, sociable young women; planners who are busy getting the skills they need to deal with the uncertainties of the global marketplace. I have to respect their ideas and their decisions, for surely the whole point of reaching maturity is that I've achieved the capacity to enter sympathetically into their plans and experiences, without judging them or wishing to make them conform to my expectations. Besides, I never look at my daughters without realising just how much they please me simply by being their lively, hopeful, affectionate selves.

'I'd be a fool not to know that my happiness depends on their being there, and that *their* freedom to be themselves frees me to be myself – not some sad person wanting to control the world by controlling the people dearest to me.'

Pressuring our children or partners, openly or covertly, to live as we do – and using our significant powers of approval and disapproval to achieve this – we take away their invaluable right to explore and discover what adds up to a rewarding life for them.

From 2500 years ago, the Buddha speaks to us of exactly this expression of respect: 'Do not believe in what you have heard; do not believe in traditions because they have been handed down for many generations; do not believe anything because it is rumoured and spoken of by many; do not believe merely because the written statement of some old sage is produced; do not believe in conjectures; do not believe merely in the authority of your teachers and elders. After observation and analysis, when it agrees with reason and it is conducive to the good and benefit of one and all, then accept it, and live up to it.'

TOLERATE UNCERTAINTY

To *know what's going on*, we need the space and freedom to be ourselves. We need time to reflect. We need time to develop confidence in the wisdom of our own experiences. We need curiosity too not to ask the familiar, dead-end question, 'Why is this happening?', but to ask more useful questions: 'What do I want to achieve here? What's the outcome I am seeking? Will my actions take me there?' And maybe: 'How can I help myself to tolerate *not knowing* for a little longer?'

The vastly underrated capacity to tolerate uncertainty does not lessen your capacity to know (eventually) what's going on. In many complex or ambiguous situations it may be your greatest asset. Relationships are ended prematurely every day because one person must have an answer to what's troubling them, and often prefers half an answer, or a negative or premature resolution to a difficult situation, to no answer or resolution at all.

But the sweet irony is that there can be a valuable increase in maturity if that impatience can be reined in – if the person who feels the rumblings of change can look first at their own part in the relationship, rather than assuming that fault or even the inspiration that might drive a solution could only be found elsewhere.

Recently I went to a noisy, extravagant tenth anniversary party for a now exceptionally happy couple who discovered this.

Grace and Ned were 30 when they met. They had both had intense, complicated love affairs in their twenties and when they got together it was with some relief that they thought, 'This is it!'

A year or two into their relationship, however, Ned quite suddenly found he was tired all the time, sluggish at work and no longer much interested in sex. He underwent all kinds of medical tests, with no clear reason for these changes emerging. This went on for several months and at first Grace was pleased to be generous and solicitous. But as time went by and Ned's interest in sex disappeared along with his good humour, Grace became tetchy.

Perhaps inevitably, she also became quite interested in a colleague at work and it was at this point that Ned roused himself enough to suggest that whether or not his medical team could find an explanation for his lethargy, he and Grace would have to accept this mysterious process, work with it as best they could, or end their relationship.

Grace says now that she *was* tempted to walk away. Ned had become a burden rather than a partner. Perhaps it would go on forever. What kept her from going was her admiration for Ned's honesty. He couldn't tell her what was wrong. Obviously he couldn't say how long it would be before his health and vigour returned. But he could be open and straightforward – even about his confusions. It was this that reawakened Grace's interest and tentative commitment.

LET YOUR IDEALS SUPPORT YOUR LIFE

Moving into the present and looking at any complex relationship as it is now; making a reasonably intelligent assessment of what you want; finding out what other people want and dream of: all of this adds up to a level of emotional and social awareness that often seems beyond our reach. Daily life already asks so much of us. Flossing our teeth can feel too much. Aren't there some things we can satisfactorily take for granted?

The answer is surely yes. But perhaps our relationships are not among them.

We can trust people and have confidence in them. We can expect their loyalty. We can offer them our trust and confidence and loyalty in return. But unless we are willing to stay awake to *what's going on with them and with us*, and *between them and us*, it becomes only too easy for the relationship to slip out of sight.

Barely noticing that this is happening, we can assume too much. We can cling to a familiar version of events long after the evidence of our own eyes should have told us something different. And we can forget not just what our values are, but how effectively those values can support us in and out of all our relationships.

One of the most talented young women I know is a musician and singer called Paris. In her early twenties, she is already strikingly interested in the big questions of life. But predictably, however confident we may appear on the outside, on the inside most of us remain quite uncertain about what we dare ask for or expect.

At the age of 20 Paris had an intense, sexually powerful relationship with Andy, an older man who is also a gifted singer and composer. She has no regrets about that relationship but says, 'The whole time I was with him I was in fear of him leaving me and fear of him not loving me. Strangely enough, he could never say that he loved me and what hurt the most is that I was so afraid to say it to him in fear that he would leave me. The thought of being on this planet loving someone, but being unable to say it, was the most painful thing. So although I believed freedom was so important to me, this was not a free relationship although it had many free elements. And that's what makes it all so confusing. We use the good bits as an excuse not to look at the dishonest bits.'

What Paris says seems generally true: that we fix our gaze on what pleases us and blot out the rest. It often takes a long time to see a bigger and more truthful picture, especially when this does not coincide neatly with what we want.

Further on into a relationship – and there is real sadness in this – we may do almost a complete flip. We may then concentrate so hard on what is *not* right, what is *not* easy, that once again we fail to see the person or relationship in its entirety.

In telling her story, Paris noticed how unbalanced our attention can be. She says, 'I had a dream after we broke up and I was pining for Andy. Ammachi [Mata Amritanandamayi, a renowned contemporary Hindu teacher, affectionately called Mother by her students] and lots of monks were in the dream. Mother came up to me and gave me my cello bow and said to me, "See this bow. Your relationship with Andy was like having only a few hairs on the bow. Yes, they are correct and lovely and free, but you have to give them all up – give up love – to one day have a bow with a full complement of hair on it."'

Months later what has Paris learned? 'I am consciously acknowledging my honest reaction to situations, not just my edited reaction. I hope I'm pulling the Bandaids of illusion off much quicker!'

THE PAST CAN CONFUSE THE PRESENT

However intently we may try to keep track of what's happening in the present, there will also be echoes of the past in almost every potent situation. We may feel comfortable because of this. At other times we may feel great foreboding: *I have been here before. I didn't like it.* This feeling of being disturbed or unsettled by the past may arise in us without any obvious reason. It can be far more amorphous than conscious memories of events or actual behaviour.

If you are someone who wants to be more conscious, or wants to feel confident that you have learned from your mistakes, then there is something particularly tough about gradually realising that you are at risk of repeating a difficult drama. Yet that happens all the time. People come to therapy in great distress because some months or years into a second or third marriage or partnership they have become aware not only of similarities between the way this partner and the previous one behave, but also of being stuck or unable to react very differently themselves. In addition to their distress, they often feel tremendous anger towards themselves, or shame and frustration: 'Why didn't I see this? How could I possibly have made the same mistake all over again?'

Romy is one woman who explained this painful trap as her principal reason for seeking psychotherapy. She told me, 'I got married when I was 21 to a man who was horribly possessive. I could hardly breathe and when I left three years later there was a real danger that he'd kill himself. I knew that – but it was life or death for me also.'

As she began her story, Romy's face was pale and tight. She was sitting literally on the edge of the chair, unconsciously tugging at her skirt, then wiping her hands on her thighs, over and over again, as her words tumbled out. 'That's bad enough. But the worse thing is that at 32 I got married again and within months knew I had made virtually the same mistake. The man I had thought was sweet and quiet and loving was possessive, jealous and actually quite dangerous. Like the first one. And I hadn't seen it coming.'

To repeat a major mistake or misjudgement is disturbing. As Romy's therapy eventually showed, it was not easier for her to get out of that second marriage. In fact, I think she would agree she felt even less entitled than before to protect herself and leave behind a wounding and unrewarding relationship.

The first time she had told herself the failure of the marriage was bad luck. The second time she began to agonise that perhaps something in her 'attracted' that kind of immature, punishing man. But if that were so, then how could she risk her judgement again? Feeling guilty and self-judgemental sapped her strength. It was only with effort, and the wholehearted support of her two sisters, that she again left a marriage she described as 'totally unsalvageable'.

Any of us should be extremely wary about staying too long in a draining relationship because we believe that we are strong and that the other person would collapse without us. People who live out the myth of their own helplessness are surprisingly ruthless about getting their own way. And surprisingly adept at finding a new caretaker. It is vital to know that *we can be kind to ourselves and not become a selfish person*. And if life requires us to risk selfishness by acting on our own behalf, we can usually do that too. And not die of it.

GROW IN WISDOM AND GOOD HUMOUR

Do we grow wiser as we grow older?

The answer to that must be, I think, no as well as yes. Certainly life gives us countless opportunities to grow in wisdom and to see more clearly what's going on. Nevertheless, it helps us to remember that at each new phase in our lives we are somewhere we have never been before. In the most fundamental way we continue to be amateurs throughout our life. What a consoling thought this is! And there are certainly times when we are especially vulnerable and *need to match that vulnerability with appropriate caution*.

At the time of her first marriage, for example, Romy was emotionally and socially insecure. She did not want to have sex before getting married. The idea of being married and settled was tremendously appealing. This desire clouded her judgement, as it might do for any of us. At the time of her second marriage, Romy was more secure and was well established in business as the owner of several thriving coffee shops. But she was again vulnerable. She had been on her own for a long time. She was anxious that she wouldn't marry again. She wanted children. Once again, *what she wanted filled her horizon* and clouded her judgement as to whether this particular person could meet her needs – or she, his.

Romy is a bright woman. Her failed relationships do not reflect any lack of intelligence or self-awareness. She is a woman with many friends, a loving family and loyal employees. So what went wrong?

In my life and my own psychotherapy practice, I find little obvious correlation between the intelligence and kindness of people and their success or otherwise in establishing committed sexual relationships. A lively interest in each other's inner and outer worlds, an explicit sharing of values, a genuine physical and sexual ease with one another, an equal and simultaneous need for a committed relationship: all of these seem crucial to building and sustaining a long-term sexually intimate relationship.

But whether or not these factors come together for two people at any given time depends as much on good fortune and synchronicity as on the valuable capacity to *work at it*, the mantra so loved by relationship counsellors.

It is, I know, quite possible to work yourself into the grave and not achieve happiness if the values in your life are not shared by the other person. Or if, despite your best efforts, the other person chooses to remain aggressive, arrogant, bitter or self-absorbed. Or if you cannot shake yourself free of self-pity or resentment.

Some people have the capacity for a loving sexual relationship in abundance, but not the good fortune. And the mystery of that absence can be more painful than almost anything.

In the face of urgent need, and especially when our need for love is narrowly focused, any one of us can easily substitute hope for experience. We can persuade ourselves of all the ways that a halfway promising situation is different from the difficulties we have faced before. And we can overlook all the warnings that, in crucial respects, it is the same.

There is a lovely postscript to Romy's story.

A year or so after ending our work together, she called to arrange a single follow-up visit. This turned out to be less because she needed therapy than because she wanted to share with me how happy she now is in a relationship with a man who is what she describes as 'a grown-up mate at last!'.

And what allowed this? Romy's solution would not be every-one's, but she decided to join a weekly discussion group for a dozen people over thirty-five. In her words: 'I needed to see how other people interact in an emotionally frank situation. Perhaps I secretly hoped I might see how someone was in a fairly raw situation before I got to know him individually. But I was also absolutely disbelieving that I could meet a possible partner. Getting to know a few new friends, and getting to know myself a bit better, truly would have been enough.

'I would not have recognised Ken as "my type". He is a furry, brainy man. Small – my height – with wide, beautiful eyes. My husbands were both good-looking sportsmen: tall, fair, handsome. I have to admit that at first I thought Ken was a know-all and only after several meetings I recognised a faint trace of my mother's insecure judgements of well-educated people. I noted that with some interest. Then I began to pay more attention, trying to see Ken as an individual and not as a "type". I tried to do that with everyone, actually. The group was a great chance for that because we had to get beyond our everyday roles.'

Did Romy also become aware of Ken's special interest in her?

'Well, gradually I found myself making eye contact with him almost inadvertently. We'd crack up at the same things, or feel exas-perated at the same time. I also noticed, though, that some of his reactions were completely different to mine. He's had lots of relationships. He talks far more freely about his feelings. He's sexually open. He likes women in a way I've probably never been able to like men. And I can get on with that.'

Romy is not married to Ken and she may never be. He does share her valuing of monogamy; they are committed to one another. But for the first time in her life this is not adding up to the version of sexual intimacy and commitment that Romy once valued above all others – yet which, in those two earlier combinations, also caused her so much grief.

UNLOCK YOUR HEART

Some of us may have been more fortunate all along than Romy was. But few of us know what's going on all of the time. How could we?

Life is moving within us and outside us. Life is acting on us and in us. Our sphere of awareness can grow only as we pay close attention to the motivations that drive our actions, *and to the effects our actions are creating.*

Becoming more aware is the most crucial activity of our waking mind. Our capacity to choose and to live 'knowingly' absolutely depends on it. Nevertheless, our waking mind exists on the margins of our immense unconsciousness, our *un*awareness – and the drives to action and response that come from that.

To find out what we are doing, to discover where we are heading, and to bring our choices into awareness, we must pause, reflect, look deeply at the effects of our actions – and not hide from them. We must know when to ask, 'Is this wise?' or 'What's driving me here?' or 'Do I like what I'm seeing?' We must know how to be honest with ourselves, as well as with other people.

We also need courage: to make changes when they are needed, to look at what's going on from a broad perspective, and to stop at once when what we are doing moves us far from love.

Some of our finest decisions are made in the name of sexual love. And some of our worst. We are primed genetically and instinctually to love and mate, to care for each other and to be cared for. With great single-mindedness we may seek out the pleasure, affirmation and release of sex, as well as the companionship and comfort that a sexual relationship promises.

Whatever our sexual preference, whether we are in a committed partnership, having casual affairs or are voluntarily or involuntarily celibate, those same instincts are in all of us. They are good instincts. When we can honour them and align them with our mind and spirit, they serve us sublimely well. But love is never fully lived only through caring for one partner or one family, or in one way.

Love, says contemporary poet and mystic Andrew Harvey, is 'a way of unlocking the heart to the whole world and to the shining of the divine mystery in everyone and everything'.

Unlocking our hearts to the whole world will help us to love more and to fear less. With or without an ideal relationship, with or without a sexual relationship, with or without living parents or children, the ideal job, body or income, *we are not nothing. We are not incomplete.* We can still and just as fiercely live as loving beings; find our way through life as loving beings; and express, through everything we are, the truth of what love is.

We reach out towards love to give us something. We demand from love that it will make us someone. Doing that, we forget: in the ground of our being we already have that 'something'. Through all of who we are, we are already 'someone'.

Bringing ourselves into the present moment, treasuring what we have as well as who we are, allowing other people their freedoms alongside our own, we connect with life's bounty. And we can say: *This is what's going on.*

Know What's Going On

You want loving relationships. You want to feel that you are in charge of your life. You want to feel steady, resilient, confident. You want to trust you can choose wisely. You want to enjoy the world around you. You want to feel fully alive.

And this is possible.

To achieve this, you need only turn off the automatic pilot that may be creating your life for you. You need to look with fresh eyes at what's going on inside your own mind; what direction you are moving in; what values you are expressing; what's *really* happening between you and other people. Until you recognise what's going on, you can't make whatever changes might benefit you or others. You can't step into the centre of your life where you belong.

The power to make positive choices is the greatest gift we human beings have. Knowing what's going on is essential to that. Whatever your outer circumstances, it allows you to be the author of your own life and not a bystander.

There are many things you can do to know what's going on.

Be present – conscious of how you are affecting events and not simply being 'acted upon' by other people ('She made me . . . ').

Be aware of your 'observing self'. Learn to pause and reflect, learn from your experiences; 'choose' even on the run.

See things as they are – not through the prism of your good intentions ('I didn't mean to . . . ').

Read the language of the body (your own and other people's) to see the needs, desires, fears and hesitancies the body vividly expresses.

Move into the present moment. See what's happening *here*, right now. *Know what makes you happy or works well.* Do more of it.

Find out through simple observation the effect you have on other people. Where that doesn't reflect your best intentions – make the changes needed.

Know what makes you or other people suffer. Do less of it.

Discovering what's going on, you develop the key skills of self-awareness: reflection; resilience; awareness of choice and the capacity to make choice.

- Until you know what's going on, you will live reactively. *Value the choice that insight gives you.* It's your greatest asset always.
- *Value communication.* Many relationships end in bewilderment as well as injury. Your reality and someone else's must meet to support your relationship. Without that connection, you will inevitably drift apart. Talk. Tell. Listen. Think. Reflect. Communication is essential.
- Recognise your part in things. Take responsibility. This gives your relationships a chance to thrive.
- Be aware that you see through fresh eyes *only when you choose to do so.* Otherwise habit clouds your gaze.
- Cultivate insight by switching from 'automatic' to 'interested'. Ask yourself *often*, 'What's happening here? Do I like what I see? Does this express my best intentions?'
- Know how stillness feels. It allows you to see things in focus.
- Question your assumptions constantly. They may be past their use-by date.
- Ask other people how they see a complex situation. Respect what you hear. Take time to think about it.
- Don't let 'events' decide for you. Choosing badly feels better than not choosing.
- *Let yourself feel things.* You risk more sorrow – and more joy.
- Find out what your 'automatic' reactions are. Until you

recognise them, you can't decide which to keep or abandon. (Do you automatically say you are too busy to have fun; too needy of money to choose how to spend your time; too set in your ways to create change? Think again.)

- Let your 'automatic choices' reflect what you value: joy, gratitude, a willingness to try out something new.

- Make decisions and requests *that support your wellbeing*. (You may be shocked to discover how rarely you do this.)

- *Act courageously.* That usually means 'owning up' when things are not right and making concessions, suggestions, adjustments. Keep checking the effects.

- When making a change, talk about it in the present tense ('I'm using a more collaborative style at work', 'I am listening to my son more and talking less'). This makes the positive change real and more likely to last.

- Tune into your body. What makes you tense, angry, frozen, overheated? What gives you headaches, backache, migraine? What makes you laugh, lifts your spirits, increases your wellbeing?

- Tune into the body language of other people. Notice what makes them tense, angry, relaxed, peaceful. Take that seriously. Act accordingly.

- Look for *patterns* in the way you affect other people. These are easier to identify than one-off behaviours ('Staff seem tense when I talk to them about their work . . . ', 'Calling everything urgent is taking a toll . . .', 'My partner is thrilled when we make time for friends').

- Look deeply into familiar things, familiar faces. *Look through the eyes of love.* Experience the emotions that come with that.

- Make changes confidently. Walk yourself through them imaginatively. Put them into practice and watch with interest.

- Question whether your actions and values match up. Raise the standards of your actions; don't lower your values.

- In knowing what's going on, *don't leave yourself out*. If other people's actions or decisions hurt you, say so.

- Regularly envisage a vast golden circle of compassion. See yourself, other people or difficult situations in and through the light of this circle. It will become clear to you what needs attention. Spend five to ten minutes a day on this.

- Seeking insight? Write out your question. Then let yourself write a reply. Go back to the same question daily and write for five to fifteen minutes until you feel clear.

- In a complex situation, ask yourself, 'What outcome do I want here? How can I achieve that? What impact will this have on other people? Is this loving?' Return to the same questions until you feel settled.

- Sometimes we fear the void. If you are afraid to know what's going on, seek out a friend or a therapist to look with you, especially someone who thinks creatively and imaginatively. Remember: *all creation stories begin with emptiness.*

- Don't rush past the everyday moments of your own life. Savour them.

- Tune into nature and the seasons. Know how they affect you. Move with them, not against them.

- Pay attention to simple things: they can restore you to yourself.

- Experience your own mind as a place of refreshment: learn meditation; buy meditation tapes; listen to music; read Thich Nhat Hanh's book *Peace is Every Step*; walk with awareness; know how peace feels.

- Create rituals that help you look with gratitude at what you might otherwise rush by. Pause before eating; eat with friends regularly; call people when there's nothing 'wrong'; take time to ask, 'What's going on for you right now?'; keep a journal; give yourself a sense of living your life rather than being hurled along by it.

- Open your heart as well as your eyes.

Live

Encouragingly

Managing our power of choice . . . begins with

choosing what our thoughts and

attitudes will be.

CAROLINE MYSS

O ut on the great ocean of worry, where we bounce around on our fragile single-person rafts, we may spend a surprising amount of time attempting to second guess the effect we are having on other people.

There will be variations, but often we worry that others may find us 'too something': too old, too young, too rich, too poor, too eager, too withdrawn. Or maybe we worry that they might see us through the equally harsh lens of 'not enough': not smart enough, not young enough, not original enough, not thin enough, not successful enough, not sexy enough, not important enough.

We credit those judgements to other people. Just as likely, though, those are the harsh thoughts and judgements growing like weeds in the fertile space of our own minds. *And they are not loving.*

Even when we know how to be relatively kind to ourselves, we may continue to rehearse thoughts that are harsh, judgemental or undermining ('I shouldn't have said . . . ', 'If only I'd . . . ', 'I'm so hopeless . . . ').

Or maybe we persistently re-run situations that went wrong, rather than giving ourselves even half as much chance to recall the many things that have gone well. Or shifting our attention to what's happening here, right now, in this moment.

And the limitations and suffering don't stop there. Because we are so skilled at self-criticism, we inevitably become highly attuned to even the most subtle reinforcement of criticism from outside ourselves. Like the newly pregnant woman who suddenly notices with surprise how many other pregnant women are about in the streets, or how many new parents are pushing prams, *we pick up on what already most absorbs us.* When slights and hurts, insults and disappointments dominate our internal territory, we become acutely sensitive to any lack of interest or unkindness that others show us. Those moments grip like Velcro, while many other more rewarding moments just slip away.

Each day brings us fresh opportunities to be liked and appreciated. To live encouragingly. And we long for that. How ironic, then, that even while we are worrying about what others may think of us, and wanting them to approve of us, we are simultaneously rehearsing feelings of anxiety, distress or failure. Or we are presenting ourselves to others with a grim face, or through depressing or boring conversations, or via temper tantrums or petty complaints about matters that we could as easily pass by. Or even through accusations about how a particular person or situation is depriving us of our God-given right to happiness.

And then, despite that highly contagious outpouring of misery, we expect people still to seek out our company, care for us, forgive us, believe in us – and treasure who we are.

YOUR THOUGHTS SHAPE YOUR LIFE

Who we are today arises from our thoughts of yesterday. Who we will be tomorrow arises from our thoughts of today.

Thoughts are running through your mind ceaselessly. To feel confident that you are 'at home' in your own life, you need to know what those thoughts are. But do you? Could you say confidently whether your thoughts and attitudes are generally encouraging? Whether you routinely notice what's uplifting? Whether you are resourceful and creative in your thinking? Whether you customarily seek to find 'the good in the bad'?

Do you know what kind of incidents you return to most often, not just through your initial attention but also in your ruminations?

Do you know what kind of world you perceive and create through your gaze?

Your world may be a place of suffering and tragedy, where injustice is rampant, where evil and betrayal lurk, where other people are indifferent or disappointing at best, and judgemental, undermining or dangerous at worst.

That is a legitimate view. You can find much suffering inside and outside yourself to support those assumptions. But the world you react to – and to some extent create through your perceptions – could equally be a place of unfathomable complexity. It could be a place where profound injustices and suffering do indeed exist, yet so does much that is stimulating, beautiful, mysterious and wondrous. That world is also true.

The focus and quality of your thoughts shape your life.

Your thoughts – or the perceptions, interpretations, opinions they unwrap – are what lift your feelings or drag them down. Your thoughts are the means by which you make sense of things. They sift through a raft of experiences on your behalf. They guide not only what you perceive but also your sense of who you are in that world.

Your thoughts influence virtually everything that you feel and do. They shape and create your attitudes. They can literally shorten your life or extend it.

This is something that's been known at least to a minority for thousands of years. Yet I heard nothing much at all about it during my years of schooling. And I suspect that you didn't either.

I learned many useful things (and many useless things also). Thinking about thinking, however, certainly wasn't part of the curriculum. 'Think, girl!' did not actually mean think! It usually meant remember and regurgitate what you have been told – but may not have understood and certainly may not have experienced, even imaginatively, for yourself.

Norman Vincent Peale's famous book *The Power of Positive Thinking* was published while I was still a child but I suspect that its claims ('Eliminate self-doubt!') were too grandiose and unrealistic to attract my family's attention, so at home too we missed out on the book's strengths and its popularisations of some vital ancient insights.

Even now, decades after that book was published and when this kind of knowledge is widespread through diverse spiritual as well as psychological and motivational teachings, I suspect that the majority of people continue to regard their thoughts as rather like clouds: natural, spontaneous and beyond anything that they could change or affect.

The truth could not be more different.

We all possess the same awesome power to affect the quality of our lives through what and how we think. But until we tune into this process and make it conscious, we will be selecting both what we pay attention to and *how* we think about it, automatically rather than consciously and optimally. More precisely, we may be virtually hypnotising ourselves through our inner commentaries about what is possible and what is not – without considering whether those vital inner commentaries serve us well.

It's a simple matter to become more aware of what's grabbing your attention. And to discover what you are rehearsing and re-running in your own mind. Better still, if you don't like what you find, it is also relatively simple to discover that you can exercise more conscious choice and powerfully increase your capacity to influence your own life in the way you want to.

Eden gives a tremendous description of making exactly this kind of change, and experiencing the leap in self-awareness and self-assurance that inevitably comes with it. She is now in her thirties. She's a journalist and public speaker who is in a satisfying, stable relationship with a man she loves very much. But adult life certainly hasn't always been easy for her.

Eden's first serious boyfriend was killed in a motorcycle accident when she was only eighteen. She was riding pillion at the time. On top of that, her parents were in the process of divorcing, with a good deal of bitterness on both sides. Not much later Eden left art school because she had developed a panic disorder.

'I'm convinced,' she says, 'it was because I was so unhappy. I was by then having another relationship and had a hard time dealing with the fact that he also rode motorcycles. If he was late coming back from college – or anywhere – I flew into a panic and imagined him dead on the road. Despite being a close friend of my previous boyfriend, he could never understand or be sympathetic about my anxiety.'

Eden's situation grew worse. She couldn't study. She found it hard to ride in cars. And she hated to fly. Her solution?

'I'm a great self-analyst. If something's bugging me I find out what's causing it and work towards overcoming it. After visiting many doctors to no avail, I checked a book out of the library on relaxation techniques. Voilà! I've never had another panic attack. And, if I do find myself anxious, I try to pull myself back from that – because it's usually worrying about the future, something you can't control – and ask "How am I now?" It's like a mantra, though: you have to keep saying it for it to have an effect.'

Eden's self-help relaxation techniques were a powerfully effective means of moving from being overwhelmed by her own fearful thoughts – and the feelings of panic that they caused – to thoughts that could reassure her and leave her calm.

It was an immense relief for Eden to know that she was no longer at the mercy of a frightening and disabling disorder. Even better, it was a huge boost to her self-assurance to discover how effectively she could encourage and help herself.

CHECK YOUR HABITS OF MIND

Individual thoughts affect us less than our habits of mind do: our style of thinking, the topics we return to most often, the quality of the overriding commentaries that shape our perceptions.

The healthiest habits of mind are also the most flexible. Living encouragingly promotes a sense of curiosity, possibility and connection. These thoughts are reflected in an optimistic, positive outlook that other people in turn respond to with enthusiasm.

More troublesome habits of mind are reflected in a largely pessimistic outlook that is itself fairly static. They make themselves known through experiences of anxiety and doubt, or isolation and suspicion, or sometimes rigidity and dogmatism. Those more discouraging habits of thought generally make a person feel defensive, critical, judgemental. Unsurprisingly, that person is often more difficult to approach, and certainly more difficult to feel comfortable around.

The origin of our habits of thought and style of thinking is always complex. It's partly genetic, cultural, circumstantial. And those are the elements that are not possible to change. (If you grew up in a tempestuous household where malcontents were constantly threatening suicide, your outlook is likely to be rather different from that of the person who grew up in a laid-back household where the only rule was to let every dog have its day.)

What *is* most definitely possible to influence, however, is the key element of self-awareness: what you tell yourself about your capabilities. This would include how you describe a situation to yourself; what choices and responses you allow yourself to envisage; whether or not you dare to encourage yourself.

As long as your habits of thought remain unexamined, you will respond out of habit only. This means that in a tense situation if, for example, you are a largely pessimistic thinker, you will 'fly home' to pessimism. Pessimistic thoughts and attitudes are likely to flood you. And will probably seem totally convincing.

You will beam in on danger, betrayal and disappointment, readying yourself for disaster – even where there may actually be none in sight – because this is what you are most used to seeing and most used to feeling.

But your thinking does not need to stop there.

Self-awareness can help you to dispute negative, limiting thoughts: to argue with them; to view and acknowledge them as habits of mind only and not as absolute truths that must inevitably grind you down.

What's more, these processes of inwardly disputing your own personal horror show are not much more difficult to achieve than calming any other anxious person – or a troubled child. You can soothe yourself effectively by telling yourself that *you will be able to cope*, rather than telling yourself how hopeless everything always is. (And then wondering why you are feeling overwhelmed!)

You can look for ways in which this situation is *not* like all those other disasters that have blighted your life.

You can review new possibilities (and extend your creativity).

You can make conscious and practical decisions about how to get the support or help you may need.

Using those processes you will simply be borrowing the habits of the optimistic thinker, whose more positive outlook, when faced with a difficult situation, quite automatically sustains their feelings of hope, and belief in their own survival.

INTERPRET EVENTS POSITIVELY

Pessimists use their imaginative powers to restrict their lives ('I couldn't possibly travel. Someone might attack me, steal my passport, take my money . . .').

Optimists use their imaginative powers to step beyond what other people might regard as limitations ('I'm short of funds but

I've decided to travel anyway. I hope I'll pick up some casual work, and even if I don't I will have a marvellous time').

The crucial difference between an optimist and a pessimist, therefore, is in the way they appraise their possibilities – not whether they are 'lucky' or not. Of course it may be good fortune if someone fairly naturally thinks in ways that are creative and self-encouraging. But the story does not end there.

Any halfway optimistic thinker can discover that, far from being ruled by their thoughts and living at their mercy, their thoughts in fact are not inevitable, nor beyond their power to affect.

To discover this power for yourself, you need do no more than briefly observe your own thoughts. Watching your thoughts, you will discover a precious sliver of distance between yourself and your thoughts. And that it's possible to say and to experience: *I have thoughts; I am not my thoughts.*

It might help you to put this book down, close your eyes, and in your mind's eye observe your thoughts. ('I'm not having any thoughts' is a thought!)

As you watch your thoughts coming and going for a minute or two, much as you might in any period of reflection or meditation, you will experience for yourself that your thoughts are not the same entity as you. If they were, your observing self could neither track nor watch them.

Most of us identify so closely with our thoughts that we miss that fantastic little gap of opportunity that exists between ourselves and whatever it is we are thinking. More significantly, we miss the crucial choice that this gap offers.

It's in that gap of awareness that you can begin to play with the idea that your thoughts are truly not inevitable. No matter how doom laden your family of origin was, or how habituated you yourself are to thinking grimly and feeling worse, you can learn to think differently. And you can certainly learn quite fast to be intel-ligently self-encouraging.

There will be countless times of course when you'll be so wound up or so comfortable and unselfconscious that your thoughts will simply take their course. And that's fine. In fact, it's wonderful. Breaks from self-consciousness are always welcome, which is why we love laughter so much, or sport or cheerful sex, or good times with friends, or work or creative pursuits that 'carry us away' from self-examination and everyday concerns.

But when you recognise that yet again you are at risk of falling into gloomy, pessimistic thinking, or into critical or indirect patterns of communication with other people – and you are willing to question those habits – *you can rapidly learn to guide yourself differently.*

It's not hard to see how your communications with other people also reinforce and reflect your own thinking. If you want to diminish negative habits of thought, you must hold back your criticisms and complaints – or silence them. You need to switch your attention to what's pleasing and *speak about that.* You might want to let some petty injustices pass into oblivion. And initiate and seek out conversations that are adventurous and free ranging.

Any shift in your habits of pessimistic thinking will have immediate benefits for the people around you. Just as vitally, your view of your own life will lift remarkably.

YOUR THOUGHTS INFLUENCE YOUR FEELINGS

To observe your own thoughts – and assess how they are affecting your mood or interactions with other people – may seem somewhat unnatural or awkward, at least at first. But few of the skills that are most helpful to us are entirely natural. We become skilled at what we practise. And we become skilled quickly when we experience instant benefits with little extra effort.

These are not benefits for you to experience at the thinking level only. Certainly interrupting familiar patterns of thought, thinking more broadly and with a greater sense of possibility means that your vision will extend and become more inclusive. But it's not possible to think about thinking in any meaningful way without also thinking about feelings and emotions.

What we pay attention to – and how we think about it – profoundly influences what and how we feel. Emotions may seem more powerful than thoughts. This is perhaps because they are often experienced more directly than thoughts are. And it's clear from how quickly we learn something when our emotions are engaged, or how vividly we remember events when we were profoundly elated or disturbed, that thoughts and feelings are in a constant process of interaction. Nevertheless, in thinking about living more encouragingly, it's essential to know that it is our habits of thought that more usually influence our emotions, rather than the other way around. In other words, *pay more attention to your attitudes and thoughts* – and your feelings will come right along with them.

Consider this: can you remind yourself of all your unfinished tasks and feel euphoric? Can you think about a recent hurt you have sustained without feeling sad – or numb? Can you finish a difficult work assignment or hear from a friend after a long time without feeling delighted? Can you remember a time when you 'talked yourself into (or out of) something' and the shift in feelings that went with that experience?

It's true that if you are in the grip of a serious depression, your mood could be so low that encouraging thoughts will ring hollow. At such times, psychotherapy and antidepressant medication may help re-establish the essential inner space that allows you to think more self-supportively.

If you are grieving that's also a time when you may be overwhelmed with feelings of sadness and loss. More routinely, though, how you see and interpret events, and talk about them to yourself, will affect you way beyond the experience of the events themselves.

A client visits me for the second time. Charley is a delightful, fairly shy woman in her mid-fifties. She has given up paid work after many years and is taking on new creative interests. She has the time and financial independence to do this. All that stands in the way of a thoroughly satisfying life are her own well-developed feelings of inadequacy and insufficiency.

We talk about those feelings. We look at a couple of situations where they emerge most strongly. I invite Charley to see the feelings themselves less critically. For years she has been calling them 'bad', and has been afraid of them. Sometimes they have felt more powerful than she is: keeping her from seeing friends, persuading her to give up her classes, and making work and social situations much more stressful than they have to be.

I encourage Charley to look at those feelings differently: *to think about them differently.* A shift in the power balance between herself and her feelings is possible. She begins to observe her feelings; she isn't overwhelmed by them.

It certainly is too bad that they have kept Charley from some activities and social situations in the past. But now, in the present, I wonder if she could afford to see those familiar thoughts – and the feelings that accompany them – more neutrally: 'Here they come again. And soon they will be gone.' From that stance the thoughts may be as persuasive and the feelings may be just as uncomfortable, but they don't need to determine what Charley can or cannot do.

Before we get to that, though, I am curious to know more about the content of the thoughts that drive those feelings.

Charley makes herself comfortable on my big yellow sofa. She closes her eyes, thinks for a while. Then she tells me that, as a child, she wasn't good at anything. She pauses, then corrects herself: 'I was good at sport and good at school, but I wasn't good at anything else.'

'What else was there?' I ask.

'Things at home, with my mother. I was clumsy. I did every-thing wrong.'

I ask her for an example. She explains that her mother would want her to cut the cheese, but she always cut it clumsily and incorrectly.

I ask her, 'Did the cheese taste any different because it wasn't cut well?'

Charley laughs. And immediately gets the point. Her fear of cut-ting cheese – which became in her adulthood a fear of doing almost anything that could be assessed and judged by others – had blinded her to the lovely experience of eating cheese, tasting it, enjoying *the process* of eating it, and *the process* of many later experiences also.

Over a few more meetings, Charley and I returned to this theme several times.

Habits of critical or self-negating thought are not corrected in a moment. They need to be regarded with patience, even curiosity.

It's curiosity that reminds us of the useful distance between the thinker and the thoughts: the space where new thoughts can come in; where discouraging thoughts and attitudes can be disputed, or where more inclusive and encouraging thoughts can be tried out.

Each time she practised, Charley became a little more curious and a little more confident that she could step back imaginatively from her most judgemental thoughts, and – when she could sense that they no longer held her in their grip – lose her fear of them.

There were situations when she still felt fearful no matter what she told herself. But she learned not to blame herself for this. Nor did she fight her own thoughts or attempt to ban them. Instead Charley practised paying them less attention and turning her atten-tion instead to the process she was in, reminding herself when she needed to of the sharp, memorable pleasures of tasting cheese – however imperfectly it has been cut.

Expecting and opening to happiness is no small thing. It is the foundation of a spiritual life built on love. At a more everyday level, psychological and social research also assure us that optimists have more friends, more fun and a more intact sense that life is worth living. They also have better sex (or perhaps just feel better about the sex they are having). They live longer, and recover more quickly from illnesses as well as setbacks. They get the best jobs and can leave those jobs most easily when they feel ready to put paid work behind them.

As alluring as that description is, however, the truth is that probably few of us are wholly pessimistic or wholly optimistic. You may be optimistic about your work, for example, and less confident or hopeful about your private life (does that explain most workaholics?). You may be creative, adventurous, successful – yet continue to fret about whether you have locked the front door, turned off the iron, written your assignment well enough or remembered to tell your partner to heat their own casserole.

Wherever we are in the scale of things, it is helpful to return repeatedly to this simple truth: that the crucial difference between a pessimist and an optimist lies in how they perceive life itself and *what they tell themselves about it.*

CREATE YOUR HAPPINESS

To discover that you can lose defensiveness and mistrust and achieve the loving connections you long for, it is essential that the core beliefs running through your mind support and enhance your life. 'The effectiveness of your being in the world depends on the value you give your own existence and the existence of everything else irrespective of how it behaves,' says Gestalt teacher Howard Adams. 'If you present as a fool, people will believe you, especially if you also act like a fool. But the fact is that you exist, that you are alive, and *you have the potential for bliss and wisdom.*'

Listening over many years to the labyrinthine ways in which

people put themselves down, limit their dreams, talk at length about what's bothering them and fleetingly or not at all about what pleases them and brings them joy, it seems all too easy to forget the innate 'bliss and wisdom' of our own natures.

I wonder sometimes if most of us know how to be even as encouraging to ourselves as almost any coach of an under-twelves neighbourhood soccer team would be. Do we even feel *entitled* to be that encouraging?

Our most fundamental nature is *not* reflected in the irritations, disappointments and grievances that occupy us so intensely. But it may be that even contemplating the idea of happiness is, for many people, a greater risk than they dare to take. The contemporary Tibetan Buddhist teacher Sogyal Rinpoche has said, 'Human beings can enjoy a lot of suffering, but very little happiness.' For many people this seems painfully true.

What holds us back is not a simple question of intelligence. Nor is it an issue of how positive our affirmations are. There are times when we need to take a more global look at our lives to move ourselves along, for the truth is, we often 'improve ourselves' in tiny patches when actually we could be doing something that is simpler as well as more effective and profound.

What stands between us and happiness?

No matter how intellectually able we are, many of our conversations with ourselves are fatalistic or terminally boring. *We need to wake up to that.*

We drive ourselves like slave-owners. We rehearse failure. We replay disappointments and frustrations. We torment, denigrate and belittle ourselves. Or we pack ourselves around so tightly with cotton wool that we can barely breathe and certainly cannot meet life with strength and spontaneity. *We need to wake up to that.*

We are also fascinated by our own terrors, picking at them like scabs on a sore that magnetises us. *We need to wake up to that.*

We fear disappointment – so don't aim too high. We fear having our expectations dashed – so don't expect too much. We fear the loss of contentment and satisfaction so greatly that we avoid those precious experiences.

Wishing to save ourselves, we hide from our own potential for 'bliss and wisdom', and then wonder 'Why am I not happy?'

We need to wake up to that. Lovingly.

Parental or societal injunctions not to 'show off', 'get too big for your boots', risk a 'swollen head' or 'hope for too much' reflect those tragic fears of unworthiness and insufficiency. So does the awful notion that you must pay for whatever happiness life has brought you. Or that in the wake of happiness comes defeat.

Many people carry these deep-seated fears into adulthood and unconsciously suffer because of them throughout their lives. They may be particularly highly developed among people raised in religious traditions that emphasise humankind's original sin and tendencies to evil, or where the God of infinite compassion is reduced to a petty despot in need of continual appeasement. But even when people have been raised with confidence in their own capacity for goodness, those beliefs can still trip them up.

The sad thing is, in all its forms and whatever its origins, such thinking *is* incredibly powerful. But in the opposite way from the practitioner's intention.

We take charge of our lives most effectively by formulating positive intentions; setting goals that encourage and vitalise us and reach out to include other people; visualising successful outcomes; aligning our best possible intentions with our actions; and setting what we want in motion. *This process creates our happiness.*

Doing the opposite – rehashing old injuries and fears, allowing visions of disaster to fill our minds, telling ourselves why we can't live fully – we don't stave off suffering; we are already suffering. We are effectively creating our own limitations.

TRUST YOUR CAPACITY FOR SURVIVAL

Fear of suffering shackles our lives. Yet this too is needless. Suffering is always unwelcome, it's true. Sometimes it is horrifying and tragic. What's also true, though, is how inevitably we limit ourselves if we dread suffering or fear pain or disappointment so much that we tell ourselves we can't or couldn't ever cope with it.

There is no quick fix for suffering. Grief and devastation need to be survived first of all – not more than that – then gone beyond. Nevertheless, even in extreme circumstances, we are more emotionally robust than many of us may believe. And that is especially true when we can support ourselves inwardly.

In the living of a fully engaged life, we will all suffer. *And we can recover.* This doesn't mean that we will be unchanged. On the contrary. But if we are fortunate, the experience may teach us that we share the experiences of sorrow and loss with all other human beings. And that we share with them also our capacity for laughter, goodwill, resilience, recovery and survival.

To fear suffering less – and to break free of its limitations – it is helpful to see even the worst experiences of suffering within the context of a whole lifetime. Then it becomes possible to say, 'This hurts terribly. It's beyond me to imagine a time when this won't hurt at every waking moment. But if I look around I see others who have suffered and who have, in their own way and time, gone beyond that suffering to pick up life again.'

This movement towards recovery is something I have thought about deeply in my own life. Without consciously recognising what I was doing, each of my two novels – written more than a decade apart – turned out to be at least in part about the experience of loss and grief and the remaking of a different life from what had gone before.

I know that the obsessiveness that grief and pain can arouse may be, for a time, a version of madness. We should observe that always with great care. But even the most extreme loss does eventually become somewhat less anguished, somewhat less constant. Life itself is dynamic. Through our senses it invites us to rejoin it. Life, moving through us, moves us along quite inevitably. There is no disloyalty to those we mourn to acknowledge that.

But perhaps this is something that needs to be experienced at first-hand really to be understood. When I talked about the obsessive nature of early grief with Tom, a friend now in his mid-forties, he told me the story of a contemporary who in their last year of school together killed himself because the girl he loved couldn't or didn't love him.

The story was deeply familiar to Tom. He has thought about it often. Yet his retelling of it rocked us both. We sat together in silence first, then talked not only of the despair that Tom's friend must have felt, and the utter devastation for his family, but also of our awareness of just how extreme our own feelings of need or love also were at that same age. What made this loss most poignant for us was how conscious we were of the harsh reality that people whom he or I had loved or longed for during our teens or twenties were now not even part of our conscious memories.

The causes of depression and hopelessness are always complex. But to have ended a life over a love affair that might by now have been largely forgotten adds up to an especially bitter loss.

We give ourselves the best chance of experiencing happiness by trusting that *if we are hurt we can recover.* And that we can, in this present moment, embrace and welcome happiness in all its forms.

MAKE IT EASY FOR OTHERS TO LOVE YOU

The way we think about ourselves impacts crucially on our emotional relationships. Through our attitudes and beliefs, at least as much as through the behaviours that flow from them, we are continually making it easier or more difficult for others to love us.

Here's a familiar example.

You tell someone close to you that you need to spend more time on your own. That person could hear this as a rejection. Or they could hear you say that you want to spend more time on your own.

The person who hears it as a rejection of them doesn't want that to happen. Yet it does. And why? Because that interpretation *fits the way they already see the world.*

This is not because they are stupid or neurotic. Or out to drive you crazy. It is much more likely to be because over the course of a lifetime, partly through habit and partly through temperament, they have created at least two unhelpful patterns of call and response. The first is to see everything from their own point of view ('It must be me she wants to get away from'). The second is to bring the most catastrophic interpretations of events to the fore *even when the evidence before their eyes confounds those interpretations.*

You might be shouting by now, 'All I want is some time alone. I have my own needs. It has NOTHING to do with you!' But the other person can hear only the clamouring of their own anxieties, which assure them that, no matter what you say, what you really, truly mean is 'I want to spend much less time with you.'

It is difficult and sometimes even tragic to be the person who views the world through the complicated prism of fear and abandonment. But it must be said it is also difficult to try to love that person. Consolation, respect, adoration can be poured into someone but if the dominant voices they hear are those in their own mind that warn them of disaster, then they will continue to feel fearful and horribly empty. And the person who tries to love them will continue to feel useless and rejected.

To make it easy for others to love you, or simply enjoy your company socially or in your community or workplace, it is essential that you are willing to risk receiving what they want to give you without automatically pushing it away or finding reasons why whatever it is that you've been offered is disappointing, wrong or unacceptable. It is also essential that you pause to ask whether your interpretations of other people's behaviours are *routinely* pessimistic – and if they are, that you recognise your power to change those interpretations.

In this, as in so many painful relationship issues, the crucial starting point is not with the other person and what they are doing. Much more significant than that are the attitudes, feelings and thoughts *you have about yourself.*

If you believe in a deep way that you are unlovable, or that other people are inevitably treacherous or cruel or just disappointing, then you will test, push away and punish any poor person who tries to approach you with kindness, interest or love.

VALUE YOUR LIFE – AND YOURSELF

Helping yourself to accept and hold onto what other people are attempting to give you, you have no choice but to risk a profound change in attitude. Yet what do you have to lose? You *can* learn to think about yourself more encouragingly. You *can* learn to see those self-denigrating thoughts and fear-laden attitudes for what they are: not eternal truths cast in stone but a painful, unhelpful series of habits that can be transformed.

You may want consciously to acknowledge that the time for thinking about yourself and other people negatively and fearfully is over. You no longer need that restriction. You may want to spend some time each day practising seeing yourself and other people as though through the eyes of an infinitely compassionate and accepting divinity, or an ideal friend. You may want to find help from a companion or therapist who can hold steady the fragments of your image of yourself as a lovable person until those fragments meld and you feel trusting and fully alive.

But that companion or therapist, no matter how skilled, cannot do the crucial work for you. An act of will as well as an act of love is called for here. A different belief must somehow take hold within you: 'I value my own life. I am open to receiving love and giving it. I welcome the kindness of other people.'

Jeremy is a man I worked with in therapy some years ago. From this distance, it is easy to say that his deepest and most influential problem was an absence of self-love. At the time, though, he would have described it any other way but that: difficulties with his work, problems with the girlfriends who came and went at speed, a general feeling of malaise and dissatisfaction.

His first attempts at therapy were also unsatisfying. He would come late, cancel late or appear for his sessions yet be distracted. If I suggested something he might think about or read, he would find reasons not to do it. On the rare occasions we made a connection, he would then either disappear for weeks or spend several sessions telling me how ridiculous therapy is and how he hated himself even for being there.

When he talked about the more practical issues he brought to our meetings – arguments with a colleague, whether to call a girlfriend with whom he was fighting, if it was worth sending his parents a Christmas gift – he usually did so in a brisk and somewhat dissociated tone that sought to assure me how trivial and boring this issue was. It was hard not to feel exhausted by his frantic but unconscious efforts to keep the emotional content of our time together to a minimum.

A year after our work began, Jeremy rang to cancel another appointment and to say he would not be coming back. I told him that he could ring me if he needed to see me again and that I would continue to think about him.

Two years later he called again. Almost the first thing he said was, 'I don't suppose you have ever thought about me, have you?' With total honesty – not least because whatever might or could have happened between us had remained so incomplete – I was able to assure him that I had indeed thought about him, that I would be happy to see him and that I could make an appointment for him the next week.

Our work began again.

Why did it take off this time? Why did I sense that a somewhat different, more vulnerable Jeremy was sitting with me in my office? Why did I feel that here at last was someone that I could slowly approach, who would allow me to approach, and would not automatically have to fight against me defensively or reject whatever I might have to offer?

There is no simple explanation. All that I can say is, something within Jeremy had shifted. Something had readied him to risk experiencing a little more closeness and a little more vulnerability than before. Perhaps a powerful unconscious yearning to have someone continue to think of him even in his absence, and to do so without being angry or blaming him for that absence, had been met. His own relationship to absence was complicated: his mother had been ill often when he was a child; his father had been emotionally volatile and frightening. But the psychoanalytic 'reasons' are only part of this story. Perhaps this intelligent man's own lack of satisfaction with living superficially had also reached its limits. Perhaps small, daily acts of good humour and connection between himself and other people had played their part in shifting positively his experience of himself.

The reasons why he found the courage to come back to therapy and continue that process are less important than that he did. This doesn't mean that he is now, even after a great deal of reflection and careful work, an unguarded man. He is still, and maybe always will be, quite defensive. That shows in his anxieties, his small persistent rituals, his swings of mood and confidence.

Nevertheless, something essential in Jeremy did wake up. *And he allowed that.* He can now receive affection from a range of people, even though he remains prickly. He can express warmth and gratitude, even if this is sometimes awkward and self-mocking. He does, I believe, now genuinely value himself and his own life. He is able to value other people also. And receive what they offer him without souring it or pushing it away.

SILENCE YOUR COMPLAINTS – FOR LOVE'S SAKE

Our relationships thrive in the presence of love. And soar in the presence of those magnificent expressions of love: courtesy, consideration, tolerance, delight, acceptance. We all know this – yet we behave as though we don't know it. We dump on the people whom we are closest to. We whine. We put ourselves down. We nitpick. We stonewall and sulk. And ceaselessly we complain.

As sensitive as we are to complaints from other people, and as much as we suffer from the litanies of self-complaint that run through our own beleaguered minds, we remain willing to moan and complain and verbally demolish other people, sometimes with little reason or provocation – and even when there *is* provocation, with little hope that this complaining will bring out the best in the other person or lead to greater mutual understanding.

In the early days of a friendship or relationship, we are generally more than willing to overlook petty offences; to put a good spin on the other person's weaknesses; and to accept their different ways of doing things as part of their individual charm. Further into the relationship or friendship, however, criticism or the prospect of criticism can hang in the air so constantly that each person is unconsciously in a state of defensiveness virtually all the time.

We need to remind ourselves that criticism is rarely encouraging. And *high levels of criticism are deadly for a relationship.*

A human relationship is at least as tender as a beautiful plant. Pouring acid onto a plant would seem grotesque. Yet many of us are willing to dump acid onto a relationship that we profess to care about. And the saddest thing of all is that often the criticism is anyway much less about the other person than it is *an expression of our own sense of frustration or lack of self-love*. But that does not excuse it; nor does it make it more tolerable.

Sufi poet Rumi suggests:

When something goes wrong, accuse yourself first.
Even the wisdom of Plato or Solomon
can wobble and go blind.

Few of us are Plato or Solomon. If we believe there must be criticism in a tense situation, then for the sake of love or mutual respect we should face the question honestly: 'For whose benefit am I risking this?'

Here is a fine example of thinking twice before criticising. It comes from Henry, an ebullient, talented artist in his early sixties. I love Henry's story, not least because along with his useful reflections on not criticising, he's also demonstrating how relationships are something we can improve at as we age.

Henry says, 'Over the last twenty years – the time for me of greatest learning about how relationships best function – I have changed my mind dramatically about the place of criticism in relationships of all kinds. Once it seemed stimulating, even invigorating, whether given or received. (But perhaps I thought more about ways to give it? I suspect so.) I now think that "talking things through", which is one of the names we give to an attempt to put another person right, is seldom useful and can be destructive.

'There are much subtler and far more effective ways of registering discontent with a trend in a relationship, or of finding its source. I have a friend at present who has, in my opinion, "sold out" to the official government bureaucracy she works for. She seems to me to use their language, to have adopted their way of thinking and given up a good deal of her own independence of mind. This upsets me quite a lot, but I do not see myself accusing her of such a crime. She would be outraged, disbelieving, offended – and what would I achieve? A sort of self-righteousness, I suppose; certainly not a shared reappraisal of the issues at stake.

'For the moment I am not sure what I will do. Try to steer our conversations into challenging areas to begin with, I think, so that we discuss questions of loyalty, integrity, the manifestations we both know of power manipulation. Am I trying to improve my friend? Clean up her morality? Act as her keeper? I hope not. What I think I am doing is trying to find – perhaps for my own peace of mind more than hers – whether the friend I thought I had still exists.'

To live encouragingly we must see how inevitably our own sensitivities as well as our yearnings are reflected in other people's lives. (What we don't enjoy, they may not either!) We must resist the temptation to let other people know how superior we are. Or to buy a few moments' superiority at their expense.

We help ourselves too when we decide to judge less and accept more. When we can let slights go and practise forgiveness. Our irritation with others anyway often expresses nothing more profound than that we are in need of a meal or a good night's sleep, or have taken on more responsibilities than a human being could meet.

This is what self-awareness asks of us: that we should *recognise our own emotional states and limit our demands on other people.*

EXPRESS YOUR PLEASURE AND CONCERN

Experiencing yourself as a positive presence for others, and observing how rapidly others blossom in the presence of your interest and kindness, does wonders for your social and personal relationships. Expressing encouragement is a powerful way to live. And it benefits you also.

There are no attitudes more helpful than those that allow you to reach out to other people, care about them and accept their care in return. Encouraging others, you heal wounds, leave helplessness behind and powerfully support your own feelings of social integration, self-acceptance and self-assurance.

Eleanor's slightly complicated run of experiences shows this beautifully. She's a warm, likeable woman in her early forties, a skilled and enthusiastic administrator who gives every appearance of confidence, yet like many people she would say that her confidence has been hard won. She grew up with an alcoholic father who lived with her family until she was 6 and then, from 9 onwards, she and her older sister lived with a 'belligerent and sadistic stepfather' as well as her fairly weak and ineffectual mother.

Learning to read the emotional climate, and to minimise the eruptions that came her way, became essential to Eleanor's emotional survival. Even now, she says, she is extremely conscious of the emotional climate in most situations. 'This means that I tend to work hard at making things OK if I sense tension in the air.

'I am also acutely aware of other people's nonverbal communications. And my own. When I am sitting in a group of people I don't know, or don't feel comfortable with, I can find that my body is twisted around itself. I sometimes get a shock to look down at my physical self and see what a knot I'm in. I've usually relaxed somewhat by the time this happens and quietly untangle myself without anyone noticing.'

Those insights and the resilience Eleanor has gained through her early experiences have stood her in good stead. She is adamant about not being in the company of people who 'have no control over their own poisonous behaviour'. She is also careful to help her children understand that they have every right to step away from encounters that are harmful or draining.

Eleanor feels less confident, however, when the emotional atmosphere between herself and a person close to her is somehow charged, yet she doesn't know what's going on. She explains: 'Because I find emotional tension so upsetting, if I sense unease or tension between me and an intimate other, I have to know what is wrong. They are often not aware they are showing their feelings – or what feelings they are showing. My sensitivity to atmosphere and undercurrents of emotion can be a disadvantage sometimes. For example, when a loved one might be feeling a bit pissed off – but left alone would get over it. Once the tension is pointed out, they often feel they need to justify themselves, and the whole thing gets amplified.'

This spiralling anxiety will be familiar to many of us. Nonetheless, it's possible, and I suggested this to Eleanor also, that if you can look at the bigger picture ('Is this person usually someone I can like, trust, respect?') *and* recognise that your own anxious response to the tension can only increase it, you can generally imaginatively step back and make a more conscious decision about whether this is in fact the best possible moment to bring up your concerns.

Discussing the issue *after* the initial tension has died down is generally more productive than meeting tension with more tension. We talked about this and about the choice that Eleanor had, which was to bring 'awareness of her own anxiety' to this matter or 'awareness of her capacity for curiosity and goodwill'.

With considerable interest, Eleanor tried the more spacious approach – looking on with curiosity and goodwill – and a couple of months later was able to say, 'To my surprise, really, I have discovered I am much more able to let things ride than I would have believed. Sometimes you just have to back off from situations. I tended to want to make things better right away, to have resolution, to have things sorted out. Tie up the loose ends, and know where I stood. I am now much more open to accepting that this is not always possible. My approach can work – but not invariably. Sometimes things have to be left alone in order to be resolved or to be discussed at another time.

'As someone who is proactive and capable, as well as driven to "make things right", this has been a hard lesson for me to learn. But a valuable one.'

It *is* easy to complain. But unpleasant to experience the negativity that comes with it. To breathe more freely ourselves we must complain less and appreciate more: speaking more openly about what others do for us and how much that means to us. Finding non-verbal as well as verbal ways to express our appreciation. Delighting – and expressing our delight – not just in what the person does but also and most deeply in who they are.

That simple shift of emphasis from thinking primarily about ourselves and how others are affecting us, to thinking much more closely about the pleasure and sustenance we get from our relationships, may seem to bring us nothing special. Nevertheless, it is what will allow many petty irritations, anxieties and judgements to slide away, revealing our precious relationships and connections much more clearly.

YOU CAN AFFECT OTHERS POSITIVELY

The power to be encouraging is formidable. It makes a fundamental difference to the way that we move through this life. It creates an invitation to happiness, as well as to a good life. 'A good person,' says the contemporary Christian writer Matthew Fox, 'is looking for goodness.' *Good* in this sense does not mean pious. And it certainly does not mean separate or judgemental. On the contrary, here the idea of goodness joins with the ideals of encouragement (looking for what is good in life).

Fox goes on: 'Some people are looking for mistakes to put people down and for cynicism. But a good person is looking for goodness and when they see it, they praise . . . You begin with what's good in people and build it up . . . '

To be fully human we need to develop a social and moral conscience based on an inclusive vision of humankind. But we cannot do this by focusing on misery and injustice only. We must also look for goodness – and find innumerable ways to encourage it.

It doesn't take a high degree of personal power to affect other people. The essential issue is not whether we are affecting others: it is *how we are affecting them*. Do we leave them better off for knowing us? Or worse off?

This has little to do with how effective we may feel on any particular day. In fact, the opposite is true. A bad mood or attitude is highly contagious. On the days we feel most undone by our own difficulties, we radiate a negativity that is often hard for others to be around.

There are no outsiders in this story.

No one is exempt from that constant ebb and flow of human influence. We may choose not to recognise how we affect other people. We may tell ourselves how insignificant we are; how helpless. But that would be our loss. Knowingly or not, we leave a trail behind us, affecting others for better or for worse.

From the Hebrew Bible we can hear Solomon, the great poet-king, reminding us: 'I also am mortal, like everyone else . . . When I was born, I began to breathe the common air, and fell upon the earth we all share. My first sound was a cry, as is true of all . . . For no king has had a different beginning of existence; there is for all one entrance into life, and one way out. Therefore I prayed, and understanding was given me. I called on God, and the spirit of wisdom came to me. I preferred her to sceptres and thrones, and I counted wealth as nothing in comparison to her.'

We leave loneliness and self-centredness behind when we too can freely call on wisdom, turning outwards to ask, 'What would be most encouraging, most *loving* here?' Or inwards to discover, 'How can I best encourage myself?'

It seems evident that we would understand how directly we influence every situation in which we find ourselves. Yet when relationships break down, or fail to reach their highest potential, it is often because the people involved have paid obsessive attention to *what was being done or said to them*, but little attention to what influences they themselves were bringing to that relationship.

OPEN TO WHAT YOU WANT FROM LIFE

Bringing your ideals and behaviour closer together, talking to other people and about situations in a way that is hopeful and open, does more than send your life in a particular direction. It reminds you that you are making constant choices, whether you are conscious of this or not. And that you can love your life most easily, and even accept setbacks with least disarray, when those choices also express your best intentions.

It makes no sense, for example, to want more friends, yet stay home watching TV every evening. It's difficult to make time for reflection if you are also commuting long distances and spending sixty hours a week in a stressful job. It's useless to complain about the atmosphere at work if you yourself are bitter or disgruntled. How could you be anything but depressed if you constantly rehearse failure or prepare yourself for loss?

Living encouragingly is not something to adopt for the big events only. A commitment to living encouragingly must find its expression in the most routine moments of your life. For it's there that your power to live encouragingly can be experienced as most transforming.

Berry is a talented composer who has had years of feeling stuck in a dismal view of herself, convinced that she will never have the partner and child she passionately wants. At the age of 38, with great personal courage and professional support, Berry has achieved significant changes in the way that she thinks about herself and her own opportunities. For all that, her story does not yet have a conventional happy-ever-after ending. That's just one reason why I believe it is worth telling.

Many of our stories do not end exactly as we would wish. Yet, stilling the voices of doom and *identifying and daring to wish for something better* is worth doing. Berry discovered this.

She is quiet and fairly introverted but also capable of moments of great liveliness and brave social experiment (dancing, drumming, hiking with groups of previously unknown people). She has worked for years as a composer of serious music. This has brought her a small amount of fame and no financial security. She has worked alone largely and has frequently suffered from feelings of painful isolation, often accompanied by physical ill-health.

Throughout her adulthood Berry has had little confidence that she could attract a loving relationship – at least not while she continued to have difficulty loving or even accepting herself. 'After a very painful relationship break-up about seven years ago, which involved many lies and sexual betrayal, I avoided entering relationships,' she says. 'I came to believe a good relationship was beyond my grasp.'

Feeling shut out from what many people take for granted or as their right was an exceptionally painful experience for Berry. She could have stayed in that same emotional space, perhaps becoming more bitter or more envious of what other people have. But she chose not to do that.

'I went into therapy a year or so ago because I recognised I needed help with ongoing depression and chronic fatigue. I had to admit that a large part of my depression developed out of my lack of hope or belief in the possibility that I could ever have a loving sexual relationship with a man.

'My belief around this – what I told myself consciously and maybe accepted unconsciously – changed through the therapy, where the focus was on the relationship between my male therapist and me. The consistency and continuity of his acceptance of me, and his encouragement for me to freely express myself around him, acted as a catalyst for me to feel differently around men generally. He gave me the opportunity to feel more alive and less fearful around a man. As I found myself enjoying our relating and feeling secure in his acceptance and caring for me, I began slowly to believe both that a good relationship with a man could be possible for me, and that it was worth my while taking the risk of being attractive around men.

'I had been very secluded. I started to go out more socially and to express myself in a livelier way. I began to dress more attractively and to wear make-up. I had my hair cut differently so that I was more open and exposed to the world. I felt more "out there". I was completely conscious that I wanted to meet someone and give myself another chance with relationships.'

Over a period of several months, Berry took increasing social risks, going to more parties and to groups where she hoped she would find like-minded, stimulating people, as well as possible male friends or partners. Relating more actively and optimistically was crucial to Berry if she was to get over her earlier self-denigrating beliefs.

At a dinner party organised by a good friend who cared enough to bring some likely unmatched people together, Berry met Will, an advertising man who had a passion for music. She says, 'When I met Will I immediately experienced a huge difference in myself around him. In my own mind I had approached this possibility quite differently. I felt attractive, interesting, and entitled to ask for and engage in a good relationship.'

Few of us are likely to inspire or attract other people, or keep a mutually supportive relationship going, when the churning of our own thoughts continually reminds us why we are unlovable or why sexual love is impossible for us. Unloving thoughts about ourselves inevitably affect the way other people think about us. Even if they don't catch the drift of those actual thoughts they are affected by the emotions those thoughts arouse. Negative thinking makes us self-critical, stand-offish, judgemental, awkward, shy, needy or uncertain. *None of that is helpful to a new relationship.* Nor to a long-standing one either.

When your worst enemy is your own negative thinking, you do yourself a great disservice. As well, you make it more difficult for other people to accept you. Your inner crankiness will flow out as criticism, distrust, dissatisfaction.

Self-love; a sense that life is delicious as well as sometimes alarming; a willingness to be accepting of other people: none of these may bring the perfect person into your life. But they will radically increase your feelings of confidence and self-acceptance.

It is vital to learn how to challenge and dispute negative thinking – to see the bigger picture, *to get real.*

'Everybody's happier than I am. *Two of my workmates are about to lose their jobs.'*

'Nothing ever works out for me. *I have three close friends who love me.'*

'I am ugly, fat and undesirable. *Actually I am tolerant and funny, I like to cook for friends, and I can play sensational ragtime.'*

Nothing is more encouraging than the confidence that you can survive unhappy endings – and bring resilience and wisdom to happier days.

Berry's romance with Will did not end as Hollywood would have written it (and as we'd have wished it). Yet Berry survived that. She was ready for something new but her enthusiasm was met by an increasing withdrawal of interest on Will's side. After just a few months together, he told her that he wasn't ready to make a commitment, as much as he liked her and enjoyed their time together. It might be fair to wonder when a 42-year-old man will find himself 'ready' to make a commitment to one woman only. But that aside, this familiar scenario presented Berry with an equally familiar set of choices.

She could choose to see Will as her 'last hope'. She could tell herself, with some truth, that commitment phobia is rife among heterosexual men of a certain age, and that her chances of finding someone who is simultaneously free and interested in commitment are so slim that she would be crazy to try again.

She could also tell herself that really there is an awful lot wrong with her, and that Will's reluctance was just his way of moving on to find a woman who is more talented, lovable, younger, et cetera, et cetera, than she will ever be.

Or she could – and did – tell herself that Will had his own demons to wrestle with, *which had little or nothing to do with her.* Her chances of meeting a man capable of making a commitment need not be in any way diminished because Will's goals and desires were different from her own.

On the contrary, with considerable fortitude Berry is telling herself that she has a *greater* chance of success than before. As she says: 'At least I know that I am desirable, and that I can feel alive and comfortable in a sexual relationship. My confidence about that had been almost non-existent, and that's changed and the change has remained intact. I am really sorry that Will couldn't work something out with me. I felt we did have a lot going for us, and I hate having to start out again. However, I'm convinced that I am starting out from a better place, not a worse one.'

In the months since the relationship with Will ended, Berry has been deliberate in her efforts to avoid the traps of anger or bitterness. She points out: 'I'm not helped if I'm angry with Will. Of course I am angry with him sometimes. I wake up crying and feeling awful sometimes. But that doesn't affect him. He hasn't the faintest idea what I am feeling! Railing against him keeps me stuck in a powerless place. That's not where I want to be at all.'

Within our own minds is a place of equilibrium. From there we can learn to recognise the fluctuations of our moods, observe the thoughts that drive those moods and create attitudes that reflect and nurture our capacities for love. From that place of spaciousness, we can also recognise how and why other people cause us difficulties. *And that many of our difficulties are self-created.*

Berry is intelligent, creative and tenacious. Despite those gifts, she was able effectively to discourage herself for many years from something she wanted almost more than anything else. What's more, she was able to do this without fully recognising how she was injuring and limiting herself – and taking effective steps to change that.

Our thoughts are like a compass, turning us in this emotional direction or that. Whatever direction our thoughts take, our emotions follow and our attitudes take their shape. The quality of our thoughts – the inner coaching that we constantly give ourselves – directly affects the quality of our lives. Like the stone dropping deep into the pond, causing circles that grow in diameter the further they extend, the quality of our thoughts also affects the lives of the people we meet and influence.

The Indian peacemaker and activist Mahatma Gandhi is just one of countless teachers who have reminded us that we have essential choices to make about how we regard ourselves, other people and life itself. And whether we dare to live encouragingly. 'Man often becomes what he believes himself to be,' said Gandhi. 'If I keep on saying to myself that I cannot do a certain thing, it is possible that I may end by really becoming incapable of doing it. On the contrary, if I have the belief that I can do it, I shall surely acquire the capacity to do it, even if I may not have it at the beginning.'

There is awesome responsibility in 'becoming what we believe ourselves to be'. Yet how infinitely rich our lives become when we can take up that idea – and live by it through every day of our existence.

HOW TO

Live Encouragingly

There is nothing more attractive than the capacity to be enthusiastic, hopeful, affirming and encouraging. And this can improve and grow with age! Everything you do, each encounter that you have, benefits remarkably when you can approach it with a clear determination to make the best of it and to find the best in it. Your intimate relationships will be sustained even during times of difficulty when you can fearlessly express love and encouragement through simple words and acts of respect, delight and goodwill.

Living encouragingly also means that *you can walk away from situations that are unhealthy* – trusting in your capacity to recover and find sustaining relationships elsewhere.

It is literally life changing to discover how powerfully you can encourage yourself and influence other people by doing not much more than curtailing old habits of negativity and instead *thinking positively and supportively*.

Encouragement is not expressed through words of praise only. Those are usually precious and welcome. But living encouragingly goes much deeper than that. It creates an attitude towards life itself that is tolerant, generous, respectful, trusting, resilient; that allows you to believe in other people, trust in their goodness, want the best for them – and no less for yourself.

- Know how powerful your own thoughts are. Nothing influences your outlook, mood or relationships more than the quality of your thoughts.

- Notice *how your feelings change* when you think positively, look for solutions, notice what's pleasing, or allow yourself to be stimulated, enchanted or inspired.
- Know what makes you happy, relaxed, delighted. Do more of it.
- Look for what's affirming, possible, fascinating, positive; talk it up; make it happen.
- Know what your persistent internal messages are. Listen in. Write them down. If they breed pessimism, *change them.*
- Don't blame other people for messages that limit your life. Move on.
- Create positive *inner* messages ('My life is precious. I love my life. These are my gifts. I can learn from what life brings me. This risk is worth taking. My efforts have value. I can let go of hurts. I can open my heart to others').
- Believe in yourself – and something greater than yourself.
- See yourself as someone good to be around. Easy to like. *Be* that person.
- Practise commenting positively ('I love the way you . . . ', 'Thank you so much for . . . ', 'Congratulations on . . .', 'What a beautiful . . . ', 'I have been so helped by . . . ', 'It was such fun when . . . '). Make this a way of life.
- Notice how encouraging others benefits you. Everyone wins.
- Give freely *because you can.* Not because you need rewards. That keeps you a slave to other people's whims.
- *Never* miss a chance to express gratitude. It's sublimely encouraging.
- Let slights, small hurts, unintended insults or losses go by. You will feel amazingly liberated. (And so will everyone else within your orbit.) This alone can transform your relationships.
- Don't blame others, whine or criticise. Turn your attention to what's rewarding; to what you can appreciate; to what others have done for you; to what you can do for them.
- Encourage others to talk to you about what's going well in

their lives – what excites or deeply interests them. *Listen.*

- Don't wait for other people to 'make things better'. Do it yourself. And discover that you *can.*
- Allow yourself to be inspired. Lift your gaze.
- Pay attention to what you *already* have. Praise what is *already* pleasing. Comment out loud on what is *already* satisfying.
- Taking someone for granted? Remember: that's profoundly *dis*couraging and distancing.
- Notice how other people affect you through their moods and attitudes. Recognise you affect them similarly – *no matter how powerless you feel.*
- Avoid negative people and situations whenever possible.
- Cut regular complainers short ('How are you planning to change that?').
- Ask a friend or partner to stop you short if you routinely complain about a situation you can't change or influence.
- Use habits of criticism, self-pity or self-disparagement like a meditation bell, reminding you such thoughts are habits only. Stop at once. You *can* live encouragingly.
- Challenge your defeatism ('This situation *is* different', 'I know more than I used to', 'I can get help', 'I am moving on').
- Avoid saying 'should', 'ought', 'must' or 'have to'. Those words make you a slave. Use 'will', 'can' or 'want to'. Or see the task neutrally ('There's a deadline for this project', 'It's time to pick up the kids').
- Avoid negative ruminations. Read something uplifting. Call an enthusiastic friend. Tackle something physically demanding.
- Find ways to say what *can* be done, what *can* be learned, what *is* enjoyable, what *is* possible.
- Record what you are *learning from major or recurrent disappointments* ('I need to focus and define my goals, perhaps with the help of a friend'). Turn dust to gold.
- If you catch yourself 'catastrophising' ('I never get what I

want', 'I always screw things up'), *dispute that* ('Today I really enjoyed . . .').

- *Do what needs to be done* even if you feel low. Your feelings will change as the task or event progresses. Often the hardest step to take is the initial one.
- Identify the strengths you are developing. *Value them in others* ('Your patience was great with that difficult customer').
- Think creatively ('How would my hero or ideal self respond here?'). Simple tasks done creatively, with a note of beauty, are powerfully uplifting.
- Talk about solutions not problems. Ask yourself, 'What would help? What am I aiming to achieve?'
- When you have a difficulty with another person, speak about it collaboratively ('How can we work through this?').
- Recognise the body language of anxiety, depression or despair. Don't slump. *Move.*
- In a disappointing situation salvage whatever's instructive or pleasing ('The store was closed – but we had a great drive', 'We didn't win – but we've refined our pitch').
- Act 'as if' you're already skilled at living encouragingly. Soon you will be.
- *Believe in love.* Allow love to awaken and encourage you freshly every day of your life.

Jim's Story

Jim is an inner-city youth worker in his twenties: a tall, thin man with bright, dark eyes, shaved head, a contagious sense of fun and an inspiring commitment to his work. The young people he works with have long ago been abandoned by the educational system. They are unlikely to find paid work and the status that comes with that. They are exceptionally vulnerable to the ill-effects of drugs, prostitution and despair.

Jim has more reason than most of us to see contemporary society solely as ugly and unjust. Yet he is able to model for his clients a tenacious, energetic belief that life itself is good even though it inevitably throws up many challenges – and more to some than to others.

This modelling of a tenacious belief that even a difficult life is absolutely worth living – and has value – is probably far more helpful than anything Jim could say.

It's easy to love humanity from a distance or to be high minded about your principles where there is no personal cost. What impresses me are people who can work in difficult situations while maintaining their personal humility *as well as* their confidence in humankind. Sometimes that arises from conscious spiritual values or a belief in the divinity within every human being. In Jim's case, this isn't so.

'I don't have any worked-out spiritual or religious beliefs as such,' he says. 'But I'm not ready to give up on young people who've not had much chance yet.

'Also I'm helped because I've got a really fanatical belief that a lot of streetwise kids who've had to use their wits to survive are in a really good space to learn some of the tricks of positive self-image. Or the encouragement you're talking about. I don't mean "tricks" in the bad sense of getting something across other people. I mean it in the sense of feeling more empowered than you are supposed to feel when your family's dead or doesn't want you and the youth refuge is pretty much a dump!'

I asked Jim to give me an example of what he means.

'I teach them that what matters most in trying to get along with other people is realising how much in control of the atmosphere you are. They don't realise that until they are told. Well, most people don't realise that. People almost always think the other person holds all the cards. It's not so.

'If you come on aggressively, that's the atmosphere you have to swim in. If you come on like a victim, then the atmosphere all around you is tainted. If you're open and friendly, except in really foul situations (when you should just get out fast), that's how you get other people to see you too. We see this as a mind thing and a body thing. We use role play to illustrate it. We get the guys to test out for themselves how different they feel when they are playing the role of someone in a powerful position – a banker, say, or a really centred martial arts master. Girls and guys do this. We make no differences here.

'We literally coach them, step by step, to experiment with what kinds of thoughts they imagine run through the mind of someone like that. We talk about "fuelling the walk with the talk". We coach them far less about the physical gestures – they seem to pick up on that really easily! These guys have watched thousands of hours of TV. They know what repertoire of body language, facial expression and gesture belongs with this or that set of attitudes. The only thing they don't know, at least until they are told, is how to experiment with using a much greater range of body language themselves –

and then playing around with the kind of inner monologue or way of thinking that they imagine goes with it.'

As simple as it is, what Jim's describing is a partial answer at least to chronic feelings of powerlessness in anybody's life.

Jim says, 'There *is* real powerlessness in these guys' lives. Abuse, neglect, violence, racism: you name it. It's a question, though, of either giving up hope that things could be different, or of realising even in a small way that you can tilt the power balance: you can be as much a "person" in any encounter as anyone else, even though that other person may have advantages you don't. We say, "You don't have to respond from a weak place. *You can be the one to set the tone.* You can guide the quality of the interaction."'

Jim's work with his clients does not ignore the harsh social realities that they are facing. It is extremely tough to be young, tense, hostile and socially and educationally disadvantaged. *Those obvious difficulties are increased when the inner monologue of that person is also self-defeating. And when their physical posture reflects a sense of hopelessness.* This might happen through body language that is arrogant, abusive or aggressive. It might happen through a physical attitude that is collapsed in upon itself and is heavy, slow, sorrowful, self-pitying or excessively shy.

For almost anyone, whatever their age, social or cultural background, experiencing a physical shift in that posture of helplessness supports a sense of renewed hope and potential. It short-circuits the inner monologue that goes with a sunken or defended body. And it expresses an upbeat note – a sense of possibility – to which other people can more positively respond.

Trust

Others

Self-preservation is only the second law of life.

The first law is that you and the other are one.

JOSEPH CAMPBELL

I know! I know! Give people an inch and they will take a mile. Only a fool would leave himself wide open. You can't judge a book by its cover. A bird in the hand is worth however many in the bush. All cats are grey in the dark and most grapes are sour.

For all that, the capacity to give and to receive trust, to extend to others the benefit of the doubt, to wish other people well and to assume they wish you well also is the essential good oil that keeps the wheels of our relationships turning. Where trust is not present, suspicion rushes in to fill the space; doubt erodes good-will; faults and disappointments are all that we notice and moments of delight or satisfaction are quickly tainted.

Trust begins and ends with how we think about life itself. It thrives when we can lift our attention away from the cracks and fissures, the disappointments and frustrations of human existence, and relish the thought, 'I can survive this.'

Your partner has left you. Your mother has dementia. There are serious problems at work. The dog has gone deaf. But, somehow or another – during a walk early on a crisp morning, listening to an old Bob Marley track, celebrating the joy of a friend, writing a long letter to someone you care about – you find a few moments in which you can rally and recognise: life continues.

You also remember: the gift of life is infinitely precious. You can trust that.

Trust builds openness, stamina, flexibility, resourcefulness, resilience, strength of character. (That's quite a list!) It fosters optimism. It deepens your connections with other people. It sets you free to think the best of them – even when this is not immediately convenient or to your obvious advantage.

Just as crucially, when trust is something you think about and value, you can be confident that you are giving other people reason to trust you: to experience you as thoughtful, reliable, a keeper of confidences, good humoured, truthful, supportive, kind.

DISCOVER THE SPACIOUSNESS OF TRUST

Love requires that you should be open, even vulnerable. Love makes it possible to risk that ('Better to have loved and lost than never to have loved at all!'). Opening to a more loving way of life, you may find that the most radical change you can make is moving from a mind-set of anxiety or suspicion, of worrying routinely about the worst that might happen, to a more spacious state of mind that allows you just as routinely to expect and look for the best, aware that *if something does go wrong you can and will recover.*

This shift in attitude depends much less on other people and how well or badly they behave than it does on self-trust: the way that you think about yourself ('I can face what comes'). It also depends on your own capacity to move beyond disappointment or judgementalism to see what is honest, satisfying, rewarding: what is worthy not only of your trust but also of your positive encouragement.

Because it's self-trust that largely sets the tone of your encounters – rather than whether other people are agents of good or evil! – trust of others can extend way beyond your intimate connections to the most banal and everyday interactions with others. Trust does not mean blind faith. Nevertheless, as you begin to think about trust itself more generously, you are likely to find you lose the need constantly to second guess situations and other people.

Through your own positive attitude, and especially through the resilience that brings, you *create* a more trusting environment.

Trust deepens a crucial belief: 'Good things happen to me.' (The smell of springtime jasmine from a neighbour's vine; the taste of butter on crusty bread; the purr of the cat as it makes itself at home on your lap; the hilarity of a shared joke at the office water cooler; a difficult job successfully completed; an unexpected opportunity opening up.) Just as vitally, a trusting stance *invites* good things to happen.

The attitude that you bring to your encounters significantly enhances or limits your opportunities for rewarding interactions. And attitude is certainly something you can consciously affect, not least through noting what you are thinking, and changing towards a more encouraging way when that's needed. Simply by reminding yourself that other people's intentions are generally benign, and that anyway you are free to recover from loss or disappointment, you will inevitably feel safer *and* much more adventurous.

The child who pulls herself up from a crawling position in a brave attempt to stand for the first time is driven by her genetic impulses to become a fully mobile human being. *To the very end of our lives we have equivalent opportunities.* But we are free to take them only if we believe in ourselves and in life itself; only if we have sufficient trust that 'falling to the ground' even a hundred times is a small price to pay for a dramatically increased awareness of our own capacity to connect with other people, expecting the best of them and expecting the best of ourselves.

A trusting person is not a fool. On the contrary, that person is wise. And especially wise to the fact that the occasional misunderstanding, crushed hope or even betrayal will affect them far less than living in a state of constant watchfulness, caution and suspicion.

Giving others the benefit of the doubt, assuming the best about them and recognising that you can afford to be generous and encouraging, rather than defensive, not only feels fantastic, it is also extremely attractive. It lets other people know that they can be relaxed in your company. The 'best in you' brings out the best in them.

Your good intentions may never be articulated. These crucial messages are generally subliminal as well as instantaneous. But this openness of mind and spirit is something that people easily warm to.

TRUST AND LOVE GO TOGETHER

If you love or care about someone, it is vital to trust them. An absence of trust undermines any relationship. It sets traps for the other person. It pushes you to look for what might be wrong rather than to see what's right. It activates fear – and the illusion that someone else must behave in proscribed ways for *you to feel safe*. It tempts you to interpret even the most innocent situations in a way that will feed or confirm your suspicions.

Trusting others reflects and consolidates the positive way you think about yourself. It becomes possible also to use your instincts more freely: to know how to avoid the worst, *because you don't automatically see it everywhere*. And how to expect and welcome the best.

Trust is tested often. And never more than in times of upheaval.

A mother comes to see me. Her 16-year-old son wants to go to live with his father in a distant city. Why is that a problem? The father has barely seen the son since he was four. The father himself is childish, feckless. The mother suspects he takes drugs. She doesn't trust his values. She's never liked his friends. But the boy wants to go. He is desperate to go. With her, he lives in a secure environment. He goes to a good school. He is well liked in their neighbourhood. Despite that, he is fixed on this opportunity. She wants to warn him his actual father may not be the father of his yearnings. She wants to suggest a compromise. He's a teenager, though. His world is black and white. He doesn't want a compromise. That feels like a loss to him.

The mother and I talk more. We talk about trust. Her trust of her son; her difficulties trusting his father; her anguish about whether she is making the right decision even when it feels as though it is not her decision to make.

There seems no choice but to let him go. Holding on, she would be placing a noose around her boy.

Maybe it will go well. And if it doesn't? If her son's hopes of his father are dashed, if he falls in with a cynical crowd or takes drugs himself: what then?

Even then, somehow, that mother will need to hold onto and cultivate her capacity to trust. She may need to trust more broadly. And, like every other parent of a near-adult child, she must learn how to disentangle issues of trust from issues of control. She cannot impose the script she most wants her son to live out. She is about to experience his separateness abruptly and precipitously. Perhaps for many months her capacity to trust will go underground. But at some point she will need to retrieve it because, without trust, hope and intimacy are also absent.

We think too narrowly about trust, I believe, and confuse it with control. And then we risk everything on whether just a few fallible people turn out to be worthy of the mighty gift that we are giving them.

'I'll never trust another man,' a young heterosexual woman says in the heat of a raw break-up with her boyfriend of five years. 'I'll never trust another woman,' says a father of two little children, bitter at the way his wife has become a stranger since they parted. 'I could only do business with my own family now,' says a middle-aged entrepreneur, hurting from a financial betrayal. 'You don't know how agonising it is not to be able to trust your own children,' a mother says to me when she discovers that two of her three young adult children have been stealing from her to finance their drug habits. And when he discovers that his father has left all his wealth to his two brothers, a wounded man berates himself: 'I must have been such a fool. It never even crossed my mind he would do this. Now I feel as if he never cared about me and that I have been lied to all my life.'

It is always possible that someone will betray us. It may happen repeatedly. People can let us down even though they are not particularly bad but simply thoughtless or trapped in their own self-centredness. Sometimes they are 'bad' of course, in the sense that they are ruthless, self-serving, bitter or aggrieved.

Breaking someone's trust knowingly is an act of aggression. If you are on the receiving end, it hurts.

Yet to live an emotionally healthy life, you need to trust people *and* relinquish the need to control them. You need to feel open to others, willing both to like and expect good things from them, *and* to accept that their choices and yours will not always coincide.

Most of all you need to surrender your own desire that people should behave in specific ways to make you feel safe.

Of course we all want other people to be predictable, reliable, trustworthy. That's quite reasonable! And we should certainly cultivate those capacities ourselves consciously and deliberately so that other people can experience them from us. But the safety of our inner world, and our stance in the outer world, need not depend on other people's behaviour.

Because trust is such a crucial element in the way we see the world, we need to build it on something more substantial, more universal and more deeply rooted than the reactions or behaviour of the people moving in and out of our immediate orbit. Trust can be given most freely when it is seen as an expression of belief in humanity and our innate goodness, *no matter how some individuals behave*. In that context trust can be given for its own sake. Then whether it has been sufficiently appreciated or honoured in return becomes far less relevant.

A NEW FREEDOM TO TRUST

Trust can be given – *because we are free to give it.* We are free also to think the best of ourselves. And the best of other people. And when they disappoint us, as inevitably they sometimes will, our capacity to trust reassures us we can recover from that *and move on.* Trusting others itself expresses love and tolerance. It supports a desire for the best possible outcomes between ourselves and other people. It makes possible all kinds of adventures, conversations, insights, shared experiences. It soothes misunderstandings. It heals. It bridges difference and it allows us to relish difference.

Trust does something else that's quite wonderful. It requires us to recognise and take note that no one in our lives – no matter how precious – is a possession.

We live alongside each other. We care for each other. Our lives are enhanced by the existence of other people. But trust demands that we bring to our own lives its essential meaning. Doing that, we free ourselves also to see others as who they really are: people linked to us but also with their own destiny, their own spiritual and psychological lessons to learn, their own unique gifts and failings, their own lives in which we can, at best, incompletely share.

Our children are not our possessions. Whatever it costs us, we must see them as distinct people, not as our children only. We must, in appropriate stages, let them go, let them become themselves. And we must do so *because we love them.*

Our employees are certainly not our possessions. They have every right to interests and commitments outside their paid work; yet, increasingly, employers behave as if this were not true. The demands of many workplaces are now so excessive that when employees ask for time that actually already belongs to them, the employer or the manager often behaves like a betrayed lover. But they have no right to do so.

Our partners are also not our possessions. We diminish them

when we see them only in relation to ourselves. We confuse neediness with love, trust with control, self-interest with interest.

Issues around trust are particularly delicate with sexual partners. And with good reason. We feel emotionally and spiritually as well as physically naked with sexual partners: stripped of the masks of invulnerability we put on to move through everyday life.

Trust supports sexual intimacy. And so do fidelity and commitment. Yet here too trust must be patiently disentangled from the wish to control or limit. Trust is an expression of love, and love is not love when it is not freely given. This does not mean that either partner is free to abuse the trust of the other. On the contrary, each is *free to be trustworthy* not out of fear, but for love's sake only.

Preparing to write this book, I found a hunger in people for the giving and receiving of trust that surprised me. 'I could trust him (or her) with my life' emerged as a passionate expression of gratitude as well as love. People spoke too about their longings to create and be part of communities where trust could extend to strangers and where strangers could be trusted like friends. Women and men talked of the exceptional sense of connection and possibility that they associated with trusting and being trusted.

'My partner absolutely trusts me,' said Hermann, a successful, unusually outgoing man who travels widely in his work as an art auctioneer. 'This means that I can engage totally with what interests me without wondering how my wife might interpret my meetings with other people or my decisions to stay on an extra day or go on to another city. I'm quite sure this straightforwardness benefits us both. When we married I had more difficulties with trust, or perhaps it was with my jealousy. Trudie's example won me over completely. I came to see how it degraded me too to question her suspiciously about how she was spending her time, or who she was talking to at a party, or whether she had enjoyed herself somewhere "too much" without me. How petty! She would say, "There's no need for this", and move right along. And she was right. There is no need for it. I have silently thanked her many times for showing me that.'

Knowing that many people long to be more trusting but believe that it is too difficult, or that they 'naturally' have a suspicious or jealous temperament they can do nothing to alter, I pressed Hermann to be even more specific about what he has achieved.

'I had been to a couple of motivational seminars in relation to my work,' he told me. 'I knew from those quite clearly how to identify what I want and how important it is to direct my attention towards that. If I want to trust myself in relationship to Trudie – or any close friend or even someone I am doing business with – then I do the worst possible thing if I go over in my mind what might be wrong. Doing that, I move myself in the worst possible direction. Instead I simply talk myself into paying attention to what will support what I want. Here's an example. I'd like Trudie to feel quite free to talk to anyone she likes and not have to put up with a 40-year-old husband sulking in the corner or spying at her over other people's shoulders. So I tell myself, frankly, how free *I* am to talk to whomever I choose. And once I get going of course I like that very much. I tell myself how much I am looking forward to gossiping with her on our way home. And I lose myself in what's going on; not my dreary suspicions. If I am away, and I notice how old habits of jealousy or possessiveness are creeping in, I again direct my attention to a specific goal. In this case it could be to make the most of time on my own. If I am at a gallery where there are paintings that I love, I am already not only fascinated by the paintings and absorbed in seeing them – rather like old friends – I am also anticipating with what pleasure I might talk about this to Trudie. In other words, I identify how free I am to pick my goals; to do what's needed to achieve them; and to see how utterly enhanced my life is by Trudie. But for all that, I am also master of my own destiny.

'I have come to see that trust is an acceptance of nothing more or less than that. When we mix it up with neediness, we do ourselves the worst disservice. We betray ourselves. I have a twin sister, for instance, who is crushed still by the breakdown of a marriage that happened nearly eight years ago. Nothing that has happened to her since has been half as important as that betrayal. Her ex-husband, who is now married to someone else and has a perfectly nice life with his new wife and their children, is more powerful in my sister's mind than her own thoughts are. She swears that he betrayed her. Is that true? Only in part. She has not taken back her own power: she is not mistress of her own destiny. I would go so far as to say that she has unknowingly betrayed herself and continues to do so. That's worse than anyone else's betrayal could ever be.'

In the relationships that most easily encompass change and facilitate growth, high levels of trust exist for both people. What's more, trust is expressed and experienced broadly: 'I can trust you to have my best interests at heart at all times.' In those relationships each person can generally trust that the other shares or at least respects their values; that the other will behave with genuine consideration; and that when an issue of importance comes up each can and will say what's on their mind.

Each can also trust and value their own autonomy. This gives them freedom to develop as an individual as well as part of a couple, family or friendship, or as a professional or workplace partner. And they know that they can afford to support and nourish the other's interests – regardless of whether they share those interests.

That kind of continual living out of trust is possible wherever goodwill exists. And it provides a blueprint for a loving relationship. Difficulties can be worked through and learned from. Difference can be experienced as stimulating, not threatening. Outbursts of frustration can be acknowledged and regretted – but not inter-minably punished. Petty irritations can be passed by because, in general, interactions are reliably courteous and rewarding.

It is exceptionally steadying to perceive how trust *gives* free-dom; it does not take it away. This has certainly been true for Joanna, a surgeon in her late thirties who is professionally ambi-tious and has a burgeoning practice that takes most of her time and attention. Joanna also has a marriage that is extremely important to her. Rory is her second husband. They have been together for almost a decade, work in different fields and value the time they spend together, including trips to countries new to each of them.

Joanna believes that the best basis for trust is 'complete honesty between people'. She goes on, 'What I mean by that is allowing yourself to be yourself. I have friends who have traits that I don't care for but I like the whole person.'

Joanna's vision of 'the whole person' appeals to me greatly. I welcome the inclusive reality of it: that we can trust ourselves to like someone despite the odd imperfection. That we can be will-ing to take on the complexity of the person, their contradictions; *what we like less along with what we like more.* Doing that, we can more readily trust that we too are likeable – even when our flaws are on show or we have dissimilar experiences or attitudes to the other person. This opens up all kinds of possibilities. It makes the outer world safer and also more exciting and accessible.

A more conscious way of experiencing trust has been a tremendously positive force in Joanna's marriage also. Rory grew up in a family that overtly valued trust, loyalty and commitment. They talked about it. Praised it in others. And unconsciously 'coached' each other in it through the attention and value they gave it. Until she married Rory, Joanna didn't know how impor-tant it was for her to be able to trust her partner and feel trusted in return. What she truly appreciates is 'The trust or faith that he loves me for who I am and that he will be there tomorrow, that he will still be my husband tomorrow, in the same way I know that my mother will still be my mother, no matter what happens today. The reason I think this is so important is that it gives me the freedom to be myself. I don't have to play games with him or with myself, trying to be someone I've convinced myself that he would desire more than me.

'Growing up in my family I felt I had to be perfect. That was the role I had. I had to succeed in all that I did. I could not let my family down. In relationships outside the family I felt I had to keep up that illusion. I knew I wasn't perfect but I felt if anyone else knew that secret they would not love or like me.

'In my first marriage I was not able to discuss any doubts or concerns I might have about the marriage because that would have been showing weakness. Our lack of communication on serious issues was what split us apart. We probably never were well matched but we never talked about it and thus never got beyond those differences. What I have now is a relationship that is close and secure enough – trusting enough – that we can talk about doubts and problems. That allows us to work out differences without a feeling of personal rejection.

'I'm not saying that it's always perfect. We have hurt each other's feelings from time to time, but we both have the confidence that it is not going to escalate beyond a reparable point.'

TRUST YOURSELF AS WELL AS OTHERS

Through much of my own early adult life I regarded trust – as I did love also – too narrowly, as something that I could bestow, but only on people who passed all kinds of tests about which I was only half conscious.

Not trusting trust, I was probably rather more defensively independent than I needed to be. Leaning on someone else was frightening; more frightening than being leaned on, although I also had real apprehensions about that. Yet the truth is, some degree of dependence is present in all our various relationships. We need each other *and* we need to know that we can also take care of ourselves. Those realities can and do coexist.

And the irony is clear: in overvaluing independence we are demonstrating that we can't trust ourselves to survive the hurts or disappointments that other people might cause us if we were to let down our defences and get too close.

The balance between intimacy and independence and the balance between each person's differing needs for intimacy and independence, is central to the complex process of negotiation that must continue throughout the life of any committed friendship, work partnership or intimate relationship. That was the theme of my own book *Intimacy and Solitude*. And I continue to see that it is most likely to succeed not where two people's needs are always in sync – if that's ever possible – but where *they increasingly trust themselves as well as each other*. Then they can, like Joanna and Rory, afford to work out differences without assuming that either one is being covertly attacked or rejected by the other.

In other words, they can take for granted that there will be a satisfactory outcome, even if on the way there is disappointment and difficulty. Trust emerges from knowing 'We can work this out.' And from believing 'This can be survived.'

Locking up someone else so that you can feel safe, or limiting the development of another person because you can't trust the changes that freedom might bring, is no way to save a marriage (or any other interdependent relationship). Those attitudes promote distrust and also ferment resentment, anger and frustration.

Confusion around issues of trust and dependence undoubtedly make us vulnerable. The tiny child who wails in grief and horror when his mother has momentarily disappeared from sight is expressing an urgent need to know that she will come back and comfort him; that he can look to her to regain a place of safety for himself and to know that he is still alive and 'someone'. As an infant, and even into middle childhood and adolescence, he is developmentally unable to trust that he can provide that sense of inward safety for himself that says, 'I am someone. I can trust in my own existence.'

As we develop psychologically, we discover through trial and error that we can trust ourselves to meet some of the needs that once only our parents or caregivers could have met. And this includes the need to provide our own inward experience of safety. But we don't always make this discovery easily.

Even as adults many people feel hollow, inauthentic, unsure of who they are outside specific roles or functions. Their place of safety invariably seems to be somewhere else or in someone else. This may be expressed through that agonising cry, 'I can't live without you. If you leave me I will die.'

An absence of self-trust, and the inner balance and self-love that comes with it, makes them feel painfully needy and dependent. Even when they do find someone they could apparently trust, this feels dangerous. And why wouldn't it?

To believe that the power to make us happy – or just to feel real – is in someone else's hands is horribly unsettling. And because such feelings are unwelcome, the people who feel them may disown them and turn them around to be punishing as well as controlling of the very people they believe they need most. This then worsens their feelings of insecurity as it destabilises the relationship. And it may even make them as 'difficult to love' as they fear.

The presence or absence of self-trust and trust of others has all kinds of social and political ramifications as well as personal ones. People who lack a secure sense of themselves, and who find it troublesome or even impossible to trust others on a more universal basis, may join rigidly structured churches, cults, political groups, armies or gangs that implicitly promise them an emotional home: a place where they can pick up at the door that urgently needed sense of 'being someone'.

This is not automatically a bad thing. Such a structure may be helpful for a time or even for a lifetime. Hasty judgements are not useful here. Problems do tend to arise, however, when the ideology of a group promotes a version of exclusiveness and of splitting, so that people who are 'not like us' are seen as bad, dangerous, evil or untrustworthy in an exaggerated or grotesque way. This characterises all hardline or sectarian thinking. When this happens, the group often seizes upon a rabid form of judgementalism as its principal source of power – and energy. More truthfully, though, they are demonstrating a deep-seated mistrust of their capacity to tolerate the contradictions of their own complex human nature.

Your uncertainties about closeness, intimacy and trust may push you in another direction. You may recognise your own neediness or perceive how needy other people are, but hate that. You may even despise it: neediness or even relying on someone else is something to suppress or get over. You tell yourself how self-sufficient you are. You push people away or keep them in tidy boxes. You write KEEP OUT in big letters across your heart, not comprehending that you also are not trusting.

To live fully – or even to enjoy working alongside other people or having brief, pleasant interactions with your neighbours – you must risk a little vulnerability. Or even a lot.

You must risk that other people may be less than you hoped for. And it's not 'other people' only who might cause you problems here. Very often people hold themselves aloof or apart from the connections they desperately want because they fear their own insufficiency. 'He thinks I am the elegant party guy and yachtsman he's been longing to meet all his adult life,' said 30-year-old Donald to me, less than two months after he had met and fallen madly in love with 24-year-old Warren. 'But you know what a wreck I am. How confused I can be. How fake the whole "doing well" thing can sometimes feel. I feel as though I will wake up one day and Warren will pass me my glass slipper with that adorable look in his eyes that tells me how much he loves me, and the foot I put out will belong to the ugly stepsister: huge, bunioned, wrecked, deformed. He will recoil in horror at who I really am. And I will never see him again.'

Donald expresses with great eloquence what many of us fear. (Although it's nice to be able to add that almost three years after facing those particular demons, he and Warren are living together in a version of committed bliss that is delightful to witness.) We fear being found out. We find it hard to trust – even imaginatively – that *who we are really is all right.* The grand irony is, of course, that while most of us worry that we must hide our imperfections, or fret that it's our imperfections that will in some sly way reveal our true, flawed nature – 'give us away' – it is actually our imperfections that often allow other people to love us or feel at home with us!

Warren makes this clear: 'Donald was so impressive. I was knocked sideways! I remember ringing Mum and Dad and blurting out to them that I had to keep pinching myself, thinking how could this fabulous love affair have happened to me. They were so tolerant of my ravings! I loved everything about Donald's life. But the funny thing is when I began to see the tiny flaws, or really how much effort he puts into doing things well and what it personally costs him to be Mr Successful and Mr Wonderful, then I loved him more for that. It aroused a tenderness in me that I experience, anyway, as a truer way to love than admiration. It's not that I don't also admire Don; I do. But that's not what drives my love. On the contrary. It's almost the least of it.'

Perfection (or the illusion of perfection) *is* distancing. It is also static and unreal. Imperfection, on the other hand, is wonderfully human. More often than we realise, it is those imperfections that open us up to another person's character and reality: to what makes them unique.

Ambivalence around issues of self-trust and self-acceptance affects all your connections, not intimate relationships only. It makes you touchy, often when there's no reason to be. It can certainly make you underestimate others' care, even when that's on offer.

I had a sharp reminder of this when I left Britain in my mid-thirties, having lived in London for most of sixteen years. During those years I shared with close friends a period of exceptional social change and remarkable shifts in political and personal awareness. But even that search for insight and understanding hadn't let me really understand – or trust – how embedded I was in my friends' lives or how precious they were to me. Undervaluing myself, and certainly not trusting that I could possibly make a significant difference in their busy, far-reaching lives, I had not allowed myself to recognise how much those people valued my friendship. Overvaluing my capacity for independence and for change, I had also failed to recognise how dependent I was on them for love, support, fun and a precious shared history.

My sense of loss and regret felt acute for years. Worse than that, because I hadn't understood those ties of love that bound me to my friends in Europe, I was somewhat a stranger to myself. This doesn't mean that I regret leaving Britain and coming to Australia. I don't. What I do regret is that I could not have understood my needs for friendship and constancy more realistically. Trust is at the core of that difference. I wish that I could have been more aware of what I valued and needed. And much more open to my own simple value as a human being.

Assume the best – always

Trusting is something we need to practise in small matters as well as large on a daily basis: both trusting and being trustworthy.

Opportunities arise every day that show us how everyone benefits when our interactions are based on trust. Or show us how quickly even a trivial situation can deteriorate when a basic sense of trust – and the essential goodwill that comes with that – is absent.

Take a most banal example. Someone in a shop gives you $40 less change than she should. Do your thoughts at once convince you that this is deliberate? Do you react angrily, and call her a thief? Do you threaten to tell her boss or the police?

Perhaps you don't make any fuss at all but inwardly you are seething. It could be that this person also fits a category of humankind that you feel uneasy about. Perhaps she is too black, too white, too old, not old enough. You tell yourself you should never have gone into this shop! And you never will again. Nor any shop like it. Your mistrust spreads like flood waters over 'shops like that' or 'people like her'.

Unsurprisingly, this exchange leaves you agitated. You dwell on it, talk about it. Days after it happened, you are still reliving the same scene. It may even be that you take this 'insult' personally. It isn't just that this woman is a thief, it is *you* she chose to cheat. That wily shop assistant could see you coming! It's just your lousy luck. People take advantage of you constantly. It's no good hoping for better things. Better things will never happen. Not to you, anyway.

Another view is possible of the same experience.

Someone in a shop gives you $40 less change than she should. You stop, count your change, look at the person, smile and say, 'Can we check this together?' You assume the mistake was genuine. Maybe the woman has a lot on her mind. Maybe it was a simple moment of human carelessness.

Either way, you see that her action affects you, but *it is not directed at you.* 'I'm so sorry,' the woman says. 'My son is getting married next week and I'm in a total spin. Thank heaven you pointed it out. Have a great day!'

Perhaps it is not someone in a shop who provokes and disturbs you. Perhaps it is your partner who yet again is late home for dinner. He has been late home several times this last month. He is short-tempered when he does come home, less concerned with the kids than usual and doesn't have any interest at all in sex.

Anyone would recognise this as dangerous, wouldn't they?

You might never have thought of yourself as especially imaginative, but now your mind fills with images that would do a film-maker proud. There is your partner with another woman, younger and more beautiful than you are. There is your partner leaving, on his way to live in bliss while you remain in agony. There is your partner forgetting you, the children, your shared life, your future together.

Of course you once both believed in commitment. But people change, don't they? Better to prepare for the worst, surely, than to be taken by surprise?

One last example. Your son is 11 years old. He's a bright and lovely kid but not a great scholar. You are an ambitious parent. You believe you are ambitious for his sake. After all, times are tough. You stress this to him. 'It's a rough world out there, son. You need to start doing well now. Otherwise people will have it all over you. You'll be the one without a job, without anything you can feel good about.'

Your son comes home with a score of 100 per cent in a history test. He's never had a score above 70 per cent before this. You are pleased, but also uncomfortable.

You say to him, 'Hey, that's great!' He beams. Then you ask, 'You did do this paper on your own, didn't you?'

Your son turns red. He is about to cry. Instead he runs from the room, slams the front door hard. You are left with a whole mix of emotions. None of them is comfortable.

Can you trust your son to get a good mark on his own?

Can you trust yourself to worry less about his marks than how he got them?

VALUE AND TRUST YOUR OWN EXPERIENCES

Questions around self-trust sneak out like tentacles into all areas of our lives.

What is a trustworthy person? Am I one?

Does my behaviour invite people to trust me?

What values do I trust and rely on?

Are my values expressed in the life I am living?

Am I a trustworthy spouse? Partner? Friend?

Am I the kind of worker I would want to employ? Or the kind of employer I would want to work for?

What kind of community am I creating through my attitudes and values?

These are profound questions. They ask us to think about what we have already learned and to face with honesty what we can't yet answer.

The experiences we gain through our everyday relationships can teach us more than the most brilliant books by the wisest teachers ever could. When we behave badly, we can learn from the discomfort or pain this brings, and *we can trust ourselves to do things differently.* When our behaviour enhances the lives of other people, and we feel good also, we can deepen our awareness of what we are doing and *choose to do more of it.* Learning from our experiences, and learning that we can switch to more life-enhancing attitudes or behaviours when we need to, *we grow in self-assurance.*

Our confidence in the value of our own life need not rest on other people's decisions. Other people's responses can give us significant cues about who we are: 'My team won the sales trophy for the sixth year in a row', 'My wife is as devoted to me as on the day we met', 'My daughter raised more money than any other kid for the Save the Planet marathon.' And there's nothing wrong with reading such cues positively. On the contrary, it benefits us to tune into what's positive.

What happens, though, if our self-image is a little too dependent on other people's judgements and reactions? Or if we can only trust the self that we see reflected back to us through other people's eyes?

Would our self-image as a good worker survive if our sales team came last? Or if our company went broke? Could we continue to see ourselves as lovable if our partner fell into midlife madness and eloped with their chess coach? Would our sense of ourselves as a devoted parent survive if our child grew up to adopt a lifestyle very different from our own?

These are all issues of trust.

ENCOMPASS SEPARATENESS AND DIFFERENCE

We want people to behave in ways that suit us and *reflect well on us*. The more intimately we are entangled, the more passionate our wish for that will be. It's no surprise, then, that when agendas clash and someone cannot or does not behave as we hoped or expected, we may feel not only outraged but diminished by that other person's choice. Or, more accurately, by our own beliefs about how their action reflects on us.

So how can I say this nicely? *Often the events that hurt or affect us most have relatively little to do with what we want or even who we are.* They affect us; there's no denying that. But those events that perhaps crashed into our self-image and hopes like a 10-tonne truck may not have been in any significant way 'about' us. We did not cause them. We could not prevent them. We were not uppermost in that person's mind when they happened. Surprisingly often, people's actions or decisions reflect what is stirring in them only.

This *is* hard to understand; harder still to accept. Our feelings get in the way. Our egocentricity also makes it difficult for us not to see ourselves as the cause or the victim of someone else's behaviour, especially when it's someone with whom we are intricately and intimately connected. It is a stretch to trust that much separateness. But the truth is, people are complex, changeable, never entirely predictable – even to themselves.

Let me give you an example.

Some months ago a former client called me. He is a physics genius in his thirties. He called to ask if I would see him once only with his mother, who is an observant Jew. This man intends to go to India to enter a monastery as a novice Tibetan Buddhist monk. From the moment they walked into the room, it was clear that this was an agonising situation for both people (and especially agonising as it might under other circumstances have been truly joyful). His mother was in grief, devastated that he could want to 'do this to her'. She saw it as a personal betrayal of herself, and as a public betrayal of the religion she passionately values. Her losses were huge: the loss of a son; the loss of the continuity of her faith; the loss of grandchildren she will now not have. From that stance she was quite unable to experience anything but her own loss. She could not glimpse that this decision had little to do with her, and everything to do with how this thoughtful, highly conscious man believes he should be living his own life.

Here is another example, less painful, but more morally ambiguous. This story was told to me by Morgan, a friend and writer in his forties who has been married for eleven years to a woman he loves very much.

Before his marriage Morgan had been used to a life where affectionate but fairly casual sex with a number of women at any one time was quite normal for him. Yet since his marriage he has been mostly monogamous. In our conversation, we quickly moved to issues of trust. This provoked Morgan to say, 'I guess what I have been thinking about is the need to accept the limits of honesty and realising how much pain too much honesty can cause.'

At this early point I was already looking sceptical, despite my best intentions! Morgan moved into an illustration of what the limits of honesty may allow.

'A couple of years ago,' he said, 'I was on a business trip to take part in a symposium. At the end of the first day, the group got together for drinks and dinner. On the way back to our rooms, the group gradually diminished in size until it was just me and this woman I had barely spoken to. At her door she turned around and said something utterly corny like, "Have you seen the incredible view from the balcony?" So we enter the room, walk to the darkened balcony, look out over the city of twinkling lights for approximately thirty seconds. She turns to me, wraps her arms around me, gives me a passionate kiss and within no more than a minute we are fucking, standing up. This goes on for about an hour. We don't sleep together. I go back to my room and apart from a brief comment the following day, we never talk about it, never fuck again, the symposium ends and everyone goes their merry way.

'At the time (and still now) I was living with a wonderful, kind, trusting, funny, talented woman. I was convinced I was madly in love with her, but I had not thought for a millisecond about fidelity, trust, betrayal, when confronted with the opportunity to have spontaneous sex with a stranger. So the big lesson was the realisation and acceptance that I am not monogamous and, in all probability, never will be. By accepting that, I could begin to think about my attraction to women in a different way. More objectively? I don't know. We are all so diabolically clever at fooling ourselves, but I felt that at that moment I saw part of the truth of who I am. Who knows where wisdom comes from, but I got some on that balcony that night.'

Understanding himself better may benefit Morgan. But you might be wondering about his wife. Did Morgan share his wisdom with her? Should he have? Or do you believe it would be kinder and wiser for him not to do so?

Morgan continued: 'It made me think about fidelity in a new way. I never told my wife about the incident. I didn't want to cause her pain. I decided that it was something for me to deal with. I wanted to embrace the experience and there was never any interest in sharing it with anyone. It was like a gentle slap in the face, telling me that I am free to do whatever I want and to follow my instincts whatever they might be. To accept responsibility for my behaviour and not try to convince myself that it is anything other than what it is, for better or worse. This was a very comforting realisation. A painless sort of surrender.'

We paused there. Then, without any apparent need for self-justification but with real interest, Morgan said, 'But one other thing: as a result of that encounter, the simple realisation that I was free to engage in that sort of behaviour lessened my interest in doing so. I don't know what it all means, but I felt much more comfortable with myself. In terms of the relationship, I never felt the slightest urge to share this story or the insights with my partner. I thought it would have been a cruel and destructive thing to do.'

TRUST, FIDELITY AND LOYALTY

Morgan's story seems to me to be usefully disturbing. Perhaps his wife is better off not knowing; only she could say. Certainly I have known wives who were adamant they would not want to know about a husband's sexual infidelity. And Morgan's wife is unknowingly better off now that Morgan's own interest in casual sex has so unexpectedly diminished. Still, Morgan is right also to say that 'We are all so diabolically clever at fooling ourselves', especially when our sexual temperature is rising. Yet there are health risks involved here also, which make 'not telling' a far from simple issue.

For me, trust and sexual fidelity in committed relationships have come to be inextricably linked. The freedom not to act outside the sexual commitment seems every bit as precious to me as the freedom to act. I believe trust and commitment, mutual respect and delight provide the richest mix in which love can thrive. And that whatever sacrifices commitment asks are repaid a thousand-fold in the joy of knowing someone increasingly deeply.

Intrinsic to the sacredness of love is the knowledge that another person regards you as trustworthy. That knowledge is precious.

But in a world where there is so much hypocrisy about sex, so much fear of pleasure, and so much money being made through the idolising and living out of violence, I would still say there are worse abuses of freedom than falling into bed or onto balconies for no grand reason. To deliberately injure someone within what should be the safety of an intimate relationship; to condone murder in any form; to perpetuate racism, ageism or sexism; to stand by while millions die of starvation or as a result of wars they did not cause: all of these strike me as a far greater dishonouring of love than having casual sex.

As for telling? I know that when I was younger and living through some version or another of the sexual revolution, the moral imperatives were to do what you wanted and *tell everything*. Now, rather like those wives who say frankly they don't want to know, I suspect as much pain was caused by the latter as the former. Yet not telling certainly undermines the ease on which trust thrives.

Between people in any form of a close, loving relationship, a version of a *temenos*, a sacred space, comes to exist. This is built in part through conscious acts of loyalty. *Disloyalty endangers that space.* Disloyalty may be letting a friend down; breaking a confidence; trivialising someone in their absence; undermining someone in private; making light of someone's spiritual yearnings; or turning what could be acts of love into acts of revenge or humiliation or indifference. These may not be major things in themselves, yet their effect on the *temenos* can be tremendously disturbing.

There is a crunch point here: we do well to offer loyalty, and to think about the ways in which we can express and live our loyalty, while also understanding that *loyalty is something we can only give unconditionally*. It doesn't buy us any rights.

Standing back far enough to accept someone's need to live differently from the way you want them to can be difficult. There is loss in that situation. Loss of control, certainly; loss of some illusions of sameness; loss of your centrality in that person's world. Yet if we can trust the right each person has to create their own journey, even if we cannot understand it and wish it otherwise, there need be no end to love.

In the case of the man who wished to become a monk, it became clear during our painful hour together that his mother hated what she saw as the eccentricity of his choice. She was afraid of what she imagined her friends might say about that; or worse, that they might pity her. But all of that was secondary to the agonising loss of the daughter-in-law she would now never welcome to her home and the grandchildren she would now never hold in her arms.

There is no easy relief for pain on that scale. She may eventually be consoled by her son's contentment. Yet that cannot be predicted.

Questions of trust continue to hang in the air.

When someone dear to you has behaved differently from the way you wanted, or even very badly, should you cease to love them? Should you cease to trust them to make the right decisions? Should life itself now appear diminished in its glory?

FORGIVENESS IN YOUR OWN TIME

The presence or absence of a capacity for forgiveness, and for recovery from the pain of disappointment or betrayal, makes or breaks relationships. In acute moments it may be impossible to think with much love or understanding about someone who is causing you pain. And it may be false to try. Where forgiveness or understanding is sought, it may be most helpful to bring to mind the relationship itself – the sacred space you have created between you – reminding yourself of its strengths, the values it reflects, and the shared experiences that remain precious.

Lily spoke about a situation like this. After twelve years of marriage her husband, Dimitri, left her to live with another woman. Three weeks later he asked to come back. Her family and friends told her she would be mad to trust him again. That he had no right to come back. They urged her to punish him. Lily explains that she saw the situation very differently.

'He was the same person he had always been. He did something awful. But I could imagine it. I could imagine being possessed by the need to live extremely. Maybe that helped. He's rather a dull person, actually! I don't find him dull but there is this evenness of temper to him that did actually turn out to be deceptive. He ran off for love. He came back for love. I was angry. I am angry. But I also love him. And I have loved the life we had together. I found that I could encompass all the contradictions of that.'

Clearly Lily benefitted from her capacity to see that Dimitri's action was not 'about' her. It was about his 'possession', his need. She was deeply affected, but she was not the cause of his leaving and was only in part the cause of his return.

In any extreme situation, it is often the conscious valuing of what we share that can allow us to set aside outrage and find the strength to listen. At such times we are highly vulnerable to feeling insulted as well as hurt. Perhaps it is the additional pain of that insult that is unnecessary. And that we can let go.

Setting the insult aside, we may interpret a difficult situation more generously: 'He didn't do this to me. It was not nice. Not wise. Still extremely hurtful. But it's not directed at me.'

Stepping back in this way and taking yourself out of the centre of the picture doesn't mean that you have no right to reassert your value of fidelity. This may not mean sexual fidelity only. Betrayal can take many forms: spending money that you both own; talking about something private to a third person; giving something away when it's not your right to do so; acting without reference to shared interests; behaving with indifference or contempt; ignoring a concern that is urgent; overlooking kindnesses.

MUTUAL UNDERSTANDING GROWS WITH TRUST

In all close relationships, issues around trust and loyalty crucially affect the quality of what passes between people. Where the quality is lost or shattered, those values need to be explicitly renewed and shared. You have the right to ask for that. You also have the right to leave a situation where those values cannot be respected.

What is much more morally ambiguous is to insist that someone lives by your values if that person does not freely share them.

Talking openly about trust, unravelling it from the need to own or control someone, using the ideals of commitment as a reference point, wondering aloud about what love allows, two people in any relationship can discover a great deal about each other. It's just this kind of questing conversation – often extending in tiny stages over decades – that brings a depth of mutual understanding to a relationship that simply cannot happen when conversation is restricted to where it's possible to buy a decent bottle of shiraz, which movie we should see or even whether we should have two children or three. Trust encourages that continual evolution of mutual understanding. And commitment depends on it.

Sherri-Ann and Emily were two people who discovered this. They came to a workshop I ran after they had been together for twelve years. They are both lawyers who have achieved materially beyond their parents' wildest dreams, yet they were honest enough to say they felt restless and dissatisfied as individuals and within their relationship despite their strong commitment.

We met half a dozen times after that workshop, and didn't do much more in our time together than talk about what interested them beyond their work and running their home. Both began to read much more widely and intensely than they ever had. Emily cut back her paid work and enrolled for a master's degree in history. Sherri-Ann admitted to longings to travel in Jordan and Egypt, but said that she'd thought it would be impossible as it was not what Emily would ever want to do.

Sherri-Ann was right about that. Emily didn't want to go to either of those countries. But with a quite different sense of what trust allows, it was easy for her to wish Sherri well. This essential cooperation, necessary for each to develop and for the relationship to flourish, arose out of setting their minds and intellectual interests free. And also freeing themselves to see trust itself as a liberation and not a restriction.

It was impossible not to notice how quickly they grew more curious about each other's experiences. For the first time in years they had a great deal to talk about beyond daily life.

The way that Emily and Sherri-Ann talked to each other also changed. They self-evidently trusted the other one to be interesting as well as interested. And while the topic of sex wasn't overtly raised in their early meetings with me, out of these new interests their sexual interest in each other also came back to life in a way that delighted and vitalised them. This was virtually a textbook example of psychologist Alfred Adler's view that 'If the partners are really interested in each other, they will never suffer from waning sexual attraction.' (Not least because they will find a way to talk about what feels wrong, as well as finding the confidence to do so.)

Adler was almost a contemporary of Sigmund Freud, but unlike Freud he was overtly interested in the part social awareness plays in our psychological health. He was a great believer in the community benefits of strong relationships built on personal and social responsibility, and while some of his views now seem dated some are increasingly appropriate.

In Adler's experience a lack of sexual interest indicates the loss of a social (or more encompassing) interest in the other person. Sitting in front of a television set at the end of a long day of work; passing a few words along with the salt and pepper; assuming that you already know everything there is to know about the other person; talking round safe topics; quarrelling to provide a break in the routine: none of that does much to keep sexual love alive. Nor does a mechanical or habitual demand for sex; nor any routine that makes sex as banal as cleaning your teeth or spending ten minutes in the gym.

A loss of sexual attraction (or using sex simply as a means to release tension) 'always implies a lack of interest [in the other person]' said Adler. 'It tells us that the individual no longer feels on equal, friendly and co-operative terms with his partner, and no longer wishes to enrich the life of his partner.'

That desire *to enrich the life of your partner* sets the scene beautifully, evoking as it does gratitude and delight in the other person's wellbeing and an awareness of how you influence their life most powerfully through your attitude towards it.

Self-love also slips in here. Adler believed, as I do, that the attitude a person brings to their marriage or partnership *reflects their own self-image*. If the person is self-trusting, self-respectful and loyal to their values, that will inevitably be reflected in all their relationships. Trusting others expresses that.

MATURITY AND WELLBEING ARE THE GIFTS OF TRUST

Discovering what trust allows is no small thing. We are born into total dependency. Our survival depends on the willingness of others to meet our needs. Later our spiritual and emotional development depends on our capacity to build on those early experiences of trust and to become in turn worthy of other people's trust in us. Trust is a theme that runs through all our lives. But it remains complicated. It affects not only who you are but what you become. To see an absence of trust in a child's eyes is a chilling thing. By old age the presence of trust – demonstrated through a belief in life and humanity despite everything – creates a beauty of spirit that is not diminished by the presence of lines, wrinkles, white hair.

In *My Lord Loves a Pure Heart*, Siddha Yoga teacher Swami Chidvilasananda writes: 'How many times have you bumped into an old friend, someone you haven't seen in several years, and been struck by the change in him? You think, "Oh my, has he aged! In five years!" But is it really the years? No. It is what he has eaten. It is what he has thought. It is what he's felt. It is what he's done. The impressions of his actions have stuck in his system.'

Trust – but not control – is as essential to a healthy relationship as water is to a growing plant. Where trust does not exist, the relationship will be stunted. If you believe in love, you have no choice but to develop your capacity to trust, to look out for what's going well, to support what's sustaining, to ground your intentions in love and to develop the loyalty and tolerance that make you worthy of the trust of others.

Some of us have been blessed by our genes with a trusting nature. Others of us have not. We are affected too by whether we grew up in a family that was open and outward looking or suspicious and withdrawn. Nevertheless, whatever our circumstances and however difficult we may find it, a willingness to trust is vital to maturity and wellbeing.

Luisa discovered this and describes it in a way that is particularly moving. She is a graphic artist who became a mother for the first time in her late thirties. She had lived through many challenging experiences, a difficult time getting pregnant and several hard years reviewing her most fundamental choices in therapy.

Luisa could say, with honesty, 'There was a time when I thought that life didn't matter. I imagined that if I closed my eyes the eyeballs themselves would turn inwards, search my mind and see that there was nothing there. I felt that I didn't exist . . . that in a way

I was invisible. That no one noticed I was alive. It made me feel like a little child again.

'When I was small I played a game where I hid in the house or the yard and waited for someone to come and find me. No one ever noticed that I was missing, and the longer I waited the more surreal it felt. I was not of the world.'

And then for Luisa life changed. 'These days I feel much more part of things. Last year I had a baby in difficult circumstances. After he was born dozens of people sent us cards and presents. I was really surprised that so many people had thought about me and the baby. It felt like I'd been born as well as the baby. Now when things get tough I think about all those good wishes that were sent and I feel good.'

Sometimes in our dreams a baby is born or a little child appears. Those dreams are precious, frequently heralding the birth of something fresh in our lives, a sense of renewal perhaps, or the courage to see something from a different point of view.

Luisa's birth of her 'good self', along with the actual birth of her little son, was not something that could have been routinely predicted, nor could she have wished it into existence. What Luisa had been able to do, however – over several years and certainly not easily – was to move slowly towards a situation where she could begin to trust her own capacity to love and be loved by a good person, a man who could offer her the challenges of a committed, long-term relationship.

You may find this part of Luisa's story surprising. Surely virtually everyone wants a good person to settle with? A trustworthy, loving man, who is also intelligent, good-humoured and sexy, is surely at the centre of most heterosexual women's dreams of a good life? And maybe it was at the centre of Luisa's dreams also, yet what she was more conscious of was her familiarity with people for whom long-term prospects did not exist, and situations where she could be in some ways flamboyantly intimate, yet in other significant ways remain entirely unexposed.

A relationship in which we are taken seriously by the other person, where 'everything seems possible', can feel extremely dangerous. To enter such a relationship and stay in it exposes vulnerabilities and longings to yourself that more superficial relationships never would. The intimacy of that creeps in under the mask of invincibility through which you may have learned to face the world. It arouses treacherous fears of dependency. Where there is plenty, the risk of loss is also great. And what about the fears around your own capacity to love? Surely you will, inevitably, be disappointing? Better to flee that too.

Self-trust and trust of others live and grow alongside each other – and alongside love. Reading this book, allowing yourself to move through this chapter, seeing yourself in these discussions, or reserving judgement but reading on, you have needed to trust that I could take you somewhere worth the journey. And that on this journey you could make discoveries for yourself that make the effort worthwhile.

The process of discovering what trust allows is continual. Giving others the benefit of the doubt, expecting to find whatever is good in them and overlooking minor failings and disappointments; knowing that you can get up should you fall; accepting your own complexity; acknowledging and learning from your mistakes: all of this becomes routine with conscious attention. But is not less valuable for that.

SEXUAL ATTRACTION CAN CONFUSE YOU

From a point of equilibrium it is possible to see more clearly: *This person doesn't feel good for me.* My instinct tells me: *Stay away.*

Trusting others does not oblige you to spend time with people who have harmed you or who are undermining or dangerous in any way. In fact, the opposite is true. Freer access to your instincts as well as your feelings will allow you to be increasingly discerning about who lifts your sense of wellbeing and who does not; who is encouraging to be with and who is not. Where love is and where it is not.

Of course sexual attraction can be enormously confusing. And perhaps always will be. You may feel confident that you want to have sex with this person; that you feel excited by them; that you want to spend time with them. Yet you may be much less sure that this is 'good' for you, or about how the other person feels, or whether the relationship includes an attraction that goes beyond sex. Or is sex enough?

In this context, or wherever trust is floundering, it may be most useful to be tough minded. Observing someone's relationship history, and especially their current attitudes to their friends, family and previous partners, may give you more clues than listening only to how they believe 'it is different this time'.

You may need to ask yourself, 'Is he respectful of previous partners? Were his earlier difficulties all "caused" by someone else? What has he learned from those previous relationships? Does he know what he wants (other than sex)? Is he possessive as well as passionate? (*Beware.*) Does he demand more of my time and attention than I'll want to give? Is he careless about my concerns? Can I speak about my dreams, values, passions? Do I feel heard as well as adored? Is there a pattern to his attractions? Do I fit the bill?'

Those questions are steeped in caution, yet despite the truth that many people do indeed roll from one disastrous situation to the next, it is also true that people can change. A new relationship *can* be different. Each combination of people truly is unique. Maybe if you feel deeply drawn to someone, if that person is free *now* to be in a relationship, if there is no danger of physical or emotional abuse, then – for the sake of love – you may believe, as I would, that some risks are worth taking.

TRUST IN THE RICHNESS OF YOUR EXISTENCE

These are not trusting times. We are restless, greedy, easily distracted and disinclined to hang in through the seasonal changes and disruptions that mark all long-term friendships and relationships. We are skilled at reviewing our dissatisfactions. We are less skilled at valuing what we have. We expect too many of our needs to be met by other people or, worse, just one other person. We believe the answers to most of our dilemmas lie far outside ourselves. We believe we have the right to happiness, forgetting that happiness arises from the delight we take in our lives, the richness and surprises as well as the familiarity and trustworthiness of our connections. And from the precious moments when we allow ourselves some peace.

Trust demands that we think carefully about what we want. Yet sometimes, and how magical this is, it is the actual process of moving forward, even blindly, that leads us out of darkness.

Joseph is Luisa's partner and father of Alexander, the little boy whose birth allowed Luisa's birth of her 'good self'. Joseph is also in his late thirties and is a university teacher and writer. He met Luisa after living overseas for several years, and it was he who had the insight or stubbornness to persist with his belief that he and she could have a relationship that was loving as well as passionate through the many months that Luisa repeatedly came towards what he was offering, then just as often ran far away.

Joseph comments: 'Luisa says that she sees my faith in our love and our being together as a kind of generosity – especially during those earlier times when she wasn't convinced that I could make her happy – or she could make me happy. I was the one who was always optimistic, always convinced that things would work out, even when she was at her most sceptical and unhappy, and she sees this as a kind of generosity. That's a nice thought for me because I hadn't thought of it that way.

'In a simple way, I was just doing what I had to. Sometimes Luisa saw this as a kind of blind doggedness, as though I thought I could make things all right by sheer force of will.'

Joseph pauses, then goes on: 'This makes me think of a little story by Kafka called "The Silence of the Sirens". Kafka says that the conventional wisdom about Odysseus and the sirens is this: Odysseus knew that he would succumb to the terrible beauty of the sirens' song and be ruined. So he put wax in his ears, lashed himself to the mast and so, by closing himself off to the singing, was able to sail past. This version sees his invulnerability as a triumph of will.

'But Kafka sees other possibilities in the story. Perhaps the wax was no good. But the sirens, believing that Odysseus could not hear them, fell silent. Or, for Kafka, an even more intriguing possibility: perhaps Odysseus realised that the silence of the sirens was even more terrible than their song and so stopped his ears so he wouldn't be able to hear their silence.

'You can read this myth a number of ways. But another twist to it occurred to me. Perhaps it's the fact that Odysseus performs an act of surrender, renouncing control, by lashing himself to the mast, which enables him to complete his journey successfully.'

Joseph continues: 'Love doesn't mean that you close your eyes or ears and pretend that the rocks of the terrible dangers of failure or abandonment aren't there. I think sometimes Luisa thought I couldn't see the rocks or didn't want to. I knew I had to sail on through to show her some sign of determination. But at the same time I think as I started to learn how to love Luisa, I started to think love is also about surrender. Not in the sense of self-abnegation, but of giving up the self, being prepared to go with the other person to places you didn't know you could. Simply, it's about giving up control, the need to be the one writing the script all the time, without giving up the place where you stand in the world and what you stand for.

'I think this is just as important in being a parent. Although I am only beginning to understand what this means. Alexander is a stranger who I'm about to embark on a lifelong journey with, someone I already love dearly but don't know at all. And I think being a parent ultimately also means giving up control, while still giving love and standing up for who you are – even to your child!'

This simple idea of *standing up for who you are* means a great deal to me. We can certainly change unhelpful patterns, broaden our focus and concerns and learn from our failures. We can round off and soften our blunt edges. We can discover and develop the strengths of our temperament. But our spirit, our soul, our way of being in the world, is not always or inevitably up for change. And we need to trust that.

Parenting is my area of greatest vulnerability. I have longed to parent perfectly and have had to learn that I could not. In a period of painful self-doubt recently, when I was anguishing about whether I could or should have been a brisker and more resolute kind of parent, one of my closest friends said, 'You had to be yourself in this of all things. You have to trust that.'

This simple remark gave me comfort. We can afford to know ourselves. *All of who we are is not up for change.* We can trust that.

I think with gratitude about the relationships in my own life where the best is assumed always; where the benefit of the doubt is given and received; where acceptance is never withdrawn. In those precious relationships my mistakes are seen as mistakes and not as disguised attacks that must be met with counterattacks. In those relationships I can roam freely – intellectually, spiritually and socially – and return with insights and stories. In those relationships I know that *I will not be controlled.* My changes of mind or mood are seen as reflective only of my fluctuating human condition, my inner dramas, and not inevitably as comments on how I feel about someone else.

Like you, perhaps, I have had relationships and friendships where envy or possessiveness were far more potent than the capacity to trust. In those doomed relationships the urge to control was greater than the urge to love. I could see how those emotions caused the other person to suffer. But the fear that drives such possessiveness caused me great suffering also; inevitably I wanted to escape that.

If you do not trust the people you claim to love, it is never helpful to set more tests for them ('If he really loves me, he'll ring before 4 p.m.', 'If she values me, she will know *without my telling her* that I only like to make love when the sun is shining').

Until you believe you can and would challenge your demons and survive your disappointments, the important people in your life could become angels of light and paragons of trust and you won't be less frightened. You may honestly believe it's other people you are not trusting, but you are looking in the wrong direction.

A trusting person may be betrayed. *But will recover.*

A person who cannot trust may never be betrayed. *But will live fearfully.* The central question for any of us is not 'Who can I trust?', but 'Can I free myself to trust others? Can I free myself to risk building a life that is loving, encouraging and generous, aware of barbs and pitfalls, but with heart still open and spirit singing?'

Trust Others

Trusting others is one of your finest expressions of freedom. Trusting others, you discover that you are free to think the best of other people – regardless of whether they 'deserve' it. You are also free to take risks with confidence and insight – because *you believe in your own powers of survival*, in your own resilience. Your attitudes are not dependent on other people's permission or responses.

You are free to give the benefit of the doubt always.

You are free to recover and go on trusting even if something or someone lets you down.

Trusting others does not require blind faith. It is an intelligent, alert approach to life itself that gives you a priceless sense of your own inner authority, equanimity and optimism. Trusting others brightens even your most fleeting connections with other people. And gives love its best chance always.

- Recognise how attractive trust is: how good it feels when someone gives you their trust without limitations. Notice how it eases contact between people.
- Know how free you are to think the best of others.
- Risk being wrong sometimes, rather than being suspicious always. Know that 'being wrong' is something you can get over. 'Being suspicious' keeps you small.
- Recognise how unpredictable life is; how well you have already survived some hurts, mistakes and upsets.

- See your relationships as a chance to enrich the lives of other people, not limit them.
- Keep the lines of communication open. You trust people most easily when you also understand them. Listen to people. Look at them. Keep yourself open.
- Recognise that in the healthiest relationships *people do trust each other* and benefit from that immeasurably.
- Talk to *and about* people as though you trust them. That will make trust more real and much easier.
- Treasure your freedom to give the benefit of the doubt. Give it generously.
- Don't expect other people to make you feel safe. Do that for yourself by developing resilience and self-love.
- Your capacity for survival is your greatest source of strength: take this far more seriously than whether other people may betray you.
- Build resilience through thinking about what's gone right as well as what you've learned from adversity ('I dreaded those exams, but did quite well', 'That was a horrible experience, but we got through it by pulling together', 'My heart was broken when I was 20, but I feel fine now').
- Know that resilience is learned on the run. That makes scary situations manageable.
- Enjoy not always knowing what the outcome will be. Often you are choosing between win–win situations. Both outcomes or any outcome will have its rewards.
- Inspirational stories are all tales of resilience. Read and learn from them.
- Look for the big picture: it helps you feel bigger also. Talk to yourself positively; acknowledge your fears without being limited by them; view mistakes or losses as setbacks only; be open about your mistakes; learn from difficulties; take risks that interest you; value difference.

- Trust the way your own attitudes influence events. Interpret events positively. Anticipate enthusiastically. Make that a habit. It will lift your spirits *and* give events their best chance.
- Trusting others doesn't mean that you can't state your views or make your opinions known. It simply means you don't force them on another person or insist on your viewpoint or 'rights'.
- When other people make a decision you would not have chosen for them, *respect their autonomy*. Such respect is an essential expression of love.
- If you can't tolerate that someone else's choices are different from yours, act 'as if' you can tolerate them. *Your tolerant behaviour will affect your own feelings positively.* It will also lessen the possibility that the other person is unconsciously defying you or attempting to create a separation through claiming territory different from yours.
- Confront your prejudices ('People like that . . .'). Prejudice undermines trust.
- If you suffer from distrust, envy or jealousy, see those feelings as your problem. *Do not impose them on other people.* Work them out by disputing them, increasing self-love and self-respect through the way you live or with the help of a capable psychotherapist. Meanwhile *act like a trusting person.*
- Know that if the source of anxiety or jealousy is in you, nothing the other person can do will make much difference. You must rebuild your own feelings of self-love and safety and drag yourself away from what is narrow and obsessive.
- If you begin to think the worst of someone, *dispute that in your own mind* ('These are my anxieties', 'This is the kind of thing I often tell myself when I'm tired or upset').
- *Never snoop or pry.*
- If you want to know something – ask. If the other person won't tell you, ask yourself why you want the information.

- In all your dealings be unfailingly open, reliable, direct. It is difficult to trust others if you don't trust yourself.
- Check out your hunches honestly. Laugh when you are wrong.
- Remember that no one has the right to know 'everything' about another person. It's an illusion to think you could.
- Accept that other people won't always know *why* they are doing things, any more than you do.
- If you dishonour someone's trust, apologise. Learn. Move on.
- If someone you care about behaves badly, *continue to trust them.* However hard this is, and however absurd it may appear, it will profoundly affect them as the most loving gesture of which you are capable.
- Relish the freedom that trusting others brings you. Notice how it lightens up all your interactions with other people. Let that support you.
- Value the peace of mind that trusting others brings.
- In situations of anxiety or uncertainty, *send people the healing energy of love.* You can do this through prayer, or by imaginatively sending love along an invisible but unbreakable line from your heart to theirs.

GIVE OTHERS THE BENEFIT OF THE DOUBT — AND YOURSELF

Margaret's Story

Your life blossoms when you can switch from fearing the worst to expecting the best. A fine example of this comes from farmer and bush poet Margaret Perrin. As a gritty survivor who has undertaken all kinds of adventures (including riding a motorcycle solo across Australia), Margaret is well aware of her resourcefulness. But this is not always a cure for habits of pessimism. A letter to me from Margaret demonstrates how possible it is to be caught by pessimism — and move beyond it.

She wrote: 'I went walking up over the hill on our property. My daughter had gone ahead because I'm so slow now. Then I didn't ever catch up and she didn't pass me going back. When I got home her car had gone and I started thinking, "How did she get past me without me seeing her?" That became: "Why would she go past without greeting me?" On and on.

'Finally I said to myself, "You have to meditate. Go upstairs and meditate." So, following the instructions in your *Intimacy & Solitude Self-Therapy Book*, I did your imaginative walk up the path, through the forest, to the clearing, to the little gompa, and asked my Wise One to tell me what was right to think about this situation.

'I didn't get the answer immediately. You had said I may not. So I went on with what I was doing and it came to me very clearly that she had gone down to the Ram Paddock Bore. She hadn't even gone along the same road. She'd turned off and gone down a different road.

'She hadn't deliberately avoided me at all. It was a miracle.'

Listen

Carefully

. . . my soul is not asleep.

It is awake, wide awake.

It neither sleeps nor dreams, but watches,

its eyes wide open,

far-off things, and listens

at the shores of the great silence.

ANTONIO MACHADO

Working as a psychotherapist is a continual process of education. Each encounter brings you close to the heart of someone's life. People trust you with their secrets and yearnings, their vulnerabilities, the events that have caused them fear or shame, and the longings they feel for meaning, insight, connection and joy.

This trust is precious. I have learned so much because of it.

I have seen how surprising people can be in their capacities to make significant change in their attitudes towards themselves, their lives and other people. I have learned how, for all our differences of race or culture, sexuality or class, age or formal education, in the end what we want and need is remarkably similar: food on our table, a clean bed to sleep in, work we can enjoy, a feeling of safety and wellbeing, people in our lives whom we can love and feel loved by, and something greater than ourselves that we can believe in.

I've learned something else too.

Listening as carefully as I can to the feelings and unspoken stories that lie beyond the spoken word, listening to the tone in which something is said, measuring the speed or delay with which something spoken emerges, watching people's faces, the movements of their hands and bodies, the colour that rushes to their face or leaves it, the silences that give way to words and the words that give way to silence: listening to all of that I have learned this priceless thing. *It is impossible to listen deeply to someone who is willing to risk their own vulnerability without growing in respect and affection for them, and without meeting their experience of vulnerability with your own experience of love.*

In other words, after fearing that I might like some clients more than others, or that hearing certain kinds of things might make it impossible for me truly to accept someone in the way that person would need, I have learned that where there is a willingness to risk vulnerability, where there is a meeting of hearts as well as minds, then compassion and respect are always in that place. And so is a sense of common purpose.

The most consistent gift any therapist can bring to their clients is that capacity to listen with great interest: to open to the experience itself. This involves literally offering 'hospitality' to their story: accepting the person who is telling the story, and allowing the story to become part of the relationship between you – not judging it, not moralising about it, and not rejecting it.

When psychotherapy is flowing, a connection arises and takes life between two people who are doing not much more than engaging in a deep, gradually illuminating conversation where one of them is doing most of the talking and the other is doing most of the listening. At its best the listening is taking place entirely in the present moment, even when the events being remembered, and perhaps refelt, belong far in the past.

PEOPLE ARE HUNGRY TO BE HEARD

Most people are hungry to be heard. Hungry to have their feeling state acknowledged. Hungry to know that they have been at last somewhat understood.

Being heard is as different from most experiences of being listened to as it would be to enter a vast lake for the first time when your only knowledge of water has been gained from puddles. The lake can hold you. You can move through its depths.

Silence is at the heart of listening. You don't need to say clever things to be a good listener. You need only surrender your own agenda temporarily. And wait with interest and patience.

Listening carefully to another person is a vital expression of concern. When it is risked, we are for some moments leaving behind our version of the world to enter someone else's. We are saying to someone else you matter to me. Your feeling state matters to me. Your hopes and dreams matter to me. Your version of experiences matters to me. *Tell me more about what it's like to be you.*

Witness a child's delight as she describes to her parent something that she's experienced. Sharing that, she is giving a gift. When she is actually heard, when her emotions are allowed to resonate as well as her words, then she is receiving back something just as precious: the knowledge that what happens to her, and what she makes of that, is something another person can understand and care about.

When we talk to someone else about a matter close to us, we are making an offering. We are bringing into the outer world something from the contents of our inner world. We are saying 'what it's like to be me'. When that gift is respected and 'held' by the listener there can be a movement towards integration and connection within the speaker that seems way out of proportion with the simplicity of what has been offered.

This can happen in the safety of a therapeutic relationship. *But it's also an essential part of what people can learn to give and receive from each other in their daily lives.* Intimacy depends on the giving and receiving of messages from the inner world of one person to the inner world of the other. At its best this is a sacred thing, an inestimable expression of love and trust. Sacred need not imply something solemn. It may also be a playful experience, or a social one, or an intellectually engaging and challenging one. Those are all of value.

Being listened to supports our awareness of our inner reality. It tells us that who we are is real; that our experience is authentic, even if our inward state is one of turmoil.

LISTENING IS THE KEY TO INTIMACY AND HEALING

Debbie's story shows how healing it can be to be listened to with kindness and respect. Because her early circumstances were so unpromising, I find her experiences touching and inspiring. She is now in her late twenties, married to a professional footballer, has three young children and is also studying part-time for a social work degree so that eventually she can take up a career in social work. Her parents were unable to care for her beyond middle childhood. She left school when she was 15, and had a couple of difficult years living in youth refuges.

'There always has to be someone who makes a difference for you,' she told me. 'In my case, it was Bette, a single older woman who became a kind of auntie to me from when I was almost seventeen. The last refuge I was in, they more or less pushed me into this scheme even though it was really for younger kids. I had to go to stay with her for at least one night a month.

'What I noticed about Bette almost right away is that she didn't pry. She didn't need my whole sordid story to make it even more wonderful that she was taking me in. I always had the sense she was listening to what I was telling her, but she didn't have to eat up my whole story in one meal.

'Also, when she spoke, she was clearly thinking! This drove me mad at first, but once I got used to it I liked it. It wasn't the running off at the mouth I was used to. It certainly wasn't that worst social work kind of listening where you are the fucked-up client and a *solution* has to be found for you so that your file can be neatly tied and put away.

'With Bette it was, like, speak, speak, speak. Stop. Think. Speak, speak, speak. So what she said *fitted* the actual conversation.

'I didn't get it all right away. I was used to speaking – and then thinking. Or speaking and never thinking!

'You asked me if I learned to listen to myself first. No. I learned to listen to Bette first. Then to the other girls at the refuge or out anywhere on the streets. I could hear them running off at the mouth. Just like I did. It wasn't only because they were young though. The teachers at my school did it. Speaking on automatic. You say, "Shut up", and they say, "Who do you think you are, young lady." You might as well have been handed a crappy script. Learned a few parts off. And then you were doomed to repeat them until you dropped into the grave and someone else took your place.

'Bette, though, you couldn't second guess her. She almost never gave you exactly what you were expecting. With Bette it was always a stream of thinking that was much bigger than her stream of speaking. Like the speech was the light piece of driftwood going along on a river. Sometimes stopping. Sometimes fast. Sometimes slow. But always supported by thought.'

When Debbie was 22, and pregnant with her second child, Bette died of cancer of the liver. 'We'd got really close by then. She loved Damien [Debbie's husband] and was mad about the baby. Elizabeth Marie, our 8-year-old, is named for her. We were in such grief when she was going. But I have to say that she kept up that same degree of thoughtfulness. The underpinnings of everything.

'I had been copying her for years. I was afraid that when she died I'd forget who I had become. Maybe I even thought I'd slip back into a mind-set where I'd be responding or reacting on automatic. Back to the rotten scripts! I didn't, though. Damien is also someone who thinks before he speaks. Not always of course; enough of the time, though. It's not just that, either. Damien can listen to me and he knows when what I have said needs commenting on and when I am just getting something off my chest and need to be heard and that's that. That's a skill I have to really struggle with. Sometimes he tells me things and I get it wrong. I get angry on his behalf when really that wasn't what he was after. He was just ventilating. But we can say that to each other. We can be frank with each other and not ever bitter. That's what I hate most about those automatic responses. They are often bitter. And cut off.

'When Damien and I are talking, then all the time I am listening for the message in what he's saying, and I am trying, trying, trying to be clear about what I am saying. That means I can count on an honesty between me and Damien that goes way beyond anything that either of us says. It's an honesty that arises out of paying close attention. Before something is said as well as afterwards.'

People in relationships struggle to have a variety of needs met. Experiences of careful listening and of being heard may be relatively rare even when two people spend a lot of time together.

In some friendships and relationships there is only one listener. One person gets heard and is relatively satisfied. The other person does not. This is appropriate in a psychotherapeutic relationship where the roles are clearly set: two people have got together largely in the interests of only one of them. This is not appropriate in a friendship or relationship, yet such an imbalance may continue over many years, perhaps without either person being really conscious of what's going on, but with the more generous listener from time to time feeling depleted or even exploited.

Some good listeners do get sufficient satisfaction from seeing themselves as caretaking or supportive, sympathetic or rescuing, and don't protest. Or they have other friends or colleagues with whom the talking and listening is more mutual, and they can sustain the less balanced relationship because of that. But *fixed roles in any close relationship are rarely helpful* and when they are based on an unevenness of care, they are undermining.

Flexibility of roles and a conscious sharing of caretaking and responsibility for the relationship itself support both people best. Where there is a stuck pattern to the talking and listening, it may be that there are other stuck patterns; for instance, an assumption that one person's work or interests are more 'important' than the other's; or that one person should take responsibility for 'trivial' matters that are actually a considerable burden in time and worry; or even that only one person is creative, active or innovative, despite the potential that exists in all of us.

CAREFUL LISTENING AT HOME AND WORK

Relationships can be undermined when people feel that any central aspect of their current reality is being discounted. And if it's the talking and listening that is unbalanced, the listener may justifiably feel that their friend or partner has little idea of who they really are; what their present fears and hopes are; how they are coping with life's changes, or even how they feel about the relationship itself.

It is encouraging to know that people *can* learn to talk less and listen more carefully. It is a skill that feels clumsy at first. Gradually, though, with more awareness of the other person's needs – more *interest* in those – and with practice, listening more carefully becomes easier until soon it seems perfectly natural.

Yet the crucial point is that careful listening is not natural for most people. Interrupting, talking over someone, correcting them, criticising, moaning, offering unsought advice, launching into anecdotes of your own, *ignoring the other person's feelings*: all of that is far more natural or habitual than careful listening is.

Patterns of uneven communication generally arise out of carelessness and lack of awareness rather than ill-will. Because of that, insight may be slow to come. When it does, it is often accompanied by resentment. Yet gathering in your resentments about how poorly you have been listened to in the past, it's wise to pause. It is *always* useful to extend to others the benefit of the doubt. It may never have occurred to the other person that the talking and listening in your relationship are out of balance, or that you may have changed since the intense conversations you had ten or twenty years ago. Self-awareness is needed here – on both sides. And a cheerful request for change, rather than blame. After all, until people *experience* that they are listening at a superficial level only, they cannot make the changes needed.

In the workplace too the benefits of careful listening cannot be overemphasised – and not just because listening skills can exponentially accelerate your workplace success! Many people have work where the quality of their presence – of their capacity to pay attention and respond appropriately – is paramount. Two brief examples occurred just this week for me. In the first I watched as a young woman expressed irritation and impatience as an elderly woman had difficulty working out what notes and coins she should hand her in a suburban store. Then when she gave the elderly woman her change, she almost threw the money at her as though she couldn't wait to get rid of her. That exchange could have involved listening not only through the ears, but also through the eyes and instincts to recognise how hard it can be to be old, how frustrating it can be when your fingers have lost their agility, and when you fear being seen as a nuisance and not as a human being.

In a second example – again involving an elderly woman – it was a young man in a post office who treated her with scrupulous respect as she made her modest purchases. More than that, he found that extra half-moment to say, 'You were brave coming out in the rain today.' In that tiny exchange, her reality was 'heard' and a moment of precious human contact was achieved.

Anne Deveson describes something similar in her wonderful book *Tell Me I'm Here*, an account of her son Jonathan's struggle with schizophrenia and his eventual early death. She demonstrates how crucial it is to listen with respect – especially to people whom we may be too quick to label. At this point in the story Jonathan had experienced a hideous spasm as a side effect of his medication. Both he and Anne believed he was dying. To make sense of this story, you also need to know that like many people with mental illnesses Jonathan had valid reasons to fear hospitals and medical intervention. 'In the middle of the night the hospital was dark and silent and empty,' Anne writes. 'A nurse hurried Jonathan away to give him an injection to end the spasm. The young doctor who eventually returned with Jonathan said to him gently, "It must be rotten."

'Tears welled up in Jonathan's eyes and splashed on the arm of his chair.'

About this, Anne comments: 'Professional acknowledgement that someone is having a torrid time is such a little thing to give but means so much. When a doctor says "It must be rotten", *this is an emotional response which carries its own healing*. It doesn't happen enough. Simon, a young painter who has struggled with schizophrenia for fifteen years, says, "Doctors rarely talk to us or look at us as if we're human. All they ever say is, 'How's your medication?' But I'm not a chemical tablet. I'm a soul and psychiatrists never use the word 'soul'. They never use the word 'love' "'.

MEN CAN LISTEN

Careful listening benefits every aspect of a close relationship. I was reminded of this some years ago when I met Elliot and Tim, a couple who were then in their early thirties and had already been together for about fourteen years. Both men were well aware that changes were urgently needed if they were going to continue together, but Tim was reluctant to look closely at the interactions and communication between the two of them.

Tim's plans for renewal included buying a beach house or getting a bigger boat. He was also pushing Elliot to enrol for an MBA and was talking about taking on a couple of extra employees in his own building business. Those dynamic plans emerged in about the first twenty minutes of our initial hour together. That made my job easy. By the time Tim had said all that, and had given us a skilled sales pitch about how these changes were all that was needed, he could see for himself that while they might be stimulating and challenging they might not bring the two men closer, or renew the significant feeling of being understood and accepted that had once existed between them.

Because there was tremendous goodwill left, it was possible for us to discuss how Tim and Elliot might make time for each other – being fully present; listening for the emotions being expressed; not offering hasty solutions; and learning something as though hearing it for the first time. After two or three weeks they were able to report with a great deal of pleasure that, although they had known each other since they were just out of their teens, they were beginning to see each other in a new light.

Talking more – and more freely – they both felt energised, their sex life certainly picked up, and their confidence in themselves as a couple, as well as individually, noticeably improved. And all without buying a boat.

I remember wondering then, and I still wonder now, if Tim and Elliot were fortunate that no gender issue hovered in the air. For them it wasn't an issue that 'listening is women's business', an idea which can be divisive and painful in many heterosexual relationships.

My own experience is that some people can pay attention to whatever they are hearing well enough to be accomplished listeners; others need to learn; and a minority cannot learn. Yet that minority might be smaller than we suppose. In programmes such as the Quaker-supported Alternatives to Violence, where formerly violent or inarticulate prisoners rapidly become skilled, empathic trainers and supporters for other prisoners, the most apparently unlikely men demonstrate that they can open up in speech and in silence, in mind and in heart.

If there are gender differences around this issue, I would *cautiously* see them like this. Boys and men appear to use code more than girls and women do: much is conveyed in brief asides (which makes sharp as well as careful listening essential). Boys and men might be more comfortable showing their love through actions rather than speaking about intimate issues or offering verbal comfort at vulnerable times ('I've made you a cup of tea, Mum'). Women and girls possibly ventilate their feelings more than men and boys do, talking around and around an issue that is bothering them, whereas a man might be more likely to bottle up his thoughts, unconsciously prohibiting himself from speaking until he has a solution. This particular dynamic can have tragic consequences for the person who cannot find a solution – or get the help he needs to go beyond the point of emotional impasse.

Boundary issues – feelings of inappropriateness and trespass – also increase the difficulties of intimate talking and listening that sometimes exist between girls and women on the one hand, and boys and men on the other. Women and girls, for example, may feel that they have less right to insist on their agenda than men or boys do; or *men* may unconsciously feel that women and girls have less right to describe or determine what is going on.

That too makes for painful complications, especially when a girl or woman feels that she doesn't have the right to say no or to refuse to do something that is asked of her (from a trivial request about making lunch to a more serious request about sex); or when the man or boy cannot hear 'NO' and insists on his agenda even when it is clearly something that the woman is protesting about.

Knowing you have the right to say no without being punished for that, and feeling confident that you can hear someone else's no without punishing, withdrawing or sulking, are essential for mutual feelings of safety and wellbeing. If you have problems with this, it is important to seek professional help to affirm boundaries and find clear, effective ways to communicate.

When identifying difficulties, men and boys also seem more inclined than females to show that they feel emotionally invaded by what they are hearing (especially when they interpret what they are hearing as an attempt to control them). Men may become quickly reactive in an attempt to fend off what they are hearing. They may do this in a way that seems quite out of proportion to what has actually been said ('I only wanted to know if this year he'd like to come to my family for Christmas'). Those difficulties are likely to be worsened if the man is in general resistant to suggestions from other people or is single-mindedly focused on finding solutions.

Intimate listening does not require a solution. The 'end' is found in the process itself. Intimate listening is also not about making suggestions: it is about hearing someone express something that matters to them from their own point of view.

Those are easy differences to identify, yet it is unwise to create too many distinctions on the basis of gender. If you think about your own friends, there may be some wonderful listeners among the men and some poor listeners among the women. Even if the majority of people do seem to fall into the conventional gender categories, we need to be exceedingly cautious about apportioning skills on the basis of gender alone. Temperament, personality, the capacity to pay attention and offer empathy, cultural and social training also play a part in whether someone is willing to reflect on their experiences, talk about them honestly, and listen to someone else at a deeper level than daily conversation allows.

RELATIONSHIPS NEED STIMULATION AND KINDNESS

Many people, including adult siblings and their parents, long-term friends, and couples of all varieties, can discover, as Elliot and Tim did, that talking about talking is itself an exciting process of renewal and discovery. Many friendships and partnerships die for no grander reason than that people have stopped talking in ways that are stimulating or even interesting, and have stopped listening also.

To convince someone that listening is worthwhile, we need to have something worthwhile to say. That usually means something that is honest and deeply felt. Or something that is fresh or stimulating. If freshness and excitement are in short supply, then something must be done to correct this. Reading more adventurously; taking risks intellectually and socially; becoming involved in a wider range of social activities; approaching new interests: all that revives a sense of engagement with the world outside yourself. That renewed engagement makes your inner world more active also and swiftly spills over into the kinds of interactions that most people are longing for.

In any relationship there is always more to know. And more to know *that is worth knowing*. Most of us have been busy talking and listening (in somewhat uneven proportions) throughout our lives. This doesn't mean that our friends or partners are transparent to us. Taking someone for granted is easily done. More difficult, but more rewarding, is remaining fresh and open in the present moment; listening with all your senses; drawing the person in through your eyes; listening sometimes as if for the first time, or the last.

There are people who talk so much that their partner or friends can no longer bear to listen with any real attention. At best, they let the torrent of words pass by. That was certainly true for sisters Leah and Diane, who were born only a year apart but could not have been more different temperamentally. Diane was my client and she felt grief as well as frustration that it was so hard for her to spend time with her sister without becoming angry and exhausted by Leah's need to fill every moment with a deluge of talk.

Diane and I talked about how she might raise with Leah the possibility of finding ways to recognise that it was an anxious need for reassurance and connection that was getting expressed through this deluge of words. We also discussed how it can help for the anxious person to identify other ways of feeling connected – sitting in silence, for example, *in the presence of someone else*, or bringing to mind positive images of the person rather than seeing words as their sole point of connection – or to learn to ventilate some of their feelings in a journal. And then, through journal writing, to learn to refine their thoughts by asking themselves, 'What is it I'm trying to say here? What do I want this other person to understand?'

After some consideration, Diane decided that she could not raise the issue directly with her sister. She feared that Leah might hear her suggestions as a refusal to accept her as she is, and that it might worsen the uneasy situation between them. So the next idea we explored – this time more successfully – was for Diane to stop trying to distract Leah or ending their meetings prematurely and precipitously, and just to take the time, occasionally, to sit patiently and wait until the deluge subsided. Perhaps then, I suggested, something more meaningful might get heard as well as said.

Interestingly, that same successful outcome can also be achieved with someone who apparently has 'nothing to say'. Sitting peacefully, in a state of acceptance and without too much expectation, almost everyone does have something to say. And often has something to say that may surprise them every bit as much as it does the listener.

Careful, focused listening is the key to trust and communication, to intimacy, to knowing someone deeply and to being known. It is the key to greater knowledge, tolerance, acceptance and love. It is also the key to harmony between people.

Thoughtful speech and deep listening are the twin pillars that support all human relationships. Loving speech asks you to consider the effect of what you say on the other person. It requires you to remember that it is a person that you are speaking to, and not the target of your frustration, bitterness or contempt. To the best of your ability, it asks you to withdraw the stings and barbs from your speech and let them go. It asks you to be honest but, I would add, *not at the expense of the other person*. Sometimes kindness is needed to keep silent or to overlook what is inessential, and certainly not to pass on something that would be hurtful.

So much tragedy has come about because people speak to each other in ways that obliterate their shared humanity. In the face of an attack, the human instinct is to become defensive and counter-attack. This happens in our homes, workplaces and communities just as it does ceaselessly in political and international affairs.

Words are the means by which we break peace, and could make peace. We need to regard them with awe and respect.

Inner peace, and the quality of restraint that leads to the development of trust and tolerance between people, is not a static or passive thing. It arises from an active choice that needs remaking every day. It develops the highest skills of emotional intelligence, including self-awareness, consideration and self-control. And the rewards are exceptional.

Zen teacher and peace activist Thich Nhat Hanh emphasises how important speech is in its power to bring people together or drive them apart. He points out: 'Arguing with others only waters the seeds of anger in us . . . Do not think you will feel better if you can make the other person suffer too. This is a dangerous way of thinking. In their anger, the other person might respond even more harshly, and the anger will escalate.'

What Thich Nhat Hanh suggests is that you neither express nor repress your anger: 'The Buddha taught that when anger arises, close your eyes and ears, return to yourself, and tend to the source of anger within. Transforming your anger is not just for your personal liberation. Everyone around you and even those more distant will benefit if you succeed.'

LEARNING TO LISTEN

Little children have to be taught to listen. Left to themselves they would constantly interrupt. Left to themselves many adults would also constantly interrupt. Careful listening demands high levels of empathy and self-control. It means developing the capacity to set aside one's own urgent interests. To some extent at least, it means temporarily setting aside one's own self for someone else's sake.

The first voice you must learn to listen carefully to is your own.

This can be quite a shock. Through our voice, gestures of face and body, we are presenting ourselves to other people. But we can forget that there is an I in there, directing the circus! Our words are not caused by someone else; our voice and gestures belong to us alone.

We take so much for granted. We assume that the people closest to us will know we 'really love them' even if we speak to them like an army sergeant. But why should they know that? Why should we require them constantly to translate what they are hearing into what they are supposed to know ('Mum can't help sounding like a banshee. She does really love us', 'Dad's always going around yelling that we are born losers. But I know he wants the best for us'). That assumption makes no sense.

A young man said to me recently, 'I grew up in a house filled with "Don'ts".' His mother loved him and wanted the best for him, but what he has carried away from his childhood is 'Don't'.

In a new relationship, when you still believe that everything is possible, it is usually easy to talk and even easier to listen. There's not much credit in being a 'great listener' when you are trying to impress someone, or when you are newly struck by love and the world feels remade. The challenge comes when the newness of a relationship has worn off and you no longer feel inspired to make an effort. Then your habits of self-absorption can easily come back, along with a carelessness about whether your communications are as generous as they could be.

It's at that point that your habits of speech and listening will reassert themselves. When you are responding out of habit only, you are rarely entirely present. Your body may be there, slumped in your favourite chair. But where are your thoughts? What's capturing your attention? Whose voice are you actually listening to? Is it that other person's? Or is it your own as you re-run an event of the day, or work on something that is looming in your mind? It takes an effort of will as well as love to be present with your mind. *You must choose to be present. You must choose to pay attention.* And again and again, choose it.

VALUE EMPATHY

Listening builds empathy and sustains it. It also deepens our capacity to concentrate, absorb information and pay attention through our instincts as well as all our senses.

It is interesting to note, then, that many conventionally high-IQ people are relatively poor listeners. They may have contempt for what they regard as 'emotional matters' (despite clear evidence that emotional intelligence brings the qualities that make us 'fully human'). They may be people who have difficulty stepping out of a competitive frame of mind, or of setting their own 'important' concerns aside. They may also be uncomfortable when they believe something non-specific is being asked of them. And despite their intellectual gifts, they may be relatively unconscious of how they have learned to use an authoritative tone of voice or a dominating manner to silence others and reduce them to a sense of relative powerlessness (which reflects, in part, the speaker's own lack of social awareness).

Carlos is a jazz piano player, a father, and a 50-year-old optimist. He has sustaining friendships with other men, including his accountant brother. But he sees this as a benefit of having been born after the Second World War and coming to maturity in the 1960s. For earlier generations, the story was different.

Carlos says, 'My father was highly intelligent. Yet I believe that careful listening was difficult for him. Maybe intolerable. Quite unconsciously, he deflected opportunities to listen outside a range of topics that he did effectively control. That's how it seemed to me. Like many articulate people, he was most comfortable when he was holding the floor – he had many fascinating theories – or listening to other men holding the floor, telling well-crafted anecdotes or sharing memories that not only had been honed with time, but had been made safe by time. As a child, and even as an adult, I admired my father's eloquence, but felt put outside by it. Now I would assume that the person who speaks in this way is distanced from his own emotional or instinctual life. Dad could barely ask about anything in my life or my brother's life other than our professional achievements. I can feel sad about that and regretful about how he'd been socialised and how he wouldn't or couldn't overcome this. It certainly was a loss for him too. He was cut off from his aliveness.'

Careful listening *is* a risky business. Even when the subject matter roams over the past, it requires us to pay attention *in the present*. It is an intimate experience and it can be intense. Listening carefully, we must relinquish control of the other person's agenda. We must allow ourselves to be surprised. We must accept the thoughts and feelings of the other person, even if we don't agree with them or approve of them. *We must tolerate another person's reality and show it respect.*

SIMPLE CHANGES, GREAT RESULTS

Andrea has become a mother for the first time at the age of thirty-eight. Her baby was born after several years of marriage and a long, arduous time on an IVF (in vitro fertilisation) programme. Andrea's husband, Daniel, wanted a baby as much as she did, and is passionate about their little daughter, Chiara. This family is a very contented one, but Andrea is self-aware enough to recognise how often her tone of voice has come to express a mood of impatience and irritation that actually does not reflect how she feels about Daniel.

Talking about this, Andrea said, 'I've taken on the role of organiser in our relationship. I'm someone who likes order and action, and Daniel's a bit of a dreamer. Part of him likes me to organise him. But part of him resists it, and the more I try to organise, the more he seems to be forced to dig himself into a hole of inaction, irresponsibility, etc. (and of course the opposite is true – I get stuck with the role of "straight man" too much). Anyway, with my organising hat on I see it as my responsibility to see that the business of the baby's "maintenance" – feeding, cleaning, changing, et cetera – happens quickly enough so she can get to bed on time. So every evening when Daniel comes home, and is desperate to have some play time with her, I'm always in the background chiding him relentlessly about time – "Daniel, give her to me, I need to feed her now"; "Daniel, can you stop playing with her and change her now, it's getting late"; "Daniel, she has to go to bed now . . . now . . . now!"

'I read a little pamphlet where someone recalled their unhappy experience growing up with their mother, and said she was always so driven to keep to this unrealistic timetable that she set for herself that she was terrified that any of her children should express any kind of spontaneity, lest they should throw her schedule out. This really frightened me – I could see myself so easily doing this – and I started hearing how I was haranguing Daniel about time whenever he was playing with Chiara. He loves her so intensely, and he really gets so little time with her in the hour or two between his return from work and her bedtime. I realised that the greatest gift I could give him would be to ease up a little, especially when they're having a really joyful moment together. Also that I should stay away a little bit, not interrupt them and distract her from him. And if she goes to bed fifteen, twenty or even thirty minutes late, it's not a disaster.

'I feel very generous when I can manage to do this – I do feel like I'm giving him a present. And I get one too because I feel a lot more relaxed, and not crushed beneath my responsibility.'

However hard we try to cultivate generosity and restraint, our reactions on occasion overpower the voice of reason. We feel compelled to behave in certain ways, say nagging, bitter, blaming or angry things, even when the voice of experience is telling us how fruitless or even counterproductive such reactions are. *We are listening to ourselves. And we don't like what we hear.*

In those difficult moments it is helpful to wrench yourself physically away from the situation, even if it is only to go into the bathroom where you can catch your breath (long breath in, long breath out) and challenge those feelings of inevitability.

Andrea acknowledges just how tough it is to move away. It may feel as though all thought has stopped. Or as though your feet are glued to the floor. Or that you've been sucked into a whirlwind from which there's no escaping. Yet, as Andrea points out, when you can fight those powerful feelings and take back self-control the rewards are tremendous.

'I think I am often aggressive when I am doing something that I don't really want to do. But it takes such an effort to step back from myself, get perspective, and see that it's often self-imposed, and that I need only speak up clearly and calmly and say that I don't want to do it.

'More often I just do it but become resentful, with a lot of buried anger escaping and being directed at Daniel. He would of course say, "Just don't do it!"

'He has a wonderful philosophy of "Stop and smell the roses" – enjoy the moment. Whereas too often I am so focused on getting to the next moment that I can't enjoy any of them. This is probably a key issue underlying most of our exchanges. I need to plan less, and he needs to plan more. Instead we're attracted to each other because we are opposite and complementary on this issue, but we end up forcing each other into more extreme positions.

'During my pregnancy, and in the months after having our baby, when I was focused almost entirely on getting enough sleep, I became aware that Daniel and I did not really laugh a lot any more. We did not seem to experience those moments of pure fun that we used to. It was a bit of a shock to see this suddenly. I tried to keep my eye out for moments that could blossom into laughter, and instead of cutting them off (in order to get on with the business of running the house, organising the baby, et cetera) I let them bloom. And I discovered something really interesting. I realised that Daniel loves to make me laugh. It seems to make him feel very good about the person he is. And I remember now that this was very much part of his self-image when I met him. He was the one who made all his friends laugh. It moved me very much to see that it was especially important to him that he make me laugh. It's sort of like a tenderness that I was completely missing. So laughing is something that we do more now.'

Listening carefully, it is often true that we don't like what we are hearing. As we listen we become angry, resentful or insecure. We feel pushed to stop listening and start speaking. And believe – or so we tell ourselves – that we have every right to do so!

That burst of self-satisfaction should be noted with caution. Reflecting on the changes achieved in her life through devotion to the contemporary Hindu teacher Mata Amritanandamayi (Ammachi or Mother) – writer Amanda Lohrey says that she sees her teacher as 'the lens, the prism', adding 'All my relationships are refracted through her and through the perspective that the guru–disciple relationship takes.'

So how might this help Amanda in a situation where, for example, she doesn't like what's happening externally or doesn't welcome a reaction that's arising inside her?

Amanda explains: 'I probably take things a lot less personally than I used to do, so that when someone lets me down, as someone did only this week, instead of getting hostile and upset I tend to think, after only a brief tantrum, OK, what's the lesson here? Someone I was relying on to help me said she couldn't come to this event. She couldn't help me. And I thought – after not all that much reflection – well, OK, it's probably time for me to do this on my own without her help. Am I up to it? Yes I am. It's probably good for me to do it on my own. The moment's come and that's fine.'

That capacity to glean an insight, even from a difficult situation, is immensely soothing. Better than that, it's empowering. You move from feeling that what someone else is doing is causing you horrible unrest, to a more balanced view that 'I don't like this, but what can I make of it?'

The process Amanda is following is as psychologically strengthening as it is spiritually. She explains: 'The guru [Ammachi] says that everyone is your spiritual teacher and especially the people you don't get on with or who frustrate you. It all sounds Pollyanna-ish when you put it like that, and it doesn't prevent you from still having tantrums, being disappointed, having all the usual range of negative emotions. But it does temper them. It does mean that they are not as strong as they might otherwise be. And that they last less time. It means that I am less egotistical with people, less defensive, more detached. I'm not talking about detachment as in "I don't care", more the detachment that comes from minimising the involvement of the ego, maximising the involvement of the heart, and the intelligence of the heart. There's a lovely line in one of Mother's (Ammachi's) books, talking about Western rationalism and reason, where she points out that *the role of reason is to support the heart.* That's a favourite line of mine.'

MOVING IN AND OUT OF CAREFUL LISTENING

Making notes about listening, thinking about some of the many conversations I have treasured, and noticing too what an incredibly strong impulse there is in us to communicate and feel understood, I decided to call several friends who are long-time therapists. Somewhat provocatively I asked them if they listen well outside their work.

Predictably Frieda, my post-Freudian friend, asked me, 'How do *you* experience my capacity to listen?', and then laughed before she said, 'I only listen well when I need to. I don't want to be analyst to my friends and most of all I don't want to be analyst to my family. In normal conversations I know I do all the usual gross things. I interrupt. I talk across. I shout. I contradict. I think my own thoughts when someone is boring me. I shut off. I don't necessarily ask the "right" questions. In fact, I sometimes pay next to no attention! Yet the skills are there. I can trust that.'

Down the phone I could hear Frieda warming to the theme. 'Maybe it's like singing. I have an old friend from school days who's a brilliant tenor. If I hear him at the opera, his voice is divine. He's divine! But if he's here for dinner and we are all trying to remember how Frank-N-Furter's opening song in *Rocky Horror* goes, he's not going to give us the full-scale opera voice. We know it's in there. But it doesn't go out with him to dinner.'

Thinking about that conversation, and how closely Frieda's views match my own experience and that of the other therapists in my small and unscientific sample, I realise how helpful it is to know that we don't need to be perfect listeners all the time.

People in family or long-term relationships may back off from this style of listening, afraid of what is being asked of them. Will the relationship become too intense? Will people feel too exposed, ashamed? Will they be asked for something that they can't provide?

It's reassuring, then, to discover that deep listening is rarely needed on an everyday basis. It's not what happens on a rushed morning as everyone gets ready for work; or in the moments when someone has pressing assignments to finish, homework to complete or a distracting situation in another part of their life.

It is also reassuring to be reminded once again that for deep listening to be mutually relieving and satisfying, solutions are not needed either. *To listen well is enough in itself.* Once someone feels heard, their emotions often feel less turbulent. Having been heard, they are likely to want and need less.

The significance of good communication and listening is widely acknowledged. But I wonder might there be too much emphasis on listening as a skill and not as an experience? When you can set your concerns aside, allow yourself to be available and moved by what you are hearing, then the listening will be rich and true. Listening deeply, giving the other person your attention, restraining yourself from judging, reminding yourself that *you are not there to fix anything*, you give something that is priceless.

RESPECT BOUNDARIES

Mark is a registered nurse and counsellor. He's in his mid-forties, and has been married for sixteen years. He values listening but, like most of us, finds aspects of it extremely challenging. 'I think "perfect listening" is part of some "perfect relationship",' he says, 'and is reflected in a feeling or an habitual belief that I can't attain it. I can't have it.

'Much of my listening is affected by a sense that I was not heard when I needed it most, as a child. In intimate relationships I do find it hard to ask for what I need. It's as if I wasn't listened to then, so how can I be now?'

Listening to what he's saying, Mark laughs. 'That creates a contradiction when I am listened to! I sometimes find I shy away and
then don't speak!

'Conversely, while I see myself as a "good listener", I know I can
be most defensive as a listener when someone intimate is talking. There's some kind of self-talk going on about what's being asked
of me, and am I capable of giving it?

'As for those times when I do listen without preparing my next
statement or judging, when I am giving complete attention, then
that person opens up so much. A space is created where vulnerability and truth can emerge. And the same is true for myself when
I receive the same level of attention from another person.

'It is harder to do, the closer we are related. It's as if we are taught
to not listen and to not give true attention to each other.

'I am aware of how presence and listening go together. In listening and in being listened to, the issue of presence is strong.
Even when we have those flashes, those rare flashes of truly listening from our stillness, we do so with a presence that is still
uniquely our own, I believe.'

Mark's honesty about his difficulties in accepting that someone
could listen deeply to him – and his almost involuntary withdrawal from that – strikes a chord with me. Listening deeply
expresses interest and concern. It directs attention away from the
listener and back to the speaker. *To receive that level of attention from
another person is difficult for many people.* We may want the experience and seek it out, yet find it, in reality, unbearably exposing. It
may expose to ourselves our own neediness ('I will never get
enough of this. I'll want your attention forever'). It may raise our
fears and issues around trust ('If I tell this person too much they
are sure to take advantage of me'). It may confront an unconscious
drive to be in control ('Only weak people reveal their deepest
emotions and thoughts').

It might also require us to re-examine some deep beliefs: 'No one cares about me. No one could understand me. No one can help me. I'll always be alone.'

The person who has difficulties being listened to should respect those habits of caution. To be told it's now safe to say whatever you want may not placate your anxieties. You may need to discover slowly the safety and relief of being heard.

In psychotherapy it is often the case that when someone has difficulty making connections through talk and self-revelation (and many people do), progress towards a more trusting relationship will be quite uneven. And that is understandable. Following a meeting that has allowed for a deepening of intimacy, there may be a withdrawal, perhaps a rejection, either of the therapist or of the idea of therapy. The person's own anxieties may flare up. He might imagine all sorts of reactions in the therapist's mind that perhaps more exactly reflect his own difficulties with self-acceptance and self-love. In that uncomfortable state, many of us would and do lash out, expressing ourselves aggressively, even violently.

In intimate relationships similar patterns can occur. A wonderfully close night together may be followed by silence or withdrawal for a week or two; a far-reaching conversation may be followed by what seems like an entirely unnecessary outburst of criticism; plans to move in together may be followed by a heated argument 'over nothing'.

Moving closer into someone else's soul space through talking and listening requires patience, consideration, kindness. Boundaries need to be strictly observed. Differences in personal style need to be respected. Few assumptions should be made. There is no timetable for the way in which an intimate relationship should develop. In careful listening, less is more. Less interference; less judgement; fewer assumptions, but closer attention. Above all else, when someone has set aside their defences, even by the smallest degree, to allow you to glimpse their inner world, this is not the time to push your way in to criticise, to be demanding, to be moralistic or to lecture.

'I've learned the hard way,' a mother told me. 'With my first three girls I've always been quite unselfconscious about what I would say. When my fourth and last daughter hit puberty, it was a different story. It was only when she threatened to leave home to live with a friend from school that I was shocked enough to realise that I had to change my style of relating to her. I believe I was being loving and interested. She believes I was an interfering monster.

'I can't recognise that reality. I adore my girls. It's horrible to me. But I must respect it. Otherwise we'll be in constant conflict. Or she'll go altogether. I've learned I must bite my tongue. I must swallow my usual attempts at reason and logic and just listen to her, acknowledge what she's feeling with the bare minimum of words. And never, ever imply that I have a possible solution unless she specifically asks, "Mum, what do you think . . . ?"'

NEW SKILLS ON THE RUN

In each of our close relationships, different skills will be required: different patterns of communication, different emphases. We might find this disconcerting – especially when what 'works' with one person falls flat with another. But it also allows us to develop our capacities for flexibility and resourcefulness.

We cannot even begin to meet other people's emotional needs unless we learn to read their cues ('What's this person wanting now? Am I going in too close? Asking too much? Pressing too hard?'). Crucial to that will be a conscious willingness on our part to respect limits and emotional boundaries, *even when they make no sense to us.*

Individual perceptions of intimacy and autonomy vary enormously. To cross someone's boundaries is an act of trespass. To respect another's boundaries – no matter how eccentric we think they are – is a vital expression of love.

If someone lets you know verbally or through their emotional reactions that 'You are coming in too close. You are asking too much of me. I am feeling overwhelmed by you or by your demands', *it is essential to hear that and to act on it.* Not with grudging unwillingness. Not with self-pity. Not with a moralistic outburst ('I thought you'd be the kind of person who'd make time for her friends'). Not with any attack whatsoever.

Unsurprisingly, anyone who experiences discomfort about other people coming in too close will be driven further into their own shell by emotional outbursts. Their fears will be eased only where there is no counterattack, no 'punishments' and no miserable revivals weeks later ('I remember the time when you said . . . and now you expect me to . . . ').

In any relationship that is halfway intimate, we need the freedom to be ourselves. It's impossible to overemphasise the importance of that. But that freedom is not always readily given – or taken.

We may enter a relationship already less than comfortable with who we are. So when someone we love and respect demonstrates through their solidity and commitment that they can be comfortable with us, usually our gratitude matches that of the angels.

A sense of timing in all our relationships matches in importance that crucial awareness of boundaries. And it requires much the same levels of self-control and respect. Lu is an editor in her thirties, newly and very happily married and stepmother to a child from her husband's first marriage. 'This relationship is more than I dared to want,' she says, touchingly.

Lu is conscious of how she uses silence as well as words in a relationship where a high value is placed on close communication, humour and trust. She explains: 'I find that I use silence as a code to my partner that something is bothering me. It's a kind of passive-aggressive ploy. Usually we're very vocal with one another, and when we're in good moods we often good naturedly tell each other off in this exaggerated manner that allows us to let off steam in a humorous way. So, when we're not playfully having a go at each other with mock-violent threats and good-natured put-downs (I know it sounds weird – but it works for us), silence very loudly warns the other that something's up.

'When my partner detects my silence, he can then ask me what's wrong and thus open up a discussion that will enable me to express my feelings.'

You might wonder why Lu needs to be relatively indirect in this way. As she explains it, the subtlety of this interaction strikes a note of real respect. 'I guess I do this rather than just come out with it because it's a way I can make sure that he's ready to confront what I have to say to him. When he says, "Is there something you want to tell me?", then I know that he's ready to listen.

'Being heard is really important to me and the time and context have to be just right. By "making" him raise the problem, I can ensure that both of us will give it our full attention.'

Timing is important to me too. Like many parents whose children's activities are spread across a large, dense city, I have come to value any time spent in the car with just one of my teenage children. Side by side, looking ahead, caught in familiar proximity, half listening to background music, the experience of speaking and listening, and of shared silence, seems wonderfully sustaining.

There are equally familiar occasions, though, when your intention to be accepting and close is thwarted. Perhaps you hear something you didn't want to hear and you interrupt precipitously. Or something said irritates you and you jump in reactively. Or you are tired or overwhelmed, torn between the tasks waiting for your attention. Your concentration splits and can't rest.

Those are not the moments to invite someone to pour out their heart to you. Tell the person honestly, if you need to, that you want to listen to them but now is not the time. If they can't wait (or if they are too immature to know how to wait), tell them you will do your best to listen now, but that you will need time to think about what they are saying once you have heard it.

The space 'to think about' doesn't take anything away. On the contrary, it allows you to give a measured response. But you must honour the trust that you will return to the issue soon; and that you will do so as a 'listener' still, and not as an 'expert consultant' on someone else's life.

Of all the skills required by intimacy, listening can seem one of the most difficult. It is useful to remember, then, when you don't know what to do and you are tempted to interrupt or withdraw to relieve your own tension, *just to be present.* Think of a figure of love who inspires you: Christ, Buddha, the darling grandmother you loved. *Listen with their ears. Listen through their heart and mind.*

LISTEN INWARDLY

Just as our outer relationships benefit from – and need – careful listening, so does our relationship with our inner world, with our soul or with our God. Every aspect of our lives is supported when we know how to listen inwardly. Taking time to sit in meditation, or 'doing nothing', or taking time to write your questions in a journal and then to write answers without judging them: those are all invaluable listening activities that make your inner world a familiar and trustworthy place.

And listening inwardly need not stop there. Paying attention to everyday activities, *listening in to the hum of our lives,* we have a chance to transform those activities and tasks into things that connect us with ourselves.

Artist Meinrad Craighead expresses this same thought: 'The simplest actions should be done with a full realization of their significance . . . Ordinary, daily life is weighted with mystery and beauty. The smallest observation or activity can startle the imagination to wakefulness and a sense of wonder at the significance of being.'

Like so many of our most precious capacities, careful listening can improve with age. Our need to talk may feel less urgent; our capacities for acceptance may grow; our perspective on life may become more generous.

As we trust what *we can bear to know*, we become steadier. As we allow ourselves to admit the contradictions of life, we become less distracted by our own agitations. We are less concerned about what other people might think of us; less fearful of living passionately. We become more familiar with the fullness silence offers.

Inner listening is available to everyone. It simply requires the same time and respect that we can offer others; the same patience; the same willingness to pay attention, to be accepting; the same confidence that *what we will learn is worth knowing*.

Listening to who we are, we perceive how our spirit is our link with eternity as well as our connection to all other living forms. It is our spirit that leaps when we hear the voice of someone we love or a sublime piece of music; when we notice how exquisite a single leaf can be or a simple touch; when we lose ourselves in the joy of dancing or singing, lying under the spread of a tree or throwing ourselves into the cold springtime ocean; when we pause to remember where we have come from and where we are going. And when we allow ourselves to be fearless.

Here is a marvellous example of this from 70-year-old Rabbi Lionel Blue, talking in Naim Attallah's book *Insights* about his early difficulties with sex and religion, and his crucial discovery of the inner voice that not only lives in us, but also liberates us to experience our lives joyfully – if we are willing to hear it.

'To begin with,' Rabbi Blue explains, 'I thought I had to sublimate all the sex for religion, and in trying to sublimate sex I found myself back in my childhood again being neurotic, and I thought, no, no, no, it can't be like that. Then through the Quakers I developed a kind of inner voice which told me to break out. At that point I felt I had had enough so I decided to say yes to everything and I went to Amsterdam, which was the sort of Greenwich Village of Europe at the time. And there I found religion again because I discovered that people are very vulnerable, especially with no clothes on. I found out a lot of other things as well. For example, I went to a kind of gay sauna in Amsterdam and after experiencing the two or three seconds of relief, I began to think this was the biggest con trick ever. I thought, is this the thing I've been mad about all those years? And the inner voice said to me, "Lionel, you don't get much from it because you don't give much." I then realised that religion and sex had to be brought together. I had been a terribly repressed person, so I needed a bit of relief, but going beyond that bit of relief, you ended up in the sphere of beginning to make love. And that was a different matter.'

Do we avoid attempting to listen to our inner voice because we fear we won't find it? Or because we fear that, if we do find it, it will speak to us like a Victorian nanny? Make us feel worse about ourselves than we do already? Pull us back from enjoying what we love most? Some people may indeed experience such a voice: but I believe that voice – the one that rubs our noses in our limitations – is the voice of our superego. It is not the voice of love, of the universal heart that welcomes us with concern, humour, wisdom, and lifts us to an experience of our inner beauty, no matter who we are or what we have done.

When you listen inwardly, you recognise with increasing skill and ease what matters and what does not. You also increase by a hundredfold that most loving and liberating connection of all, which is simultaneously with yourself and in this moment, and with all of life, and with eternity.

We are the many hearts beating within the One Heart.
We are the many hearts
through whom the One Heart
finds expression.

HOW TO

Listen Carefully

Listening is the key to intimacy. It will outlive your youthful beauty and take you beyond your wildest dreams of devotion and connection. Careful listening is the greatest investment you may ever make in your relationship future.

It demands and cultivates patience, good humour, self-control, tolerance and generosity! And all of that supports love. Putting aside your need to interrupt, defend, match stories, or correct, teaches you that your own needs can sometimes wait; that familiar habits of urgency need not come between you and another person; that the more 'real' someone is to you, the easier it is to care about them – and that there is always more to know.

Careful listening can transform personal relationships. It can make your interest in other people livelier and more tender. There is no greater cure for discontent or even tension than being listened to carefully. That's what psychotherapy offers; that's how it 'cures'. Within relationships, careful listening can be a lifesaver that's just as powerful.

Workplaces also depend for their wellbeing on how carefully people listen. People who feel listened to in their workplaces develop self-confidence and loyalty, solve problems faster, treat others with respect and consideration, and feel valued.

Listening inwardly is also part of careful listening: finding and trusting your inner voice; recognising it as the voice of your own experience and wisdom; taking you deep into your own nature.

- Relax your body. Visualise your inner spaciousness. (Listening depends on a positive, open *attitude*.)
- Listen through *all* your senses. Watch the other person's body and gestures, the rise and fall of their breath.
- Observe what emotions are being expressed. Be respectful of them. Often the other person most wants you to get *the feelings that lie behind the words*. Listen for them. Develop empathy – intimacy depends on it.
- When someone is saying something that matters to them, let them speak *without interruptions*.
- Don't control or direct with nervous or intrusive questions.
- *Never deny the other person their own experiences* ('You couldn't possibly have felt that', 'You look OK to me', 'It doesn't sound that upsetting'). This is a form of trespass that kills open communication.
- Don't routinely top the other person's story with your overwhelming memories of the time when . . . That's a power game. It is not respectful or intimate.
- If you must say something, keep it encouraging ('Tell me more about . . . '). Remain focused on the other person, on their story. Your stories can wait. The purpose of this interraction is that *the other person will feel heard*.
- If you are unsure what you are hearing, check it out ('I'm wondering if you feel pushed to make a decision too early?').
- Often we want someone else to be with us while *we find out what we ourselves think*. See yourself as a companionable listener, not as a strategic adviser.
- If you are explicitly asked to advise, speak in the first person ('In my experience . . . ', 'I've been helped by . . . ', 'What works for me . . . ').
- If you are asked, 'What do you think?', ask what *they* think (or feel, fear, want or would like). Keep your interventions

or suggestions to a minimum.

- When the person's experience is different from yours or their response is different, set aside judgements. Remain present for them.
- *Never* press for more information than the person wants to give.
- Respect boundaries. An intimate or honest conversation gives you no rights to extra intimacy.
- Be unafraid of silence. When someone pauses, don't rush to speak. Let them use the space to move deeper into their own thoughts.
- If you are uncomfortable with silence, pay attention to your breathing. Simply count long, slow breaths as they enter and leave your body. This is an instant cure for discomfort.
- When someone has shared something important, *acknowledge it*. Don't leave the person unsure if you care ('Thank you so much for letting me know', 'I am really grateful to have some sense of what's going on for you').
- *Never* use something you have heard in a time of sharing against the speaker. That is a vile betrayal of trust.
- If what you are hearing is offensive or frightening, explain that you cannot go on listening. Ask the person to call a professional help line.
- If you are repeatedly asked to listen, but don't feel heard, make it a priority to discuss that. The other person may need confidence that they too could be an adequate listener.
- The dynamics of talking and listening may tell you a lot about the power dynamics in your relationship. *Pay close attention.* Make any adjustments needed so that *both* people feel heard.
- If you don't have time or you feel too distracted to listen carefully, say so. But get back to it fast.
- Value *the sharing of happiness*. Make time for that.

- Listen to yourself: not just to how you talk but also to what you talk about, your tone of voice, the emotions that drive the way you speak. Are you pushing people away or allowing them to feel safe and welcome?
- Trust that the habits of careful listening will make it easier for you to 'hear more deeply' in casual moments.
- Ask the other person what they value most when you do listen carefully. Use that insight to improve *all* the time you spend together.
- *Be* someone you would like to listen to: encouraging, tolerant, curious, warm, interesting, positive. It *is* possible!

Victoria and Carey's story

Careful listening can dramatically improve a troubled relationship. It can even save it. When neither person feels heard, and both people are resentful, hurt or frustrated, then a short period of structured listening can be exceptionally helpful.

Twenty-seven-year-old Victoria and her mother, Carey, had a long history of disappointment. They do love each other, yet far too often they would meet and soon find themselves irritable and arguing. Each would leave their visits feeling ragged and resentful.

Victoria finally took the initiative, persuading Carey to go with her to a counsellor. Carey resisted the idea at first, believing that counselling was mainly for people with 'real problems'.

The counsellor explained that difficulties in communicating *are* real problems. Without satisfying communication, a relationship cannot thrive – and will generally sour. The love each felt had no chance to get expressed until each could feel heard.

The counsellor suggested that the two women formalise a regular time to practise careful listening and to begin to experience feeling heard. During that time, she suggested, each person could talk for about fifteen to twenty minutes. There was no need to prepare what they wanted to say. It would be fine to use some of that time for silent reflection and to discover that silence is not 'embarrassing'. On the contrary, persistently superficial talk can smother real feelings. Often it's only in silence that our most truthful feelings can emerge.

- While one person talked, *the other was to do nothing more than listen and pay close attention to what she was hearing.* Questions or comments were off-limits.

- At the end of the agreed time, *without discussing what had been said*, they would swap roles.
- When both had talked and both had listened, they would go about their day. They would *not* analyse or talk over what had been said. They would simply go away and think about it.

'It did feel a bit fake at first,' Carey commented later. 'But that's true with any new experience. The hardest part is that you wanted to rush in and comment. It seemed very hard to be encouraging *without* commenting. But that's what wasn't working. Also the benefits have been startling.'

What are the benefits?

Both Victoria and Carey found that they could offer a quite new level of attention to the other person. Because they weren't finding a 'solution', they could listen and accept with a welcome sense of freedom.

Each woman said that she felt heard and genuinely understood, even without the usual comments or responses. They also noticed they felt tender and interested rather than irritable and defensive towards the other one.

'I've got a much clearer sense altogether of what's going on with Mum,' said Victoria. 'I've always loved her, but now I feel I am seeing her with new eyes.'

Carey's comment was also striking. 'I feel accepted by Victoria as I never did before. I am surprised that's what I wanted so badly, but it's true.'

Victoria and Carey continue to chat on the phone in the usual way and to have unstructured meetings. However, those times together have also softened and become less reactive, less advice driven and much less tense.

Complain Effectively

Complaint is a burning issue in many relationships. Our difficulties with it reflect our longings for acceptance. No wonder, then, that hurts go deep. When someone criticises us even mildly, we often feel as though we ourselves are *not all right*. We may even feel endangered.

We tend to hold onto criticisms and remember them when kinder moments have been long forgotten. Despite this, our own deep fears of being criticised may not give us pause before we criticise others!

Love is not readily expressed through pointing out what is wrong. Nor does love gives us 'the right' to be someone else's judge and monitor. All relationships benefit from a culture of encouragement rather than complaint. *Criticising someone will arouse their defences.* (They may hate you as much as what you are saying.)

These rules need to be followed in relationships of every kind.

- Keep criticisms to a minimum.
- Never criticise when you are hoping to pass on the hot potato of your own bad mood. Nor when you envy someone and want to cut them down.
- Never criticise the person, their family or their beliefs. Stick to actions or attitudes only – but with caution.
- Don't return to the same dreary criticism. If you have already told your best friend that her choice of boyfriends is the eighth mystery of the universe and she has chosen not to

listen to you, *don't go back there*. (Actually, don't go there in the first place.)

- Never 'go global' ('You always . . . ', 'We never . . . ', 'I'm the only one who . . . '). Be absolutely specific.
- Think constructively. Bring a suggestion or inquiry along with your complaint. And speak collaboratively ('What about if . . . ?', 'Do you think we could . . . ?').

It is also true that believing you have no right to make a complaint can be uncomfortable or disempowering. Here is an effective way to complain – if it is *absolutely* necessary. This formula is one I have adapted from a psychologist called Haim Ginott, whose principles of mutual respect and encouragement are developed in this book.

Use the letters ABC as your guide.

Instead of saying: 'I can't stand the way you leave your cups in the sink/you never get home on time/you are always talking about yourself/you dump your dark washing in with the light' or 'You're a selfish shit and I don't know why I put up with you' or 'No one in this office/study group/committee is capable of seeing the nose on their own face.'
Say: 'When I see A (stating the source of your complaint), I feel B. And I'd rather you did C.'

The strategy here is easy to remember. A: you state the problem. B: you state how you feel about the problem – not the person or people. C: *you make a positive suggestion.* Then it helps to check that out with the person.

Here are some examples.

'When you won't sit down and go over the bills with me (A), I feel really unsupported (B). I'd like you to give me a weekly summary of your spending and outstanding accounts, and I'll handle the rest (C). How would that be (checking out)?'

'If I hear you resenting my request that you wash up (A), it makes me feel resentful also (B). What about if you wash up one week and I'll do the next (C)? Or can you think of some other way we can avoid this trivial task becoming a problem (checking out)?'

'When you don't directly suggest we make love and I'm anyway feeling tired (A), I feel confused as well as pressured (B). Can we make regular dates or set aside time when making love is our priority (C)? Would that suit you (checking out)?'

Like any skill, this can feel awkward at first. But it's a method that is surprisingly simple to learn. It's clean. It promotes clarity as well as respect. And it can end whining, belittling, attacking and resentment.

However – life does not always respond well even to the wisest recipes. Your partner, friend, boss or work mate may not be listening to what you are saying. They may be *responding to what you used to say or what they believe you are saying.*

If their response is aggressive and self-defensive ('The bills are your business . . . I'm already worn out . . . '), *drop the matter.* Your timing may be out. They may be feeling overwhelmed. Or they may need some time and understanding to adjust to the Benign New You.

Choose a different time to say, 'I'd still like to know how you think we could sort out the bills. Is this a good time for you?'

If your efforts to communicate and problem solve continue to be stonewalled, then the problem goes deeper. Seek professional help – even if it's a workplace issue. Skills can be learned fast. A trusting flow of communication within any relationship is crucial to openness – and worth every effort.

Hear Complaints, Express Regrets, Keep Your Power

All but living saints will rush into defence mode when they hear someone voicing a complaint or criticism of themselves or someone they love. It feels awful. You want to push the awfulness away, often back onto the other person with a counterattack that then lifts the emotional temperature in thirty seconds or less.

Knowing how to hear criticism – and keep your power – relieves your fear of it.

- When you hear someone complain, *acknowledge the complaint.* Even if it seems ridiculous or outrageous, just acknowledge it ('You're saying you don't feel supported in your new venture').

  Once the person has voiced their complaint *and feels heard,* they will often let it go – especially when you clearly take it seriously. Their tension is about getting something said. Your challenge is to defuse that tension by hearing what they are saying and simultaneously keeping yourself cool.
- If it's something serious, acknowledge it and say you'd like time to think about it. When you make that time, talk collaboratively. See it as a shared problem ('What do you think *we* should do about it?').

Here's an example.

Complaint: 'You can't seem to get anything done on time. Don't you see there is an entire team being held up by . . . ?'

Response: 'That's how you see it?/Is that how it looks to you?/ That sounds serious/I'll need to think about that – let me get back to you.'

Here's another example. This time the person criticised is someone you love.

Complaint: 'Your daughter is certainly wearing some peculiar clothes these days. In my day no one would have dared to go out looking like . . . '
Response: 'It's true that times change.'

Now you are making a totally neutral statement that does not agree with the complainer, or defend your daughter or express disloyalty to her. This simple process of acknowledgement is exceptionally steadying. Alternative defusers may be 'Some things are hard to understand', 'Isn't life mysterious?', 'There are so many trends in the world', 'That's certainly one way of looking at it.'

Learning how to express regret can be an equally powerful defuser of anger and healer of hurts. This can be done when someone accuses you of wrongdoing or wants you to express regret for something. Perhaps you have done wrong. And you can say so. Or perhaps you yourself may not believe that what you or a group you represent has done is in fact an offence.

You may feel that you are in the right. Or that the issue has nothing to do with you. Nevertheless, *someone else is distressed.*

You could rush to your own defence and tell the other person how wrong they are. Or you could again try simply acknowledging how that other person feels.

Here are two examples.

Complaint: 'You never noticed how miserable I was during

that whole year.'
Response: 'I am really sorry that it was hard for you.'

Complaint: 'You have no idea how much we have suffered.'
Response: 'I deeply regret there has been so much pain felt.'

That's all: 'I am really sorry that it was hard for you', 'I deeply regret there has been so much pain felt.'

Respond to the distress.

Express sorrow for that.

This is a pure act of compassion that makes no comment whatsoever about who is right or wrong. It is truly a practice of the universal heart.

We all know what it feels like to be hurt, sidelined, misunderstood. *We can acknowledge how that feels.*

Our personal and communal lives would be infinitely more harmonious if people everywhere could do this simple thing: respond to a person's or nation's distress without questioning whether the person or nation is 'entitled' to their feelings or self-defensive argument about whether they have caused it. In the most real sense this allows everyone involved to reach beyond themselves; to acknowledge how they can influence each other for the better, heal hurts and continue with their lives in peace.

Value Truth

as Your Ally

All human beings deceive themselves

about the way they operate.

KATHERINE ANNE PORTER

The emotions that we associate with love are beautiful. The principles that we associate with love are also beautiful, wise, strengthening. It is love that brings us lasting happiness. It is the affirmation, commitment and care that arise from love that we want beyond anything.

We may go looking for love in different ways. We may even look for it where it can't be found. But this search for love – this need, this yearning for love – is what we have in common. It fuels our lives, keeps hope alive, has us dreaming and dancing into eternity.

How is it possible, then, that we could behave unlovingly – even shamelessly – a great deal of the time? That we would hoard love: giving it out in small, tightly wrapped parcels to a few people only? That we would use love like a commodity to control people? Or that we would allow love to vanish, leaving contempt, envy, disparagement, hatred or indifference in its place?

What would it take for us to plunge into a wholly loving way of life, spending love recklessly and abundantly, and discovering how much more we have to spend? Acting as if we really do believe that love is our highest value? Allowing love to move through us and bring us closer to all kinds of people: caring about their experiences; tolerating their differences; rejoicing in their joys; demanding less from them; observing how intricately their wellbeing is connected with our own?

Animals, insects, even plants, thrive in the presence of love.

How could we fool ourselves that anywhere from prisons to palaces human life can do well without it?

A lifetime ago the poet T. S. Eliot wrote these lines:

Between the conception
And the creation
Between the emotion
And the response
Falls the Shadow.

I learned those lines at school. They are from 'The Hollow Men', one of Eliot's best-known poems, and I remember clearly my intense pleasure as I stood with my classmates in neat rows at the front of the school hall, saying them out loud, relishing their gravity and morbidity but not having a clue what they meant.

Now I have some idea at least. Or anyway I see how those lines could illuminate the fact that the intention to be loving is a fine thing but it is also limited. It is not enough to want to be loving. Or to intend to be loving. To be loving, to know love, to allow love to express itself, there can be no shadow or splitting. Intention must flow into action. What we *mean* to do is what we must do. Otherwise we are fooling ourselves.

BEYOND GOOD INTENTIONS

The way we act towards other people is our primary expression of love. Love can come alive only through our attitudes and actions. It lives in *who we are*. And it is expressed through *what we do*.

That seems clear enough. But observe people in their intimate or family relationships, or observe your own intimate interactions, and you will see that sometimes – even frequently – *who we are* is not loving. At least not if it's measured by *what we do* and the effect of that on other people.

We behave in tragically unloving ways sometimes. And we may do this repeatedly with the people we profess to love most. We may use our dear ones as the target for our worst frustrations, uncertainties and limitations. We may even act hatefully sometimes, squandering love. Yet we continue to be surprised when people read our actions as the measure of our intentions. Our mouths drop open with amazement when they say that they don't feel loved. Or that they can't trust us to be kind. Or that they want to leave us. We are stunned, horrified, often angry – yet also oblivious to the simple truth that while we judge other people by their actions, when it comes to ourselves, our actions matter much less to us than our beliefs about ourselves, and our own good intentions. *Between the conception and the creation . . . Falls the Shadow.*

'Rude? Angry? You know I'd never deliberately hurt you . . . '

'I didn't *mean* to be late. Why on earth should you be upset?'

'I assumed you would want me to save you from looking foolish . . . '

'I was only doing this for your own good . . . '

We expect other people to know that we mean well, and how well we mean, *even when our actual behaviour is leading them in another direction altogether.* We can read our own minds. We like what we find there. So we are amazed and defensive when other people can't read our minds and read our actions instead.

When it comes to judging others, though, those criteria do a peculiar backflip! Now our focus is likely to be much more direct. *We judge others by their actions.* We use the other person's actions as the sole measure of their intentions. (Actions, we tell ourselves, speak louder than words.) And we make our judgements accordingly.

'Why shouldn't I find someone else? You're always too tired for anything but sex.'

'You want to change everything about me.'

'You haven't called for months . . . How was I to know you were still interested?'

To grow in self-awareness, we must reverse those usual habits. We must give others more of the benefit of the doubt, and ourselves rather less. Observing our behaviour, recognising that we have choices, and making rapid decisions about them, we free ourselves to ask, 'Is this loving? Whose interests am I serving here? Would I like to be treated this way? Is this *encouraging*?'

We might also stop to observe and to ask, 'What attitude is my actual behaviour expressing?'

Here are some more painfully ordinary examples.

You might profess to love someone – yet sulk when you don't get your own way. You might undermine that person in public. Or show them through your behaviour that you don't trust them.

You might tell someone you love them – but have tantrums to control them.

You might dump your daily irritations on them – excusing yourself on the grounds of stress, illness or overwork.

You might parade your infidelities, or require your partner to put up with an addiction that you refuse to recognise or to end.

You might subject them to your work fixation. To your need always to be out. Or never to go out.

You might insist that they should be braver than they are. Or cleverer. Or harder working. Or less wrinkled. Or tidier. Or more amusing. Or sexier. Or richer.

Is that love? Could those behaviours be excused in the name of love?

I don't think so.

Love should soften our demands, dent our defences, make it much easier for us to be accepting. All the great teachings of East and West invite us to recognise the same insight: that *the quality of our lives is determined by the quality of our actions*. Whether our actions are loving is entirely up to us.

USE LOVE AS YOUR REFERENCE POINT

The route out of self-deception is clear. If you profess to love someone or to care about them, or if you want to live as a loving person, then your actions must demonstrate that. Otherwise your good intentions are meaningless. And it's that meaninglessness that pulls you into the quicksands of self-deception.

'An inability to notice our true feelings,' Daniel Goleman writes in *Emotional Intelligence*, 'leaves us at their mercy.' What this means is sobering. If we tell ourselves that we feel or believe in something, but behave in some other way, then *our 'true feelings' are expressed through our actions* – not through our excuses, however polished those may be.

We are all vulnerable to self-deception. But the universality of that doesn't help us. Our lives grow strong when we have the courage to face all of who we are and all of what we do. Not before.

Self-deception is more serious than deception of others. Deceiving others, there is at least some awareness, even if the choice we make is wrong-headed. But when we deceive ourselves, we miss a chance to do right *and* we close our eyes to what we are doing, stunting ourselves in a way that no one else could.

Framing worthwhile intentions, valuing them, *using love as your reference point*, checking that your intentions are reflected in your actions, making changes as they are needed: these small acts of consciousness may add up to the most demanding of all the ideas in this book. But they are also the most far-reaching.

Certainly they most directly confront our selfishness – and that faint, familiar hope that the big challenges of life can still wait a while! Talking to a friend this morning, I heard her say, 'I feel so needy sometimes, and I hate that.' Yet the truth is, we are all needy. We are biologically programmed to be needy, self-centred and selfish. Our survival as a species has depended on that.

But now, in the twenty-first century, our survival as a species may depend on something quite different. Our planet is so crowded, and its resources are distributed so grossly unevenly, that to live with any degree of peace we will have to develop our capacities to think broadly – to think long-term. And to include in our thinking all races and cultures.

Those changes do also have their personal rewards. They can push us to discover how to postpone some desires, how to discern which desires are worth pursuing, how to consider other people's interests as if they were our own. And find what's true in that.

You might not feel important enough to be part of such an enterprise. You might find it hard enough to think about yourself, your own family and your friends, without also wondering how you are affecting other people in your neighbourhood, or in some country with a capital city you cannot even name. But those modest efforts, multiplied by billions, are really all there is.

In his immense novel *A Man Without Qualities*, the German writer Robert Musil expressed this when he wrote: 'The sum total of everybody's little everyday efforts, when added together, releases far more energy into the world than do exceptional heroic feats. This total even makes the single heroic feat look positively minuscule, like a grain of sand on a mountaintop with a megalomaniacal sense of its own importance.'

In giving up (some of) the seductive pleasures of thinking of no one but yourself, it helps to remember some of the finest moments in your life. Weren't at least a few of them when you felt swept into some version of community with other people: laughing or singing together; talking across a table with your mouths full; listening together to a glorious piece of music or something that made your hips roll; solving a problem together; or focusing on something that united you in a cause that was inspiring and good?

We need those moments to remind us what social beings we are. And to remind us that our survival depends on how meaningfully we acknowledge that. This to-and-fro process of caring for one another begins and ends with our capacity for self-awareness: observing our behaviour, and checking out its effects on other people. That's not such a burden. Because we want to be liked, most of us are doing that quite automatically much of the time. The trick is to move from automatic to consciousness: to notice more, hide less and experience greater choice.

It's not a secret. When we behave thoughtfully, it is easier for others to love us. And easier for us to respect ourselves.

But sometimes we will be way out of line.

We intended to be loving, but we are not. We are sour instead. Or maybe we are abusive, denigrating or humiliating. Or maybe we are mean: punishing someone with silence; making ourselves some coffee but no one else; using up the last of the hot water in the shower; killing someone else's joy because we can't contain our envy; not going home early to help out at the kids' bedtime; pointing out something hurtful that we could have overlooked; refusing to accompany someone to an event that means a lot to them.

Some of those things are what used to be called 'sins of omission': the good things we choose not to do, which are often more hurtful or far-reaching than the wilfully bad or unkind things we choose to do.

There's something calculated about those missed opportunities. We have seen them. And have turned from them – often justifying this with self-righteousness.

Yet turning down any opportunity to show concern or to express generosity is a loss of love. And if we wonder if we can truly 'help' our worst or most hurtful behaviour, then it is instructive to observe how selectively most of us save the worst for the people we most despise – or for the people we claim to love best.

ESSENTIAL TRUTHS CAN BE REDISCOVERED

The ideals of love are simple, as well as sublime. From the words of Rabbi Hillel the Pharisee, Christ and Mohammed: *Do no harm. Do good. Love one another. Wish for others what you wish for yourself.* As a reference point for all our actions no message could be clearer or greater.

But still our willingness to marry loving intentions with loving actions remains ambiguous. We want to be loving – but resentment stops us. We tell ourselves that life hasn't given us what we most want. Or that we are overwhelmed by demands. Or that we are too hurt to offer something worthwhile to another person.

As powerful as resentment is, however, it is only an obstacle, a state of mind that can be circumvented. Even in the most unlikely situations, and even after living through a seemingly unsustainable period of loss and tragedy, strength can be found. Essential truths can be rediscovered.

This emerges clearly from Georgina's story. She is now 48, works in a high school, and is the mother of two adult children. She values honesty, sexual fidelity, self-responsibility. So far, so good. But Georgina has suffered, endured, survived through the kind of dramas that most of us would shudder to think about. From the age of 9 she saw her parents for only about twelve weeks a year. The rest of the time she was in boarding school. She married, had a daughter, left that marriage and remained good friends with her first husband. She then remarried and was pregnant again when her first husband's subsequent relationship ended and he killed himself. Georgina lost the child she was carrying at the same time as her daughter lost her beloved father – and Georgina herself lost a former intimate and good friend.

Some years went by. With difficulty Georgina became pregnant again. Her son was born thirteen weeks early. During that pregnancy she had discovered that her second husband was having an affair with a close friend. Her discovery of this led her husband to be furious with her. Georgina explains: 'He was angry with me for giving him the ultimatum of me or "her".' Then a couple of years later when her daughter, Rebecca, was 13, Georgina became concerned about her husband's behaviour with Rebecca. A year later his sexual abuse of Rebecca was confirmed.

Georgina says, 'I was told it was rare for a mother to support her daughter in these circumstances, which I found incredible. For me it was not a choice, it was instinctive. My husband was, after all, supposed to be an adult.'

While supporting and protecting her daughter, Georgina also tried to keep the family together. Despite this her second husband killed himself. 'In the weeks before doing so,' Georgina remembers, 'he rang me several times from some unknown place on his car phone "to say goodbye" with the engine running. A particularly awful form of torture.'

Some years have passed since that second death. Georgina has been in a positive, rewarding relationship for some time, and while the scars for everyone can only be guessed at, even out of this tragic chain of events clarity has emerged.

'My father's love was pretty special,' Georgina says. 'It came with a guarantee of truth, which he always expressed openly. He expected total honesty from his children and gave it unstintingly. If he had a problem with something he would tell you honestly and openly, which to me is an adult, responsible way of behaving.'

Georgina may have exceptional reasons to value honesty and truthfulness, but even in much less dramatic circumstances what she says makes sense. 'Knowing someone will always do their best for you is hard to beat. I used to think that sexual fidelity was not necessarily an essential thing for a marriage but I have learned from experience that nothing destroys trust and intimacy faster than sexual infidelity – because it destroys the intimacy which is required for total trust and honesty.'

And the most valuable lesson she learned from this awesomely tough run of experiences? 'That we only become adults by understanding we are responsible for our actions. I think this has been the most valuable thing and also the hardest thing to learn because I had so much of the opposite to *unlearn*. My [second] husband was about 4 years old emotionally and quite unable to comprehend the consequences of his actions. For so long I didn't understand that the choice of how you will respond to what happens "to" you is yours to make. When we are children, others make decisions on our behalf. That has to change. The freedom of that is both exhilarating and terrifying!'

DO WHAT NEEDS TO BE DONE

Waking up, looking around us, we see how through each day opportunities present themselves to bring love to life through actions that express tenderness, good humour, affection or delight. What's more, if we take those opportunities as our guide and respond to them intelligently, we don't even need to worry about whether we 'feel like' doing those things or not. Or, indeed, whether the other person is sufficiently 'grateful' or not.

We can do those things *because they are worth doing.* (Our feeling state *may* change as we do them. We *may* get the thanks or appreciation we would enjoy. But that is not the point or reason for doing these things.) We do them simply because they express the way that we value love; that we value our connections. This leads to the most exceptional experience of freedom.

What needs to be done can be your guide in almost all situations, rather than your feelings about it. How routinely we hear variations of 'Could you please sweep up the leaves?' And the automatic answer, 'No. *I don't feel like it.*'

Responding to what needs doing, rather than to the changing state of your own feelings, doesn't mean that you ignore your trusty instincts or make a martyr of yourself. Absolutely not. *In the circle of compassion, you will always include yourself.* This approach leads away from martyrdom, not towards it.

But when your feelings are your primary or sole guide about whether you'll do something, you remain in danger of falling into self-deception. After all, haven't you noticed how transitory your feeling states are? Or become aware of how routinely you begin to do something that you did *not* feel like and, in the process, come upon a different mood entirely – especially when you have allowed yourself to be absorbed by the task or demand, and have allowed it to soothe you?

Some forms of psychotherapy, and an increasingly narcissistic public culture, invite us to worship our own feelings and the personal needs that reflect them. Wanting is often confused with needing; needing is often confused with entitlement. And the potentially tragic effects of that clearly emerge in Georgina's story. Taking up the invitation to worship at the altar of our feeling states delays our emotional development (sometimes terminally); it fosters egomaniacal power trips as well as inward powerlessness; it produces more loneliness and unhappiness, not less.

Our feelings are not who we are. They can change in less than a second. They are not even our most reliable guide as to how we should behave. ('Could you please sweep up the leaves?' 'No. I don't feel like it.')

All kinds of trivial things affect our feeling states. We may feel quite different after a cup of coffee or a night's sleep. We may feel quite different when we get a new team leader at work. We may feel terrible when we are about to menstruate or have a hangover, and fantastic if we've just won first prize in a lottery. Those feeling states are all legitimate. But they don't create the most reliable base for considering how best we can move through life.

'When we adapt ourselves to the needs of this moment, we become part of the moment itself,' says Zen psychotherapist David Reynolds. 'Life takes on a special meaning as we go about living it attentively.'

That's true in my experience also. And it's been the liberating experience of many of my clients. You may be surprised to discover just how unshackled you become when you choose to respond in an uncluttered way to what needs your attention (leaves need sweeping/baby needs changing/music needs to be turned down/bills need to be paid) without overtly personalising it ('I'm always the one who gets stuck with the leaves'), or wondering whether it suits your wishes at that point.

You may also be delighted by how powerful you feel when you psychologically progress beyond the vantage point of a stormy adolescent: 'Other people should take care of things. I will take care of only those things that arouse my interest or attention.'

THE TRUTH OF LOVING KINDNESS

Loving kindness – even our wish for honesty – competes for expression with all kinds of other feelings.

Our ambivalences, inner hesitations, feelings of irritability and distance seem at times to be more accessible than our feelings of love. Does this mean we are not, then, truly loving? I don't believe so. Again, what's needed to bring our inner feelings into balance, and love into the foreground, is an act of awareness that is in line with our values ('I feel tired and grumpy. But this is still the person that I love'). However, that's not always easy to achieve, especially when we feel wrung out – or in some way 'lost' to ourselves.

Inner conflict is certainly the experience of 34-year-old florist Elizabeth. She feels as though she knows exactly how to behave. Yet something powerful and familiar stops her.

Elizabeth has been at home for seven months with her first

baby, Jesse. Her partner, Thomas, is working full-time. We had been talking about generosity for a while when Elizabeth paused, then said, 'I know that little things can easily change what's going on. I find it much easier to notice the "negatives" in any person or situation and that causes me trouble, especially with Thomas. For instance, when he's at work all day I get lonely and want him to come home. However, when he walks in the door and kisses me hello I always feel very reluctant. I don't know why. It would be easy for me to just kiss him back in a friendly way because I am pleased to see him, but I rarely do. It's so different to the way I deal with the baby. I've noticed feeling much more generous with Jesse than I've ever done with anyone. I hardly ever feel impatient with him and always want him to feel that I love him completely.'

The challenge here is not Elizabeth's capacity to love; it is finding an ease of expression with Thomas despite the inevitable ambivalences that arise in most relationships and particularly in the wake of the kind of changes that parenthood brings. I asked her what change she could see herself making to show Thomas the more loving attitude that Jesse effortlessly elicits.

She thought about this. 'I have noticed that I can make things easier by being more positive towards Thomas. For instance, we did the gardening this weekend. Usually we argue in the garden because I lord it over him and criticise [remember Elizabeth is a florist!], but this weekend I gave him a job that I knew he was good at and told him so. We actually enjoyed ourselves for once and hopefully that'll make it easier next time to get him to do some gardening with me! I felt really good about turning the situation around and he said that he'd had a good time, and I liked that too.'

Making a promise to yourself that you will not only *be* more loving, but will *act* more lovingly, sets an essential process in train. This can release you from the habit of holding love back, or requiring someone to guess that really you are pleased to see them even if you have no time to say hello or even to glance at them and become aware: *A person I love has just walked in the door.*

It also helps again to recognise that your more grudging behaviour is not inevitable. It's nothing more than a cluster of habits. You make it much less powerful through simple awareness.

Love is a way of living. It is life itself. It is not an excuse for bad behaviour. Yet in the name of love it is peculiarly easy to be controlling and critical – even when this is experienced with pain by the other person. We may actually be quite aware of the distressing effect we are having on the other person, but still continue on this deceptive path of conviction and righteousness.

Lauren's experience shows how this unhelpful pattern from childhood is affecting two siblings years after they both left home. Lauren is 40, smart, funny, a former interior designer who is now a mature-age, full-time student. Her brother Joel is a year younger.

Lauren comes from what she describes as 'a family of worriers'. Concern in her family was often expressed by family members telling each other how they should run their lives. (How familiar is that!) Lauren finds this pattern is still basic to her interactions with Joel, the only member of her family who lives in the same country that she does.

'My mother was like me,' Lauren explains, 'worrying and fretting all the time. She knew her son – my brother – was a master at getting himself into deep water, and she was right. Whenever I am with him, I expect him to say something to confirm my belief that he is passive and dumb and destined to fuck up.'

Lauren tells her stories in a rapid-fire, self-deprecating way that is so disarming it is impossible not to laugh with her, even while recognising that what she is saying may cause her difficulties – and other people also. When we stopped laughing together we agreed that she might try something different. What we settled on was that she would 'listen for difference': try to pick something out of her brother's behaviour or speech that she could focus on and respond to more positively, and let the rest fall away. I was intrigued to know how this might work out.

A few weeks later, Lauren reported back: 'I went to lunch determined to hear something different. To go with another mind-set and another ear. The result? I won't say I heard anything different. I just didn't hear anything to confirm my worst fears. I went open minded, up-beat, determined to be encouraging rather than impatient. And I succeeded in passing five lovely hours with my brother and others, noticing how sweet and lovely my brother is, and enjoying how affectionate and mellow he is with children. He even told a story that I found interesting and entertaining! (He usually says pretty little.)

'I went home relaxed instead of frustrated and worried about him. I didn't ask him how he was or how his business was going because he might have replied something which would echo my belief system. I just let him be. Interestingly, he called me today after my new "listening" yesterday. He has not called me socially for some time because he knows I disapprove of how he conducts his life.

'And I have to tell you, this is no surprise to me. Whenever I decide to change my attitude to get different results, I *get* different results. The fact remains, though, my brother is in big trouble. All I'm doing now is separating myself from it. This leaves me intact and less frustrated, but really worrying about him would, I believe, better reflect the heart of the matter.

'I guess I have a deeply felt belief that if you care about people you should do whatever you can to help them. But I'm exhausted from it. I just can't be bothered any more. I'm learning to care less from my boyfriend. He stays quite detached. I'm not sure what's better. His way or mine or something in between.'

PUTTING RESENTMENTS ASIDE

Every relationship is ambiguous. Or, more precisely, the emotions that swirl around it and through it are ambiguous. Keeping track of your intentions – and living up to them – takes real presence of mind. The rewards are great, however, because as long as your intentions are clean and sweet, it's in acting them out that you can recognise your choices and honour your commitments.

Trouble comes when you forget those good intentions, perhaps when you are distracted by unacknowledged resentments, as Elizabeth may have been. Or by a need to 'make things right', as Lauren was. Those common traps are compelling. But they don't support love and nor do they express it.

'I didn't mean to . . . ' is a familiar cry of anguish. It's also a clear signal that we need to pay closer attention to how we are behaving. (Not to our good intentions only: we need to watch our actions *and* their effects on other people.) Elizabeth, for example, does love Thomas very much. That's obvious when you see the subtle, precious signs of affection and interest that flow between them. But getting home at the end of his day, which has had its own frustrations and setbacks, Thomas doesn't always feel loved. Occasionally he doesn't even feel welcome.

Elizabeth's story is also complicated. She passionately wants to be home with Jesse, and is dreading the time when he will go to childcare and she'll go back to paid work. Simultaneously with being a devoted mother, however, she is self-doubting and bored sometimes with no adults to speak to through much of the day. That contradiction needs to get heard. Otherwise it will continue to be acted out through those expressions of resentment that obviously lead Thomas to feel hurt and sidelined, and cause Elizabeth to feel 'mean and horrible'.

It might help Elizabeth to speak frankly to Thomas of her mixed feelings about being the one to stay at home with their baby. This doesn't mean that Thomas then needs to rush in and find a solution for Elizabeth. On the contrary, he will support her best by hearing her out and not rushing to solve anything at all.

It would also help both people if Elizabeth were to speak with

Thomas about the more diffused difficulty she has with transitions from one situation to another – including that particularly vulnerable end-of-day switch from being alone to togetherness. Many couples find this a raw moment. (Many single people also find it hard to move from an initial experience of aloneness as they enter their home to feeling 'at home' and more relaxed.) It helps to *recognise the time of transition for what it is* and find a way around it, if the evening is not to be spoiled.

Once Elizabeth has clarified her experience and feelings, Thomas will more easily understand that he cannot always expect the cheerful greeting from her that he might want, but that later in the evening, if he has been able to deal with his own feelings about that and not make too much of it, they can probably both relax, talk, joke, make love, and feel significantly reunited.

The way you talk *about* people reinforces your view of them. Lauren's relationship with her brother would also be helped if Lauren could think more coolly about that telling gap between her intentions and her actions. Lauren does want to be loving, and she's quite intelligent enough to notice that her efforts at controlling Joel – or getting him to live in the way she thinks best – have not been any more effective than their mother's were.

Joel is a grown man. Lauren is his sister, not his keeper. It's true that she wants to save him from himself. And she wants to save herself from feeling more contempt for him than she now does. But she will need to switch her focus to find a more supportive way to talk to him and *about* him (to avoid reinforcing her poor opinion of him). And she will need to check out with Joel whether he even wants overt support from her at all.

WHEN LOVE BLINDS YOU

Love is the paramount wake-up call, pulling and pushing us in the direction of wholeness. But our longing for love can also blind us.

In the name of love we sometimes fall for our own delusions, despite the warnings of our instincts, and certainly despite our best intentions.

Caught in the maze of our longings, we are vulnerable. Far from judging other people by their actions, we ignore any of their actions that don't suit our purposes. We ignore whatever we know but don't want to know of their history. We ignore the pains in our stomach, the rashes on the backs of our hands, our back pain, the headaches we can't explain. Instead we make facts out of hopes and we create certainties out of wishes.

'She has promised she'll stop drinking. She just needs to get her life in order.'

'I know he didn't mean to hit me.'

'This time it will be different.'

'They'd never give me the sack.'

'He's leaving his wife any day now.'

'After the sales conference, I'll be coming home early.'

These are the raw times when facing the truth feels too hard. We create an encouraging story – out of unlikely evidence – to make ourselves feel better; to protect ourselves from something we fear; or to shelter illusions we fear to unpick.

This process offers testimony to the agility of our creative minds. The trouble is, no matter how brilliantly encouraging the story is, if it doesn't fit with the facts, or if it is a way of postponing what we already half know, then we keep ourselves in a state of psychological suspension, neither getting what we want nor benefitting from the sense of reality that only the truth offers. Believing in something in defiance of the evidence seldom makes it happen.

Rosalind lived with this version of heightened anxiety for most of two years as her intense sexual relationship with Troy waxed and waned, largely following his moods and his needs. Rosalind is lively and talented, with a gusto for living that allows her to hurtle herself into one volatile situation after another.

She is now 35, mother to a 15-year-old, and a successful public relations consultant.

Talking about how agonising it was to live in a state of uncertainty, she says, 'At the most deliciously intoxicating moments of intimacy, Troy would always announce that he was feeling anxious, wobbly, or that he was "drifting out to sea". This would occur within twenty-four hours of the most pure, gentle acts of loving. My immediate reaction was to panic and grab, to reassure, to remind him that the most loving gesture I could make was to love him through his terror. I thought of him as a tortured genius who was prone to these bursts of trauma.'

Rosalind's need to idealise Troy, and her intense desire that their relationship would continue, persuaded her to overlook clear signals about Troy's ambivalence. 'In retrospect,' Rosalind explains, 'I believe I should have just let go to let him catch his breath without any pressure. In fact, I did attempt this and told him to let me know when he needed to contact me. I became aware that what I was doing was an act of suffocation and it was a serious love addiction. This need for constant contact and, in turn, reaffirmation of who I was and what I was in his eyes: beautiful, loving, lovable. Not having him near would cause me an endless tangle of terror and distress. I felt I was on the verge of losing the most magnificent person in my life and that to be without him was like losing all the colour in my life.'

That heightened sense of danger that Rosalind describes is horribly painful. It throws off balance our inner feelings of personal safety. We may even come to believe that without that other person our life will lack meaning, or 'colour' as Rosalind put it. Such passionate intensity is what many people associate with true love; but the truth is, an experience of love is more likely to survive when each person feels secure, can compromise and negotiate difference, and is delighted by the love of the other, rather than starved for it.

Still, that's the reasonable ideal. For many people life is somewhat more hazardous.

When she began having boyfriends, Rosalind says she was 'ridiculously romantic and even though I thought I understood the concept of compromise I was too pig-headed and opinionated to make way for many things I didn't like. I also thought that a fair degree of trauma was necessary and commonplace in loving relationships. When things soured, my tender feelings would disintegrate and almost always never return. I found it impossible to hold onto loving feelings if troubles began to arise.'

Rosalind's love life has taught her many things, the most important of which, she says, is that 'compromise and good humour form a crucial backbone to any lasting relationship, coupled with an ability to give affection with an open hand and to do as best you can to reduce the flow of expectation.'

That sense of openness, and a longing to be able to express herself honestly, has been hard won by Rosalind as she has emerged from the loss of her relationship with Troy. 'What I really wish could have happened was that I could have been truly open with him about how I was feeling. I was always so concerned that by telling him about my profound fear of losing him, I would push him further away or trigger a break-up. So I tended to clam up at the time I needed to express myself the most. I felt stifled and misunderstood and that I was fooling myself we had a true union.

'Looking back now, the only trouble was I could not see the blinding obvious. In the quiet moments, late at night, lights out, he would speak quite eloquently of his terror of not being able to meet me and love me in the way I wanted, needed, deserved. He would mutter something about different rhythms.

'And so, in time, it ended. Swiftly, painfully, irrevocably.'

GO BACK TO BASICS

It is a truly human thing to deny what we don't want to see. We all see selectively, even at the best of times. To discover whether we are perceiving the truth in any particular situation we need to use our experience, tune into our instincts. We need to notice what's happening in our body. We need to weigh up what we know against what we are simply hoping for. We need to see the value in a sow's ear, but not mistake it either for a silk purse.

That instinct to know if a situation feels right, or if we are in some crucial way deluding ourselves, is never more needed than in our decisions around sexually intimate relationships. Yet it is precisely from that arena that all wisdom can flee.

This is, in part, because we choose partners or lovers for all kinds of unconscious reasons, no matter how honestly we believe we are being strong minded and sensible about what we want. Our hormones confuse us; echoes from the past certainly confuse us; loneliness, anxiety and fear also confuse us. The opinion of friends and families too can push us in the wrong direction as we respond either to their encouragement (wanting to please them) or in reaction to their discouragement (wanting to defy them).

When there is something major at stake – a marriage, a decision to live or have a child together, to change country, house or job – you can be drawn by a powerful ideal, moving towards it much as a sleepwalker moves to the rhythms of their dream, paying little or no attention to whether the facts of *this* person, or the facts of *this* life, meet your desires in any real way at all.

Contemplating a lifetime commitment, most people do not spend even a single hour asking themselves the most fundamental questions: 'What do I really know about this person? Does the idea of being in love make me happy – or this actual person? What interests and values do we share? What does each of us value most? Do I see that reflected in this person's life? Will we have things to talk about ten years from now? Can we laugh, have fun, pray, cook, tidy a house together? Do we share social concerns? Can we solve problems cooperatively? *Do I feel totally safe?* Am I free to be myself sexually, emotionally, spiritually? Can I be vulnerable? Am

I willing to accept this person – and not attempt to change them? Are we battling issues of control? Can we both compromise? Is there anything here that disturbs me? Anything that I am hoping will "improve" with time?'

Those are the questions that most people caught up in romance, and the delicious drama of feeling special, ignore. Sometimes at their peril.

SHARED VALUES DEEPEN TRUST

To ask – or answer – the big questions of life, it is necessary to know or discover what your values are, what gives your life its sense of meaning, what you believe is most important. Where those values are secure and inspiring – and shared – they can provide balance and ballast to a relationship. I have found this in my own life. And talking to many people who have moved from difficult to satisfying relationships, I have heard repeatedly what a difference it makes when a relationship is built on a sharing of values and an explicit concern with each other's wellbeing.

Here's a fine example. Michele Sierra is a couples therapist. Her husband, James, is a homoeopath and yoga teacher. They've been together for ten years and openly value each other's freedom and individuality. They believe this enhances their commitment.

Michele is confident that 'Commitment needs to be based on shared values and ethics, common interests. It's not a sentence to imprisonment for the rest of your life.'

James explains his view: 'My attitude to first relationships was romance, no commitment and the expectation that, once you found the woman of your dreams and got married, the rest would be easy! I was definitely not aware that relationships involved power struggles and a deep commitment to continually working through issues. Every day is different – has a different rhythm. One day it can be like living in Antarctica – cold, unfeeling, detached – the next day, a total meltdown.'

James goes on: 'It's important to respect each other's spiritual beliefs and sometimes contradictory points of view. Without spiritual values, life is too superficial. Compatible values give the relationship depth. Like a business, if you work together with a vested interest, for the wellbeing of each member, with cooperation, tolerance and generosity, you all get to share the profits. A power struggle usually reflects a lack of cooperation, self-centredness, pride. We want to avoid that. I expect to do the day-to-day stuff together – with a generosity of spirit. I see that we need to set goals together – whether it's time out together or encouraging each other to pursue personal goals. I regard each person as an individual. We need to work together to complement each other.'

James is positive that this helps both his marriage and himself. 'A good relationship based on respect, love and trust will enhance or magnify your good qualities and bring awareness of negative traits. Self-responsibility is required to work on those yourself.'

Michele was married previously. She has a teenage son from that marriage, and a good friendship with her former husband. In her earlier relationships Michele was a self-described 'pleaser'. Now, she says, 'I relate more to the title of a song by Sting, "If you love someone, set them free". I value my right to choose, to grow and explore life in the way my soul calls for. My commitment is to love and respecting the rights of my partner – the spirit of that person – and support them through their journey through life. I expect the same.'

Michele's feeling of trust and safety with James is essential to her. 'I couldn't be in a relationship without trust,' Michele says. 'I believe everyone has a right to feel emotionally safe in a committed relationship. Physical safety is essential too, as well as the ability to forgive. We all make mistakes or make peculiar choices at times. I expect my relationship to be a place where I don't have to hide my shadow side. Because of the constant commitment and openness within this relationship, *we are both able to show our vulnerability and know that it won't be used to hurt the other* [my italics].'

The freedom that Michele and James value allows them to recognise their power to affect the other one but that the intrinsic quality of their own lives remains in their own hands. Michele explains this: 'Something I have learned over time is that my partner is not responsible for my happiness. He can enhance it. And James does.'

Perhaps that respect for freedom also allows them to face without fear the possibility that they may not always be together. Michele: 'I used to believe that a relationship, particularly marriage, is forever. But after a divorce, and upon reflection, I see that we changed so much that we were no longer compatible. It was not a matter of cooperation or better communication – we were just not connected any more. I am aware that this can happen. We continue to evolve, especially in this rapidly changing world. That's quite natural and it is a shame that people often perceive their relationships as failures because they didn't remain together forever. They overlook the great achievements and positive attributes of the relationship. I like where I am and I will give it all I have got – James feels the same. But because we are married doesn't mean that if drastic changes occurred in our life that we would expect our relationship to be unshakeable. It is an unrealistic expectation.

'I like the ritual of marriage. I love the sacredness of it and I respect it. I do not respect the old archetypal marriage contract, though. Its origins were based on control and domination and that is what I feel we have to work through – go beyond – in our relationship. To create a balance based on the principles of love.'

Once again – and most usefully, I believe – Michele emphasises how a relationship lives and breathes, just like the people who give it life. 'I have learned,' she says, 'that a relationship evolves organically according to its natural cycles. Like a garden, it will go through its seasons. Sometimes it will be more attractive than at other times. Sometimes it will go through a dry season and may look like it won't regenerate. But there's magic in a garden. There is always life somewhere if it's continually tended. Compost is necessary in the garden and in the relationship. The so-called bad stuff is necessary to make good compost. The more energy, love and compassion that has been put into the relationship from its inception, the stronger its foundations.'

Veronica also has definite views about shared values. She and her partner, Amy, have been together for five years. Amy works in the public sector. Veronica is a bookseller. Each had a previous relationship that lasted more than fifteen years.

'When I realised that "love was in the air" and that Amy and I might be going to get together in a serious way,' Veronica told me, 'I thought the most important thing was to be up front about what I wanted. I'd felt stifled for so long. And I'd been on my own for a couple of years and really did feel fine about that. I was certain that I would rather have no sexual relationship at all if it couldn't be based on absolute honesty and directness.

'My previous partner and I never fought. She believed fighting was bad. That was it: "Fighting is bad. We must never ever fight." I knew that not fighting – or not having things out in the open and feeling that one could say whatever needed to be said – was far worse. We tiptoed around each other for most of the last five or six years of the relationship. It was bloody awful. Annihilating.'

Were there values other than trust and honesty that Veronica knew were essential?

'We are not religious, Amy and I, but we both feel a tremendous affinity with the land. That's our spiritual resource if you like. And I had to know that Amy could at least honour that and all that it involves: taking less time to work and more time for hikes, bush regeneration, activism around ecology issues and so on. As it turns out, she's more keen than I am. It's not a recreational issue only. It's a question of what you give your time to. What you think is important. Whether your backyard extends beyond the boundaries of your home. Whether you can trust something other than money has real currency. I share all that with Amy. And my previous partner wasn't interested. I'm not saying she should have been. But the absence of that interest was something I felt keenly. The sharing of it deepens our commitment and the pleasure in that sharing deepens the pleasure each of us can have in the other's company.

'Anger's another thing. Too much expression *is* a problem, I'll grant you. Fear of it, though, is numbing. Also pretending that things are all right when they're not. Now I know that Amy or I can blow up and say what's not all right, *and that isn't dangerous.* And at hard times – like when Amy's younger brother died in a very sudden way a year or so ago – we could get in the car, scoot off for a couple of days to a favourite place on the river, not saying very much, but both knowing how invaluable it was to be there. It was so great to be there *together,* getting much the same kind of blessing and comfort from the spirit of the land, even though we are definitely two distinct people. I know I am quite exceptionally lucky.'

SEX AND TRUTH

Discovering what's true for you in any situation where emotions are heightened, and your inner needs may be in conflict, is extremely demanding. Time and patience are called for, and confidence that your own experiences have taught you much that's worth valuing. If someone else is powerfully certain in that same situation, then your processes of discovery can become more difficult.

Other people's certainty can be seductive. In the face of it, the small authentic voice of uncertainty or hesitation can be lost.

That was true for Kathryn, a lively, hospitable woman now in her fifties. She is a writer and the mother of five children, four from her first marriage, and one from her second. Kathryn says, 'When I was 23, I married my sweetheart of five years without truly loving him. I liked him, admired him, loved his family, found his jokes funny and valued his companionship. Without really loving him, though, I found myself over the years unable to give him what he needed. During our eighteen-year marriage, in which we produced four children, there were many happy family times, the memories of which are dear to me. But when I look back, I realise overall I felt deeply unhappy and dissatisfied and that I did a lot of dissembling to produce the illusion of happiness.

'People around us were convinced we were happy. When the inevitable happened and my husband fell in love with someone else, everyone was astounded. Our children were devastated as we rarely fought. They had no idea until their father left, when they ranged in age from 15 to 10, that their parents were unhappy. My mother was probably the only person who ever guessed my true feelings and that was not because I ever told her. I told no one. I kept going, thinking things would miraculously get better.'

Kathryn learned something from that experience that she now values as her most important learning about an intimate sexual relationship.

'When I met my second husband, I fell deeply in love from the beginning of our relationship. Whereas in my first marriage I was always looking elsewhere. I am – eighteen years later – still satisfied with this second relationship. That's not to say that we don't fight. We probably fight more than I did with my first husband. Or that there are not bones of contention or faults on both sides that irritate. However, there is binding us an indefinably strong matrix I can (for want of a better word) only call "love" that wasn't present in my first relationship.

'The message I give to young people now never varies. Be sure you truly love someone before you commit to him or her. If in doubt – *don't!*'

Sexual attraction can be both confusing and clarifying. Intense sexual attraction can of course pull us into all kinds of situations that will do us no good at all. But equally, it is disastrous to discount a lukewarm reaction to someone with whom you are planning to share a bed and a life.

Like Kathryn, Miriam has five children. She has a loving, companionable marriage with her husband, and their sexual closeness and connection securely underpins their busy lives. 'Meeting sexual needs is so important to us,' she says. 'Stephen feels rejected if we do not have regular sexual intimacy. He is a generous, loving and patient sexual partner. For him it is a crucial expression of love. We still excite each other physically. We still talk openly and frankly and sometimes with disagreement about a huge range of topics. Stephen has taught me of the rock-solid constancy of love. He is unwavering. I was older and felt "until our love shall last" was my principle, but our relationship is tightly woven now. I have been taught to accept and love myself by Stephen. I felt self-disgust before I was sexually active with him. Now as I age [Miriam is 47] I become more sexually liberated, and we become more accepting in every other way with each other.'

This last point that Miriam makes is particularly useful: that her sexual ease with Stephen, and his with Miriam, arises from an ease and trust with each other that extends across all areas of their lives.

CELEBRATE DIFFERENCE

As vital as shared values are, there is also room in healthy relationships for conscious and welcome difference. From her experience of this, Miriam explains: 'The ease that we have with each other arises out of an acceptance of differences which are sometimes differences in taste and involve our individual self-expression. When we first married twenty-three years ago, we acknowledged a grey area in the chequebook with butts that did not need to be filled in or made accountable for. At the computer at reconciliation time respect was given to these "grey butts".

'Now, later in our marriage, we accept that we do not need to agree on many issues and can each make executive decisions without the approval of our partner, and after an initial sparring we each accept that there are balances and swings. This may involve invitations and arrangements with friends the other does not choose to see; purchases, investments; the degree of involvement with extended family; the style in which we entertain (casual or formal). But seldom involves the upbringing of our children. There is generally harmony there.'

As Michele and James Sierra do, I have found one of my most useful discoveries about intimate relationships is that even in the most ideal couplings, or the most supportive families or groupings, there are seasonal changes marked by the waxing and waning of closeness and affection. The reason may depend on the rhythms of each individual's needs but analysis is much less useful here, I believe, than noting how predictably this happens, and how helpful it is to be neither too dependent on the exceptionally close times nor put out either by the times when more autonomy is called for – and allowed.

Successful relationships clearly embrace seasonal change *and* individual development. Commenting on those seasonal changes within her marriage, Miriam says – and I very much like the warm reality of this example – 'Stephen and I know that the arm which reaches out in the night for a reassuring squeeze is seldom ignored. Although there are moments in our life together of cold anger. Sometimes in a compatible, loving relationship the loving member or loved one needs the space that cold isolation offers. It allows for a build up of more selfish energy, and a reappraisal of self.'

Sameness and mutuality are a potent force in myths of happy family life and romantic love ('It's so incredible . . . we were born in the same month . . . we can finish each other's sentences . . . his father is also a sea captain . . . It's meant to be!'). Because mutuality is so prized, there is often an equally potent reluctance to see difference positively – as Miriam does – or to speak honestly about what separates people: 'You see this one way, I see it another.'

Yet difference is not in itself threatening. The relationship may even be different in significant ways from what is usual. *That too can be valued.* But if difference isn't threatening, then the fear of difference certainly is.

People need courage to speak out against the grain of sameness, especially when that expression of difference may be misunderstood or feared. Yet, taking the risk, *most people will discover that they can survive difference*; that difference – of opinion, temperament, even belief – can be part of commitment. And that a relationship is strengthened by resilience and the intellectual and social stimulation that difference allows.

A husband develops new interests in the periods of solitude created by his wife's temporary absences.

An adult daughter comes to respect her mother's change of religious affiliation, and is grateful for the new friends and interests this brings her mother.

A father gives up his dream that his son will join him in his business, and instead takes pride in his son's independent career.

A couple separate, but develop a valuable friendship once the demands of married life have dropped away.

FIND YOUR PATH

Human beings need freedom. It's one of our greatest gifts. But in the context of close relationships, it's also a significant challenge. How we use our freedom determines the person we become.

How we respect others' freedom determines the relationships they and we can enjoy together.

The idea of freedom is complicated. It's loaded with values that belong to a particular time and place. Throw in the relatively controversial idea of being true to yourself *and* socially responsible, and you may face serious dilemmas.

In matters of love and sexual attraction, cultural pressures to marry within a particular community, for example, or social pressures around sexuality, or other people's discomfort that you are 'alone' – that is, without a sexual partner – can powerfully confuse a sense of whether you are acting truthfully or expressing your values and deepest intentions.

Sami felt those pressures intensely. He is a thoughtful man of twenty-five. He left school at 16 and by 22 already owned a panel-beating business. 'I had plenty of money. I'd been going out with my girlfriend, Irene, for five years. We are both from the Greek community. She's a lovely girl. I could feel these pressures coming to boiling point: "What are you waiting for?"

'I knew it was hard on Irene. I loved her. She loved me. But I just could not see us together in ten or twenty years' time. I don't want to criticise her. We are just different. She was very happy about the success of my business. She didn't want to have a career of her own. Fair enough. But I didn't intend to run a panel-beating shop all of my life. I want to travel. I want to study. I like being around kids. Maybe I could work with them somehow.

'When I finally called it off, it was the worst day of my life. Her mother, my mother, my father, all furious with me. Even my older brother. I can understand that. Irene, she was heartbroken. Would it have been better to have married her? I wondered that over and over. I believe now it was the right thing to break it off. She married someone else. I've stayed single. I've missed her but, to be honest with you, not that much. My family are bitter, especially my mother. That hurts.'

With effort, Sami was able to pull back from what seemed like an almost inevitable situation. This is not a comment on the arranged marriages that happen in many communities. But for Sami, what was virtually an arranged marriage was not right. His instincts warned him off. And he was able to identify what was true for him, even though the pressure on him to conform to others' wishes, to 'do the right thing' and not hurt his girlfriend and both their families, was exceptionally intense.

Justine faced a quite different situation from Sami's when she fell in love with Deanna, the woman who has been her partner for eighteen years. Justine experienced her love for Deanna arising 'out of the blue, not so much because of the instant recognition of a like-minded spirit, but because that person was a same-sex partner. It turned my life upside down as I quickly shed past expectations, shared my joy with trusted friends but continued to hide under society's (that is, work and family) accepted roles and definition of relationships.'

Now in her mid-forties and, like Deanna, a successful business-woman, Justine continues to allow the relationship to be a place of learning as well as love. It is different from the one that Justine grew up to expect, but within that cradle of difference the two women share principles and values that bring them inspiration and support them to deal with inevitable difficulties or tension. Over time, and not always easily, their ideals and actions have moved closer together. Not only that, they are now generally able to speak about unwelcome feelings directly, rather than indirectly acting them out.

Justine explains: 'I grew up in a household where arguments and anger were the most common mode of communication, mainly out of frustration. It has taken me many years to unlearn this "learned" behaviour and even now I revert to it in a family situation. We were reared as children, not trained as adults, and our adult selves were always wanting to break out.

'Today therefore I consciously try to avoid any conflict situation. In the case of work or family, I will just retreat and try and resolve it remotely, if at all, via a phone call, mail or intermediary. I can rarely deal with it in a face-to-face situation. I find the prospect confronting, if only because it means I will have to show more of myself or because I do not trust the likely outcome.

'In the case of my personal relationship with Deanna, I at least feel safe enough to open up, but she often therefore feels the brunt of my disappointment. Whereas before this would be expressed in anger, increasingly now I am able to explain it, knowing it is directed at others and not at ourselves or at our relationship. Deanna's ability to allow this is my safety valve.'

PUTTING SOMEONE ELSE FIRST

In our closest relationships we have our greatest opportunities to discover how our attitudes and behaviour affect other people. And, when any aspect of that behaviour falls short of our best ideals, to make the changes needed.

In a close relationship that is functioning well – and Justine and Deanna's is a fine example of this – the gaps between ideals and action will lessen over time. They may never be completely absent. Our intentions will inevitably sometimes be loftier than our actions. We may on occasion gloss over reality to make life more tolerable. And we may need a gentle or even a sharp reminder that our behaviour is less thoughtful, courteous or generous than it could be.

However, in all relationships based on mutuality and concern, both people can discover that *the way they act towards the other person is their primary expression of love*. I cannot emphasise this too strongly. This is the principle on which this book is built: that when we are privileged to connect through affection and respect with others, they deserve the best we can give them. And in giving them 'our best', we most fully develop the best in ourselves.

This doesn't mean that we won't sometimes disappoint them,

or that we won't have to negotiate some tough issues and confronting choices. All of that is part of loving strongly and well. So
too is the confidence that when we do fail or disappoint someone,
we will be willing to acknowledge that and do something about
it. Not because we want to, necessarily. But because that's needed
for the sake of someone else. And for the sake of the value we give to
connectedness and to love.

In a most graceful as well as realistic way, Susan Street describes this
important dynamic. Susan and her husband, Robert, are also in
their forties and are parents to two teenagers. They have been married for sixteen years. Over those years, Susan says, she has learned
'Not to crowd Robert at the end of the day. It is less acute now, but
when he had exceptionally stressful days, the children were young
and we were living in the country, I would be so excited to see him
at the end of the day for news of the outside world that I would
almost throttle him at the door with questions. I still need him to
remind me sometimes of his need for space, thinking time and creativity and not to take this as a rejection.'

Making a significant change – especially one that involves
curbing our usual instincts – is never easy. Achieving it, though,
gives the other person the vital emotional space they need. And
that's a wonderful thing. But the rewards don't run one way only.
Success also gives *the person making the change* an increased sense of
their own emotional range and the sense of personal power that
comes with that.

Susan, for example, could see that her habits of exuberance and
instant communicativeness were not working for Robert or for
their relationship. 'Robert was too emotionally drained to meet
my needs. We would end up tense and stressed. I realised that for
us both to enjoy the intimacy that sustains us there had to be a
transition time – for him to unwind basically.

'Initially it was hard because some days I may not have had an adult conversation all day. When Robert got home, I was wanting to be entertained and recognised for doing a great job at home with the children. I had to put aside my feelings of neediness and desire for recognition for that transition phase. It would come if I gave Robert that consideration.

'It was a matter for me of acknowledging what his day involved and supporting him. His job at that stage was ridiculously stressful and demanding. These changes came about with a lot of stress and jostling and then talking about our needs and how we could support each other so that we both felt appreciated.'

The fine balancing of separateness and commitment is crucial here. As Susan discovered, if someone needs more personal space, this request is not a comment on how they are feeling about the other one. *It reflects that person's own temperament and needs.* Susan's sense of personal autonomy enabled her to see that, while her deep commitment to Robert and their marriage allowed her to take positive action that helped them both – and their marriage. Blaming the person for the way they feel, or becoming angry or offended that you are being asked to consider the way they feel, is strikingly ineffective.

Susan shows no resentment that it was she who made the changes in that instance, rather than Robert. 'Robert articulates his appreciation. He acknowledges the giving of space and the love and support involved. I'm sure because I no longer feel rejected when he needs space, he feels a lot freer – and this is reflected even in his change of career [he has given up his practice as a physician and is designing boats]. He is leading a vastly more creative life now than in those early days of our relationship when the children were younger. We have talked about how, in order to be creative, thinking time, space to think, is essential. It has had a good effect for both of us. There is far less stress or negotiation necessary now for both of us getting our personal space needs met.

'It has also had ripples in other relationships because what I learned to do was invaluable – I learned to be my own best friend. To go within myself and nurture myself. The effects of this are substantial. I feel healthier, less needy and controlling. In other relationships, I think this self-nurture has allowed me to be a better friend and mother. I believe I respect others' need for space more. I can't think of any changes that I have been unable to make, although we are still negotiating separate holidays!'

Susan's grace in the face of an honest request for a change in her behaviour is a fine example of acceptance of difference, with no diminution of love. We want people to be honest and open with us. But it's a simple matter to view with hostility any request that we modify our behaviour. People in a committed sexual relationship are especially vulnerable to the myth that they should be able to read each other's minds and do the right thing without this ever being made explicit. What a shock to discover that real-life relationships are not like that!

Much more real are the continual processes of adaptation that need to be negotiated between people: sometimes through talking or simple observation of what works, in the sense of pleasing the other person or creating harmony.

I like the dash of realism here. Some might see it as resignation. I see it as a lovely example of how we can move beyond the traps of self-deception to love deeply with our eyes wide open. I also see how crucial it is in a relationship of any real closeness or interdependence that there is sufficient space and room so each person *can* ask clearly for what they want, just as Robert did.

This may not always mean that they will get what they want; sometimes that may not be possible or appropriate. But the widespread fear of stating clearly what's wanted taints and limits many relationships.

Being able to ask for what you want, and being able to identify and articulate what your needs or concerns are (and being able to hear no without having a tantrum or going into a state of resentment or guilt tripping) supports the development of trust as well as truthfulness and openness within a relationship. And the effects of that particular version of freedom undoubtedly lead to enhanced experiences of tenderness and gratitude.

Susan's partner captures this. The relationship lesson Robert believes that life has taught him is letting go of expecting too much of other people.

'I have learned that it is unrealistic and a cause of personal anguish to expect others to meet all my needs. I have learned not to expect perfection in others or similarly in myself. On the other hand, I have learned to expect the best in others and offer love without expecting it back from that person or at that time.'

This should not imply that Robert's valuing of intimacy has paled. 'I value most the warmth of intimacy,' he says. 'My partner has brought to my analytical mind an appreciation of the feminine side of nature, the beauty of language and a way of looking at life through the eyes of one who is connected to the womb of the universe. I see my intimate relationships [with Susan and their children] as the cave I come home to at the end of the day.'

It is one of the great gifts of intimacy that we can transcend self-interest – and do this happily for the sake of someone else. 'I will do anything for you' is a rash promise that we are fortunately rarely called upon to fulfil. But when we can exceed our usual limitations, or face something that we've been avoiding, this reminds us that our sphere of influence is something to take very seriously indeed. *Other people are continually affected by our behaviour; it is up to us to decide what the quality of that behaviour will be.*

Justine experiences her partner as someone who enjoys a rare level of internal wellbeing. 'One of Deanna's most endearing qualities is her generosity of spirit,' Justine says. 'Whenever she's disappointed by others, rather than judge she will actively seek to make personal contact and defuse the situation. When family members need support, she gathers the necessary resources together with compassion, not a sense of obligation. When faced with any religious, sexual or racial discrimination, she will address it but not attack the person. Very few friends have heard her talk ill of another, preferring instead to focus on the positive or just not comment. In all cases she is generous with her time, assessments and attention, despite what she herself may be feeling. This to me is one of the hardest, but most special expressions of generosity.'

FINDING INTEGRITY AND WHOLENESS

To find the truth in our lives, and to experience how living truthfully frees us, we need to recognise what choices we are making. We need to see what drives those choices. And review our actions in the light of them: 'What's my part in this? Is this kind or fair or just? Does this express my best intentions?'

The great contemporary teacher Sri Sathya Sai Baba asks some teasing questions: 'In a year there are 31,536,000 seconds. How are you using these precious moments? How many seconds are you wasting on useless activities? How many seconds do you devote to God? How many seconds to rectify your inner feelings?'

To those of us who are looking to 'rectify those inner feelings', writer Stephen R. Covey speaks of the 'four unique human endowments': self-awareness, imagination, conscience and will. He cites the exercising of these endowments as 'the most significant work we will ever do'. And it is not out of reach.

The drive to wholeness – to the integration of our highest values and intentions with our daily actions – is with us all our lives. Our impulses to love bring us home to our deepest nature. We may scarcely think about this. Yet, in those precious moments when we see something as if for the first time and move with truth, we move also towards integrity, contentment and peace.

Episcopalian bishop John Spong calls his God 'the Presence that calls us to wholeness'. This description sings to me, as free as it is from divisive images of the past, and as encouraging as it is that this complex, erratic movement towards wholeness is not a psychological journey only, but is also, and most profoundly, a spiritual one.

From her retirement village, Aase Pryor writes in the Quaker 'Seekers Open Letter': 'We are putting on plays and they have shanghaied me into making the costumes. They are putting on "The Importance of Being Ernest". "Gwendoline" is 79, "Ernest" about 90. "Algernon" is definitely 80. There are times when I don't believe what I am seeing . . . I look out over a lovely green hill and every morning I think, well now, I guess the old duck has landed on her feet again . . . '

Moving towards wholeness, we come to trust that we can be the same person on the inside as the person that others see and know. Those twin processes of self-acceptance and self-awareness hold and increase our sense of safety: *the old duck has landed on her feet again.*

Our impulses to love are deep and true. It is much more natural to love than not to love. Knowing that, supports us. Relaxing into that, we move into this present moment unhindered. Trusting that, we are uplifted. Love is our true home, our true nature. Behaving generously, lovingly and well need not be dull. Need not be restrictive.

Freedom is everywhere.

Value Truth as Your Ally

Most of us judge others by their actions – and ourselves by our own good intentions. For our lives and relationships to flourish, the reverse is needed.

We need to behave well, recognising that what we do and how we actually behave is the crucial expression of our values, self-love and care for other people's wellbeing. What's more, in behaving well (thoughtfully and with a real sense of the consequences of what we are doing), we find a solidity and stability in our lives that makes other people comfortable with us and allows us to feel comfortable with ourselves.

'Behaving well' does not mean being stodgy, pious or judgemental! It does, however, involve a keen sense of awareness that life flows best when our intentions and actions are in harmony with each other and *create harmony for other people.* 'You will know the truth. And the truth will set you free.'

- Recognise that love lives in *who you are.* And is expressed through *what you do.*
- Be aware that your 'true feelings' emerge through your behaviour. Saying you love someone or promising to support them, then hurting them or letting them down, is unconvincing. Praising love, then condemning other people or ignoring their pain, debases love. Words and intentions must be lived out *through action* to have meaning.
- Foster self-love through actions and decisions that express it.

- Show through your behaviour a willingness to make positive change for yourself, as well as for the people you love and care about.
- Know what you value (the health of your family, connection with other people, feeling good about yourself, having fun with friends, work that interests you, social concerns, protecting the environment). You can't make decisions based on your values until you know what they are.
- Value truthfulness, straightforwardness, honesty. They build character.
- Express your values through your decisions and everyday behaviour.
- Review your decisions alongside those values: 'Am I fooling myself here? Is this something I can be proud of? Is this clean, honest, beneficial?'
- When you recognise what you most want, offer that to others.
- Don't let your negative feelings get in the way of what needs to be done. Act appropriately – witness your spirits lifting.
- Give yourself permission to say no when that's what you need to do. But check out that you are not routinely negative.
- Reflect on how deep-seated beliefs affect your self-image and your experiences: 'I'm not important – people walk all over me' can become 'My life has value. I can speak up for what I believe is right.'
- Find your own truth and destiny even if this is not immediately welcomed by other people. Be patient with their anxieties or even their anger. *Trust who you are.*
- Recognise what makes you unhappy or what 'goes against your grain'. Find a way to give that up, or move on. Let self-respect and authenticity be your guides.
- Review your major decisions on a regular basis against the stark question 'Is this what I would be doing, is this how I would be behaving, if I had a month left to live?' Use that

sense of your own mortality to bring what's most important to the forefront of your life.

- Support your capacity to judge well (*your* actions – not other people's). Look at them from a trusting perspective that is also genuinely inquiring: 'What is driving this behaviour? Where is it taking me? What does it express? Am I happy with this?'
- Let yourself be inspired by the people you care about. Recognise how wide your 'circle of influence' is.
- Hold a positive picture in your mind of the people you care about. Don't think about your disappointments only. Think about what you love.
- Let go of resentment. It fosters self-absorption. The only reason you need to be kind is because you can be.
- Let go of any excuses that perpetuate hurtful or self-limiting behaviours.
- Recognise how affected you are by other people. When they contribute to your happiness, acknowledge that.
- Be loving, respectful and kind whether or not someone 'deserves' it or has created that opportunity for you. That is your freedom.
- Deepen self-awareness. Make changes swiftly as they are needed. When you hear yourself justifying hurtful behaviour, stop. Apologise. Move on.
- Beware of righteousness. You have no 'right' to hurt other people or diminish their existence. Righteousness is a defence – usually against taking responsibility for your part in a difficult situation.
- Expect less and less of other people. Free them from your expectations.
- If someone asks you to make a change in your behaviour, consider it gracefully. It may be needed.
- Learn to see a complex situation from someone else's point of

view. This teaches you empathy and opens up the world of intimacy to you.

- Value your own mistakes. You may not need to repeat the experience.
- Answer the call to wholeness. Bring your most loving intentions and actions into alignment: 'Walk the talk.'

Light up Your

Shadow

One does not become enlightened by imagining figures

of light, but by making the darkness

conscious.

CARL JUNG

*H*ave you ever felt convinced someone was judging you harshly only to discover that you were completely wrong?

Have you ever taken an instant dislike to someone? Or fallen in love on first sight (then, just as abruptly, out of love again)?

Have you ever been convinced that someone is standing you up, only to find out that they have simply been caught in a traffic jam, or had a flat tyre?

Have you ever gone home in a foul temper and started accusing other people of spoiling your day?

Have you ever noticed your partner's habit of talking while chewing as if for the first time – and decided that death itself would be too kind?

Our relationships are acutely vulnerable to our fickle, mood-driven, subjective interpretations. These may be so habitual we are virtually unaware of making them. And totally unaware that we could be wrong. They rest on casual assumptions that we make automatically in all kinds of situations.

You tell yourself someone doesn't like you – then discover that person is in the early stages of grief and isn't thinking about you at all.

You assume that you have met the man or woman of your dreams, and get furious three weeks later when that person turns out to be human after all.

You tell your partner that you've missed out on a great evening because he wanted to stay home. His mouth drops open. 'But you're the one who didn't want to go. I *wanted* to go. I thought that you . . . '

Or maybe you are feeling an emotion or are caught up in a mood that doesn't fit your favourite image of yourself. You tell yourself that the mood or emotion isn't yours exactly; on the contrary, it is 'caused' by someone else! ('You made me lose my temper . . . I would never have . . .', 'If it wasn't for you, I . . .', 'She drove me to it . . . ')

Doing that, you become a slave or a puppet not to the other person but to your own misguided thoughts. Those thoughts can't change – and your uncomfortable psychological situation can't change – until you are willing to see what's happening, to recognise the distress that *you are causing yourself*, and take a different tack: owning your own reactions and feelings (even when you don't like them); taking responsibility for your own emotional states; soothing yourself down; *waking up*.

LOOK AROUND TO CATCH YOUR SHADOW

The sense we make of the world is highly subjective. But we believe it's the truth – and are then affronted when someone disagrees with us. Their disagreement (based on nothing more sinister than a different way of seeing things) may feel like an attack. In response to that unintended attack, we may fight to the death, falsely believing that our honour is at stake.

These kinds of misunderstandings arise in part from our unexamined egocentricity ('I see the world this way so it must *be* this way'). Added to that, though, are the complex confusions caused by our shadow: our 'hidden self' that affects our conscious mind but extends way beyond it, powerfully guiding many of our reactions and assumptions yet easily underestimated in its capacity to confuse us.

The great twentieth-century analyst Carl Jung called the shadow 'the thing a person has no wish to be', 'an unconscious snag, thwarting our most well-meant intentions'. For each person that 'thing' will be different. Our 'shadow' is personal as well as archetypal or larger than life. It is cast by our individual ego, that part of the personality that we identify with and want desperately to protect. Our shadow is a different beast. It hides part of who we are away from ourselves, especially aspects of behaviour or emotion that we long ago learned to disown, discard or become disunited from – but not entirely.

Those feelings, attitudes or behaviours live on in us in disguised forms, glimpsed mainly through our extreme positive or negative reactions to other people or situations: through whatever 'gets us going'. Or through the things we *didn't mean to do* or *didn't mean to say* as well as through the misapprehensions, envies or prejudices we more openly express.

Our bodies remember, in some inchoate but determined way, the passions and spontaneities that once have been some small part of us, but got rejected and became our shadow. We heat up, or become cold, as we react to what disturbs us.

Our mouths purse. Our brows furrow. Our tongues click. Our voices rise. Our instincts stir. Fascination (often posing as superiority or disapproval) draws us back to the energy of what we've rejected. *One does not become enlightened by imagining figures of light, but by making the darkness conscious.* We remain attached to what we have rejected, drawn to it but outside it, rarely thinking to claim some new illuminated or changed version of it as our own.

CHECK OUT YOUR ASSUMPTIONS

Even with the people we know best – perhaps *especially* with the people we know best – it's easy to make inaccurate assumptions or to interpret their actions or intentions quite differently from the way they were intended. We make ourselves feel wretched because of this. Mostly, though, we don't acknowledge that's what is happening. On the contrary, we blame someone else for making us feel this bad. We do so not because we are wilful or stupid, but because we are unconsciously trying to defend our ego through a psychological process called projection. This means what it says: putting an attitude or feeling or even a whole series of thoughts 'out there' or 'over there'. It allows us to experience an unwanted or 'foreign' aspect of ourselves – or something we fear – as though it exists or originates in someone else.

You might think, for example, 'That supervisor's never liked me', because you feel unconfident about whether people in authority take you seriously enough.

You might routinely say, 'I can't stand people who are flashy with their money', as a cover for your own mixed feelings about not having enough money – or maybe having too much.

A simple attribution such as 'She thinks I'm fat' may express nothing more complicated than your own worries about your appearance. (Perhaps that other person has very positive associations with people who are not thin, but the force of your projection makes it hard to discover that. And not to think, 'She's only saying she likes chubby people – what she *really* means is that I would look better if I lost some weight.') Or perhaps a fear of being wrong, or being seen to be wrong, expresses itself through convictions that whatever you do other people will criticise you or 'find you out'. This might be expressed through a habit of thinking that tells you, 'No one takes me seriously.'

The sad thing about this common process is that, as efficient as we are at convincing ourselves that these thoughts belong 'out there', this rarely helps us. When we are busy projecting – attributing thoughts or feelings to someone else – we often feel helpless in two significant ways. Firstly, we may feel almost as though we are being controlled by the person who is 'holding' or providing the unconscious hook for our own unwanted feelings ('She makes me . . . I would never have . . . '). Then, because we haven't

recognised those thoughts or feelings as our own, we remain powerless to change them. We go on thinking about ourselves as the
victim of other people's perceptions!

Here's an example.

You are at a party. You are standing at the edge of a large room,
holding in your hand a warm glass of wine and remembering why
you never go to parties. Nevertheless, you are determined to have
a good time. Someone smiles at you. You'd like to smile back – but
instead, as you begin to smile, you tell yourself he's not really smiling at you (miserable you), but that he's laughing at you.

Why would he be laughing? Your projection might tell you it's
because you are fat, ugly, insignificant, needy, awkward: the scenario
would vary according to the particular nature of your fears.

Meanwhile, what's happening from the other person's
perspective?

As you turn away, he sees what he interprets to himself as a
bored look crossing your face. Are you bored? No. Actually you are
trying to hide your foolishness about smiling at a person who only
wants to laugh at you, but he assumes you are bored. In a flash he
is quite certain that you're bored. And he too stops smiling.

The interpretation that any of us might give to such a tiny, hurtful
chain of events 'fits' our expectations. It also 'fits' our unconscious
egocentricity: *our assumption that the other person is acting only in
response to us*; that we are at the centre of the universe even though
right at this moment we feel useless and horrible.

What's missing here is clarity. Our projections are, by their very
nature, unconscious and confusing. Beyond that, though, what's
missing is the safety that comes when love is a crucial point of stability as well as reference. With love (rather than anxiety or fear)
guiding our assumptions, it becomes possible to leap to the kindest
interpretations rather than the worst; to check things out openly; *to
freely give the benefit of the doubt to ourselves as well as to other people.*

And, in that way, to circumvent those self-defeating beliefs and return to a state of mind that is open, trusting and balanced.

Let's run that same scenario a little differently.

You've been to a few parties lately and have gone home feeling lonely and miserable. Gradually it's dawning on you that there's a pattern to this. That you hesitate and withdraw even when someone seems friendly (because you 'translate' their friendliness into something less friendly).

However, this pattern of withdrawing is now part of your conscious thinking. You've recognised a pattern and therefore made it conscious. So – bravely – *you decide to silence your suspicions that the other person is judging you adversely and is making you feel bad.* Instead you haul out your own shaky, weak-kneed inner authority.

When you see that same person smile, you walk confidently towards him. You say to yourself, 'I'm giving this a chance.' You say to him, 'Look, I'm sure we haven't met, but . . . '

You chat for a few moments and suddenly his face opens up. He says, 'I can't tell you how grateful I am that you've come to my rescue. I've been living in a monastery for fifteen years and this is the first party that I've risked . . . Everyone else looks so bored, I didn't dare . . . '

Even these brief examples show that *what you tell yourself about an event has a far greater effect on you than the event itself.* Here's another highly recognisable situation.

I am worried about a forthcoming exam. I am actually worried that I am going to fail the exam. (I invariably expect failure, but have forgotten that.) You try to console me.

You say, kindly and mildly, 'Don't worry. It's not the end of the world. Even if you don't pass, you know you are still —'

At which point I interrupt and say, with righteous rage, 'How dare you suggest that I am not going to pass. How could

I possibly do well at anything when you have no faith in me. If you had any faith in me I could do as well as the next person. You've never shown any faith in me. Whatever I attempt, you always undermine me.'

Now, if we are both fortunate, I might remove myself physically from the scene. I might sit down in my bedroom and run through the conversation again.

I could rehearse my sense of injustice. I could tell myself over and over how you *never* . . . and I *always* . . . and how *no one* . . . and how *everyone* . . .

I may still be feeling panic about the exam. But what I am also feeling at full tilt are my fears that whatever I do it won't be worth anything: and *those are the beliefs that I am attributing to you*, even though they arose in me and express my own fears, not yours. I am angry with you because I have convinced myself that your opinion of me is as low as the unconscious opinion I have of myself. So now, in addition to feeling in a panic about the exam, I am enraged with you.

What was your crime? That you tried to help me. That you were an easy target for my own intolerable feelings, which I have transformed into projections and now believe originate in you.

A more conscious and affirming scenario might go like this.

I remove myself physically. I sit on my bed. I run through our conversation. I let myself acknowledge that I've overreacted. I remind myself that you are a caring person. Your intention is to be caring. And your actions are also caring.

I may even force myself to remember that it's really *only when I myself am out of sorts* that I begin to regard you as the Wicked Witch from the West.

With some care, I run through again what you actually said. I write it down, or what I can remember of it. I realise that you didn't in fact make any comment on my worthlessness. On the contrary, you were, in your own inept but loving way, attempting to keep my spirits up.

If anyone is trying to do me down, it's myself. I recognise that's quite a pattern in times of stress. I get up off the bed, go to find you, and offer to make tea. You accept my apology. Life goes on.

Caught in the shadowlands of projection, you can easily delude yourself that your nasty moods or unwelcome thoughts are 'caused' by someone else ('You made me lose my temper', 'You don't have any faith in me', 'If it wasn't for you, I'd have all the friends I want', 'You think I'm boring').

It sounds crazy, doesn't it, that I wouldn't know if it's me who is angry or you; if you are sad or if I am projecting onto you my own sadness; if it's my fears or your unsociability that keeps friends away; if my company *is* boring, or my fear of being boring is getting in the way.

It may also seem crazy that I would believe that my mistakes or errors of judgement are *caused by you*. Or that I would pay more attention to the thoughts that I believe are in your mind than to my own fragile processes of self-assurance. *And not check that out.*

Yet exactly this kind of confusion, and the misery that follows it, undermines all kinds of relationships. The results of these confusions are often trivial. With a measure of goodwill on both sides, they can be resolved. And this is most likely to happen when we either look at the bigger picture ('Is this a familiar feeling?') or look at our wilder assumptions alongside what we know and can trust about the other person ('She seeks out my company . . . is always kind . . . Maybe *I'm* the one reading something into this . . . ').

The paranoid person believes it is others who want to hurt him, others he must defend himself against when, in truth, his own attacking thoughts are his worst enemy.

The suspicious person sees betrayal everywhere when, in truth, it's her own good experiences she can't trust.

The anxious person sees tasks all around him that are unfinished, incorrectly done or unsafe when, in truth, it's his own sense of insecurity that can find no rest.

The neurotic person assumes other people are having all the fun, all the best opportunities; that other people can take for granted their success in love and work; that good things happen – but not to her.

Those confusions exist in trace form in all of us, especially at times of stress. What's more, they shape our relationships profoundly. Unconsciously we may hope that an intimate relationship will save us from them. And it's true that the feelings of mutual understanding in a new relationship may seem to offer salvation. But often before the first weeks are over our idealisations begin to crumble and our unrecognised fears begin to attack, engage or involve the other person. Then, in our most vulnerable and undefended moments, we will see the other person through the prism of what we ourselves find most distasteful.

UNCONSCIOUS DEMANDS CAN WRECK A RELATIONSHIP

Eric and Charlotte are now in their early thirties. They are both graphic artists and are strikingly alike in appearance. They were married for two intense years in their mid-twenties and have become close friends since. Each is now in a new relationship. Looking back at their brief marriage, they seem almost mystified that they got caught up in a dynamic so damaging to them both.

The most obvious issues that tore them apart were Eric's increasing possessiveness and Charlotte's anger at the disappearance of the partner she thought she had married. Eric says, 'I expected Charlotte to be absorbed in my interests. Theoretically it was great for her to go out with her sisters or her friends, but in practice I didn't like it. I made scenes when it happened and she more or less gave up on that for the last year we were together. But staying home didn't improve anything. We both got more resentful.'

Charlotte continues their story: 'He was unbelievably kind to me when we were going out. I really did boast that I'd found a prince! But when we got married, he became so picky I couldn't believe it. He criticised everything I wore or did or said. Meanwhile, he wanted me to make *him* feel special. In the end we both felt so unspecial, it wasn't true. We'd had a good friendship. We had lovely sex – until that last year. But we could not hack daily life together.'

Listening to Eric and Charlotte, it's clear that for a relationship to be nourishing each person must have the space to grow while also honouring their shared interdependence and commitment. This delicate synthesis demands that each sees the other as a separate being and not – as a child does – simply as an extension of their own needs. Without that 'double vision', intimacy is not possible.

When Eric became angry about Charlotte spending time away from him, he was unconsciously expressing a belief that Charlotte should be there to make him feel safe (except when he had other things to do). He might have denied this. Yet his anxious responses intensified through their marriage, *even after he came to realise that it was driving them apart.*

As many people do, Eric muddled possessiveness and love – and love and control. The more needy of Charlotte he felt, the more he feared her absence (even her absence of attention) and tried to control her. This situation was not acceptable to his conscious mind so Eric interpreted his possessiveness to himself as increasing love, and his controlling mechanisms as an expression of that love!

This 'love' didn't result in him becoming *more* genuinely concerned about Charlotte or her separate needs. On the contrary, the more Eric believed he was in love, the more suspicious he became and the more he made demands that Charlotte should share his desires and interests only.

Eric's increasing possessiveness cost Charlotte her freedom. Less predictably, it cost Eric his freedom also. As he grew more frantic, he often felt angry with Charlotte. In their last few months together, he was angry with Charlotte 'most of the time'. The reasons why are not surprising. Any situation of high emotional dependency is uncomfortable for an adult. It makes you feel powerless or like a victim (and, in fact, you are a victim – but of your own thoughts, not of the other person).

In Eric's case, he became fearful and highly egocentric. And in a hopeless (and unconscious) attempt to assert himself he began to pick faults in Charlotte, finding her 'annoying, cold, argumentative, disloyal', while still demanding that she demonstrate through her constant attention how much she loved him.

Eric and Charlotte's relationship could have changed and survived only if Eric had recognised how excessive his demands upon Charlotte had become and that his escalating demands expressed *his own fears of abandonment*, rather than something that Charlotte was 'causing'. Had that happened, Eric might have been able to see that he was the only person who could dispute those beliefs and soothe the feelings that came with them. Charlotte was not *making* him feel bad. Therefore he was the only one who could *make* himself feel good.

This confusion does raise difficult issues around dependency.

The very word dependency is going through a bad patch at present. Notions of independence are highly prized (and often confused with simply being shut off). But the reality is that in all healthily functioning relationships people feel somewhat dependent. And why wouldn't they? We are social beings:

leaning together; needing each other in innumerable ways. Problems come only when the dependency demands are excessive – when one person is unconsciously asked to 'fill' the emptiness in the other. Eric needed to see Charlotte as a separate person, not as his wife only. He needed to learn how to listen to Charlotte *without thinking principally about how he himself was affected by whatever she was saying*; and how to take an active interest in Charlotte's life and goals *whether or not they directly concerned him, and whether or not they innately interested him*.

Eric is a fine man, and his story offers a perfect example of how gloriously *un*predictable human nature can be. He grew up as the youngest of three much-loved sons in a cheerful, affectionate family. There are no obvious 'dark corners' in his background. Nevertheless, in his relationship with Charlotte, his dependency needs blew out of the water (the 'water' of his unconscious longings). Charlotte thought she had married an adult. But Eric's involuntary responses were often those of the 2-year-old who becomes desperate when Mummy is out of reach. This was not what Eric wanted. And the cost for both was extremely high.

It is also true that Eric did not move through that ill-fated intimacy dance alone. Charlotte's different needs hooked Eric in initially ('She sees me as a prince'). Soon, though, those needs became as much an expression of her self-concern as of love for him ('I need him to make me feel special').

Through their two years of marriage Charlotte was aware of how disappointed and angry she had become with Eric. He was no longer as admiring as he had been and she quickly discovered that his admiration for her had been a significant part of his charm. Like many adults, Charlotte had, in good faith, married someone she believed would be a marital version of a personal coach. Whether or not that's a legitimate demand, as the marriage continued she got less and less encouragement or even comfort from Eric.

Charlotte's major contribution to the rescue operation of that marriage would have been to take back her unspoken need that Eric be a prince so that she could be a princess. Maybe even 'personal coach' was too much to ask of him, although in loving relationships a good deal of mutual motivating and sustaining does go on.

She would also have needed to listen carefully to how she spoke to Eric as well as *how she described him to herself.* After all, it was *in her mind* that he first became a prince. It was also in her mind that he eventually became the gaoler she had to escape from. His behaviour was certainly influencing those thoughts. Nevertheless, in thinking about him one-dimensionally, she lost sight of his essential complexity.

Charlotte responded first to the prince, then to the gaoler. Yet in the early days, Eric was sometimes not all that princely. And even in the grim days towards the end, Eric was not just a gaoler either. But the emotional intensity between them narrowed both their minds, making it painfully difficult for either of them to see the other person as real, complex, contradictory and whole.

INCREASE YOUR CHANCE OF HAPPINESS

People in relationships can and do also 'infect' each other positively, picking up on the other's excitement, enthusiasm, creativity. It's one of the unsung glories of relationships of all kinds that we can lift each other up when, alone, we might slide down. But the flipside is that other kind of infection: the assumption that your irritation, anger – your self-hatred – is 'caused' by the other person. That your failures are caused by others or wished for by them. Or that someone else is thinking 'horrible things' about you when, in truth, those horrible things express an absence of peace in your own mind.

Your chance of happiness is greatest when your intentions are generous and this is reflected in your actions; when you are aware of what you want and confident that you can harness your creativity and energy to make that happen, and when your 'best interests' explicitly support the interests of the people around you.

Sometimes, however, the hidden self gets in your way.

Here's a striking example of how easy it is to move with great effort but entirely counter to your own best interests. It comes from psychoanalyst Theodore Isaac Rubin's book *Compassion and Self-Hate* and describes a loss of satisfaction that's caused by an almost total absence of self-awareness and self-love in a person who would seem to be intelligent, privileged and forward looking.

'I had a patient,' Rubin writes, 'who wanted to be a doctor until the week of graduation from medical school when "I realized I really wanted to be a journalist." What he did *not* realize was that he asked me in our first interview, "Why is it that everything I ever attain turns to absolute garbage? It seems great until I get it and then it turns to nothing at all." He didn't realize for a long time that he had been using shifting goals as a key process in his behaviour for years. *This was the prime method he used to drive himself on and away from himself*, and away from the possibility of giving himself decent, human satisfaction [my italics]. This was how he acted out his self-hate. He set goals that were achievable, and then decided that they were the "wrong" goals after all.'

Rubin then goes on to say that his patient's unconscious but paramount belief was that a 'worthless person' could not achieve 'worthy goals'. 'Interestingly,' adds Rubin, the same patient 'was only attracted to women who rejected him because, here again, any woman who cared for him and respected him must have been a fool indeed for being blind to his worthlessness.'

You might then wonder – as I did – how this man could work with his analyst. What kind of a bind would it put him in if the analyst showed him respect, constancy and kindness? 'Since I realistically did see much merit in him, and I'm not sadistic, this posed a problem initially,' Rubin says. The solution he offered was this: 'I got around it by showing respect for who he really was and contempt for his self-hating strategems. My contempt [for those strategems] sustained him until he was ready to accept my respect [for himself].'

From the outside it's easy to see how misunderstandings breed anxieties, and how anxieties breed defensiveness. And how this pushes us away from self-love and happiness. We can also see how crucial those underlying beliefs are about ourselves. From the inside, alas, this is not always so plain.

Our need to deny feelings that jar with our self-image; our need – like that of Dr Rubin's patient – to project our self-contempt onto other people, and to act out our self-hatred through decisions that hurt or limit us, diminishes only when we feel secure enough to go searching through our emotional patterns, recognising that they *are* patterns, and at least halfway taming them *through making them conscious*. And then, perhaps, measuring them against the highest possible standards of love for ourselves first, and other people too.

A woman in her fifties said to me recently, weeping as she did so, 'By their relationships will you know them! It wasn't until I finally had a positive and respectful relationship that I could see how I had continually lived out my self-doubts and self-abasement through the men I was with. Even though I believed I wanted the very best for myself. Even though apart from my sexual relationships, I *was* making healthy decisions. Great career, et cetera, et cetera. Those relationships were a blatant sign of the mistrust and turmoil that drove my life from below for more than twenty-five years.' Then she laughed and added, 'It's a real case of "Blind . . . but now I see!"'

That is the challenge and blessing of our long-term relationships: seeing those things. Allowing other people to help us see those things. Taking them seriously. Laughing at them. Unravelling them. Freeing other people from our worst fears or assumptions. Freeing ourselves. Loving ourselves. Going on.

THE KEY TO EMOTIONAL INTELLIGENCE

It can seem almost impossibly difficult to pause and reflect, to lighten up and recognise the misunderstandings or hurts caused by our own thoughtless or unconscious assumptions. It can seem so much more attractive endlessly to blame others or to see ourselves as the victim of circumstances. In the short run, though, as well as the long, our happiness depends on moving in another direction entirely. For our own sake, and to relieve others also from the burden of our projections, we must come to see exactly what we are doing, and take full and conscious responsibility for the muddled creation we call our own life.

Have I given this person the benefit of the doubt?

Have I given him a chance to explain himself?

Is there another way to look at this?

For our own sake, and certainly for the sake of deepening our relationships and making them more truthful, we must question our habitual assumptions constantly. For it's only in doing so that we can grow in self-awareness.

Self-awareness untangles the knots of projection. And how is it learned? Not only through paying attention to your own behaviours – and at least occasionally scrutinising your assumptions – but also through paying close, intimate attention to *the effects of your behaviour on other people*. And making changes when you need to.

What you project – what you assume – will not be all bad. Some of it will be potential that is waiting to be realised. In *A Little Book on the Human Shadow*, poet and social commentator Robert Bly points this out: 'When one "projects", one is really giving away an energy or power that rightfully belongs to one's own treasury. A man may give his "feeling side" or "relationship mode" away to his wife. Then he is rid of it, and when a feeling problem with the children comes up, he naturally lets her handle the problem . . . '

Projecting, we unconsciously surrender aspects of our own potential. Sometimes these are the parts that we feel uncomfortable with: a man may give away his more caring or more creative side and not 'take it back' until middle age; a woman may remain a charming girl until she is widowed in her sixties and finds 'quite naturally' that she can run a successful business and relish doing so.

Most often what we disown, or recognise in others but not in ourselves, is what we have been taught to disapprove of or not aspire to – and somehow this teaching 'took'. Those attitudes, characteristics or clusters of abilities will include some that are in the not-nice category ('People like us don't talk about love/ money/sex/power . . . '). Others may be the more daring and creative parts of ourselves.

There's a key responsibility issue here – as well as one of boldness.

American writer Katherine Anne Porter said of her own creative work as a painter and a writer that 'One of the marks of a gift is to have the courage of it . . . Courage is the first essential.'

That remark feels true to me.

What we disown – by believing that it exists in someone else but not ourselves – we need not take responsibility for ('I've always wanted to write a novel . . . but I haven't had the time . . . ').

Idealisation dazzles us. With lights shining in our eyes, we can't see clearly. As long as we remain dazzled, we can't claim what we may be seeking. Idealisation of other people often reflects quite directly just that rhythm of yearning then pulling back: 'He's so confident . . . I could never be like him.'

Idealisation may seem more benign than other forms of

projection. But it can delude us that happiness is always some place else. It can invite us to overestimate the value of other people's lives and underestimate the value of our own. I notice this each time I hear an almost relieved note in the laughter of people when I talk in public about my own varied foibles. Or when, in therapy, I am moved to allude to something that's been difficult to unravel in my own life. There's a brief look as something in the air between the client and me goes back home to where it belongs ('Ah, she's human too . . . ').

Close relationships depend for their existence on a subtle blend of fantasy or idealisation and reality ('I never believed that I'd meet someone as marvellous as you . . . '). Even workplace relationships call on fantasies of how life and people should ideally be ('I've got the greatest boss ever . . . ').

For relationships to succeed, however, and incorporate all of who we are, reality must eventually form the greater part. Most people want to be appreciated for themselves, loved as an equal human being and not as a version of themselves that could be 'found out' and rejected any time the fragile bubble of idealisation bursts.

The more conscious we are, the better life feels to us. The more we own who we are – and own up to what we do – the greater our sense of empowerment and choice. But many of the negative emotions seem to limit our choices, enslave us, control our minds and devastate our relationships. Jealousy, envy: who'd want to own them?

The odd thing is, though, it's those killer emotions that give us a fine chance to become more conscious. When they threaten our relationships, or make us feel like a slave to our own feelings, we must become more conscious of what's driving them and us, or risk living in a version of hell.

What we envy, *we should consider having*. Not some other person's version of it, but our own. If I envy you your success, for example, or your financial security, and want that for myself, then I need to think a little intelligently about what success would mean *in my terms*; what security would mean *in my terms*. That pricks envy's bubble nicely, and releases you from my sourness far more effectively than if I go on believing that success actually means being Bill Gates and that financial security also means being Bill Gates.

Moving from the self-pitying stance of envy to the far more powerful stance of taking responsibility for speaking your desires out loud, and shaping them in your own way, releases you from that fake attention you are giving to other people's lives, and moves you forward in your own. The reality is you are creating your own life. Envy blinds you to that truth.

Of course it may be that what you secretly envy or openly long for, you cannot have. You may need to realise that consciously ('I will never walk again', 'I won't have a child of my own'). You may need time to mourn. Then gradually to allow the irresistible dynamism of life to move you forward.

BUSHFIRE EMOTIONS ARE POWERFUL TEACHERS

Jealousy, fears of betrayal or of love going wrong can be bushfire emotions, running out of control whatever the factual circumstances. They feel dangerous because they do indeed have their roots deep in our unconscious minds. What we are conscious of is not the origin of these emotions necessarily, but our knowledge that they are agonising to experience. We also know that they're profoundly destructive of trust and closeness. But when they are understood and made conscious, they lose much of that unconscious power. *And the destruction they cause can be halted.*

These hot, bitter emotions usually reflect a lack of self-love or trust that you could deserve or have the love and care you long for. That's sad enough. But those difficulties are made worse when you project onto a real or imagined 'rival' the good qualities that you may long for or even have. (We never imagine that our lover will run off with someone much *less* insightful, rich or charming than we are.)

The jealous person may have a partner or lover who is saying clearly, 'I love you and I want to be with you.' But the jealous person is not reassured. Instead they hear, with their inner ear, only: 'You're not good enough. I need to find someone who is better than you are.'

I witnessed this some years ago working with Gary and Elise, a tall, athletic couple in their late twenties who were being tortured by Elise's jealousy. She was literally possessed by her certainty that Gary was betraying her. That belief dominated her thinking and affected her ability to work as well as their relationship. Yet it was clear that Gary sincerely loved her.

Elise could never be more than momentarily convinced that her feelings of jealousy and betrayal were not caused by Gary's actual behaviour – that he was not 'making her' suspicious. And the really tragic part of this story is that she had no interest in self-discovery or in increasing her own self-awareness ('Where are these feelings coming from? Could they possibly be expressing my own insecurity? What can *I* do about this difficult situation?').

Elise's entire focus was on Gary. And as long as the wellspring of those feelings continued to be disowned by Elise, it was impossible for her to realistically check them out. Asking Gary if her worst fears were true did not reassure her. She may even have felt more deceived by his increasingly desperate denials.

The urgent task in this relationship was clearly for Elise to examine her own fears; to begin to explore the qualities of the imagined fantasy woman that she believed Gary was seeking, and to go some way towards claiming those qualities – or reclaiming them – for herself. To do this Elise would have needed patiently to unravel her familiar patterns of response *until she could identify them as her own patterns*. And then to begin to hear and accept the truth of what Gary was saying: 'I love you and I want to be with you.'

But Elise couldn't do this. She was determined to see Gary as the sole cause of her happiness or unhappiness and herself as nothing more than an 'innocent' victim. The tragedy is, this lovely young woman would then continue to see danger everywhere, because 'everywhere' was a suitable target for her own unconscious projections. And, as long as that kept happening, she and Gary were condemned to remain in a lose–lose situation.

When we believe our own treacherous fears are caused by someone else, we are already doing ourselves a disservice. When, like Elise, we assume that someone else, even a mythical stranger, has the positive qualities that our partner or friend wants – but that we do not have – we may also endanger the relationship we care about most. The tragedy of this is two-fold. It makes other people threatening in their perceived perfection, rather than complex and real. And it makes us much less powerful than we actually are.

Some people's lives are virtually ruined by such fears – at least until they recognise those fears as their own. Such measured recognition demands awareness and courage: 'This is how things are. This is my part in it. This is what I can offer to redeem the situation.' Alas, what's much more common than that level of self-awareness and self-responsibility is a hasty overreaction or a wild assumption. But even those don't arise from nowhere.

Being around Elise, for example, wasn't easy. Her anxiety was omnipresent and highly infectious. It expressed itself in her tight, anxious body, her high-pitched voice and the nervous coughing that interrupted many of her sentences. In that state of anxiety, naturally it became harder for her to question or let go of some of her assumptions than it would have been if her state of mind had been generally one of greater ease.

Whenever we are struggling to make sense of a complex or ambiguous situation, it's useful to know that in general the less tense we are and the less uptight our body is, the better equipped we will be to identify and cope with our negative thinking – and recognise the havoc it can cause. Anxiety narrows our vision. It makes it harder to incorporate other people's points of view or even to review other more optimistic or trusting possibilities. And, unsurprisingly, the more tense or anxious we are, the more likely it is that we will interpret any ambiguous situation outside ourselves negatively, and behave accordingly.

Sandy has a refreshingly honest view of this particular relationship hurdle. She is a medical researcher in her mid-forties. She and her partner have been together for seventeen years and have one son. They are still very much together, but now live in different States so that both can do the work that interests them.

Responding to this tricky issue of where the origins of one's distress or irritation may lie, Sandy says, 'When someone else's behaviour really gets under my skin, I will often try to reflect upon what this is telling me about myself. The way people use the defence mechanism of projection is something I find easy to understand and interpret. When I am very annoyed by my partner's behaviour in particular, I really try to consider whether it is actually aspects of myself that I am finding unacceptable. However, usually this is as far as I get. This kind of understanding rarely translates into a change in my behaviour. It would be interesting to see what the outcome would be if I allowed this to happen.'

It's no wonder that our interpretation of troubled moments within our relationships are frequently muddled. After all, our stories and experiences are open to a raft of meanings. What we make of our life story, and of individual experiences, depends on how consciously we interpret those events to ourselves. And what we are *conscious* of.

Sandy says, 'I can become very irritable and critical of those I care about most. I can lose my temper in a volcanic kind of way. I have been this way since I was a child. When I was younger

I would occasionally hit someone at these times, including my son. Although I have never caused any physical injury, I'm sure the recipient of my anger was humiliated and hurt by the experience, and the memory of these occasions causes me guilt and heartache.

'Over the years the intensity of these feelings when they do occur has diminished. I have gained some measure of control over them, and when frustrated I rarely have the urge to hit out, but I do still yell and scream. When I behave in this way I really wish I was someone else. It feels like an affliction and I guess it is.'

There is a pattern to most extreme emotional reactions. For example, many people react excessively to smaller incidents when a major disturbance remains unexamined. It's worth noting that this more central issue – a question around a job or close relationship, or an existential issue ('What has my life been about?') – *does not need to be resolved to end this pattern of extreme response.* What is necessary is only a conscious recognition that something within you is causing anxiety, needs attention, and a resolution to do that. Sandy says that for her there came a realisation that 'The build-up of anger *is* related to my feelings of anxiety about what's happening around me.'

ACTING OUT YOUR INNER FEELINGS

What we tell ourselves about events, what patterns we recognise, even the fragments of insight that drift into the sphere of our awareness, affect all our relationships. We move in tune with our own inward responses. And then we *act out.*

Acting out is a tricky idea. But understanding it or just acknowledging that sometimes we are expressing something through our actions that is not, in fact, *how we believe we see things,* illuminates and relieves all kinds of situations. Even understanding how apparently simple events or experiences are open to all kinds of different interpretations helps. So too does a conscious recognition of how subjectively we see things inside and outside ourselves, and how differently we interpret what we see *according to our emotional state*.

We'll take it slowly.

Think first of a mottled snake in long grass. You see it. Then you don't. You bend in closer. You see a stick. The stick moves. It is a snake. You look more closely than before. The grass moves in the breeze. It shows you its darker side, and then the side that reflects the light. The grass closes over what might never have been a snake. And it settles.

Looking into the metaphorical long grass of our own lives, we may never be sure whether we have seen a stick or a snake. Too much certainty can be limiting. In the same way we can limit ourselves if we are not prepared to see how we might sometimes be entirely wrong in our interpretations; or entirely misguided about what messages our actions or responses are giving to other people.

We are used to talking about how young children or adolescents 'act out' through their behaviour the feelings they don't want to or don't dare to express more directly. Often these are the widely forbidden feelings of frustration, insecurity, confusion, hostility and fear (feelings forbidden by society as much as by our individual families).

What we are much less used to talking about is how intelligent, self-aware adults can fail to recognise the incongruities in their own behaviour: how they can hold one set of beliefs and live out another.

You might, for example, sincerely believe that you want the best for yourself. Yet you routinely expose yourself to dangerous or unsatisfying relationships. Such acting out – and that's a common example – goes beyond your rhetoric to an unpalatable truth about your own lack of self-love. And that can be hard to see.

All extreme reactions – which might be physical or emotional –

tell a story. But to find out what that story is it's necessary to stand back a little, look for clues, for patterns.

Maria and I have been working together intermittently for some years. She is a kind, generous woman, with many friends. Every now and then she talks about a particular friend, Frances. Frances is, in Maria's view of her, passive, complaining, difficult. She lacks emotional strength, Maria says. She is drowning in self-pity. When Maria speaks of this woman's attitudes, she regularly uses the word 'disgusting'.

This is not a Maria kind of word. From her lips it's startling. Eventually I mention this, very tentatively. I say, 'You know, it's an odd word for you to use: "disgusting". Are you aware that when you feel really frustrated, maybe with Frances only, that word jumps out?'

Maria looks at me. She is amazed. She hasn't heard the word. She is disbelieving. 'Really?' she asks. 'I've used it several times? About Frances? And sound as though I'm angry?'

I nod. 'Yes. Really. It sounds . . . Well, of course it sounds a little *disgusted*.'

We need to act things out less and less as we recognise more and more of what drives our hidden story. Acting out is an expression of our unconsciousness. Consciousness lets us see things more truly as they are. And lets us choose.

Maria *is* genuinely compassionate. She is horrified to hear repeated back to her that word 'disgusting'. She barely recognises it. Does this mean that she is not kind? Or does it mean only that something in Frances unwittingly stirs Maria's hidden self and arouses in her a level of contempt or a naked fear of insufficiency that her conscious mind disowns? Her mouth says the word. And she means it. But she doesn't notice.

In so many ways we *all* do this: think about ourselves in one way and act in another. Say or do what we don't 'mean'. Disown our own fierce emotions. Reduce complex human beings to a single damning adjective. Condemn what we can't have. Judge harshly what we don't dare claim for ourselves. Refuse to see how things 'really are' *because we so badly want them to be different.*

UNRAVEL THE MYSTERIES OF PROJECTION

It is of course also true that some of the disasters we feel strongly about are, in reality, caused by someone else! Someone *has* goofed up. Someone has done something that disappoints and enrages us. And beyond our small, personal world, there certainly are more things to drive us crazy: wars, greed, environmental devastation, corruption, drug abuse, injustices of the most blatant kind. But, as real and tragic as those things are, it's also true that our reactions to those events vary. And those variations themselves depend in part on our internal state of wellbeing.

To rant against the world's injustices, for example, seems to me a fair enough reaction. In order to be part of the solution, however, we need more wisdom than anger. We need to be clear about our own role in breeding disharmony. We need to be willing to create positive change.

From my own life, I have learned this: when I am most angry about something 'out there' it is often because, along with my justifiable moral outrage, I have projected onto some global situation 'out there' my own more personal feelings of frustration or injustice. Sometimes too I have liked the energy rush of being self-righteously certain of my point of view. There's nothing wrong with those reactions, but there may not be much benefit in them either.

Into great matters, as well as small, we project the picture we want or need. As a young woman, I was one of millions of people in the West who projected onto China's Chairman Mao an idealism that we now know was true only in our fantasies. Similarly, as a child of intellectual, leftish parents, I was personally aware of the intense negative projections fermented by the anti-communists in the West, most brutally in the USA. During the witch-hunt years of the McCarthy era all kinds of malevolence were attributed to many people whose worst crime was to attempt to practise the very principles enshrined in the American constitution: social justice, equality, freedom of speech and thought.

In social and political life we hurtle projections around almost as freely as we do in our intimate relationships. We 'create' public figures in our collective perceptions of them. We attribute to them qualities they may never have had, or we deny them qualities they may have in abundance. We may not consciously own those larger-than-life projections, yet we believe fiercely in them, and react just as fiercely when the projection is punctured by reality and collapses.

And in our spiritual lives we behave similarly. Your God may be fierce, forbidding, divisive, certain and judgemental. Is it any wonder, then, if you see those qualities everywhere, feel ruled by them, or even claim them for your own? For others, God may be experienced as totally accepting, tolerant, the source of all love and continuous forgiveness. Small wonder that those would be the qualities such people would want to develop, cherish, recognise and – dare I say it – even promote.

BEYOND THE RESTRICTIONS OF CHILDHOOD

The nature of our projections – and the depth of their effect – depends in part on the collective 'rules' and prohibitions of our culture, as well as on the nature of the personal stories we tell ourselves about our childhood.

Those personal stories, seared with some of our most dramatic projections, continue to haunt and shape us throughout our lives. I have worked with aged clients and have talked with many friends who can recall with passion and clarity events in their earliest lives that they believe set them on a trail that they had virtually no choice but to follow. Nevertheless, as powerful as those memories are, and as profoundly as we may believe in their authenticity, for most people childhood will look very different as they age.

At 20 your childhood is still nearby. It may be uncomfortable to remember precisely because of that. Growing up, you felt things intensely. You were also less self-aware than you are now, more egocentric. The stark judgements of adolescence were still in the air: parents were right or wrong. The childhood itself was wonderful or terrible; rarely both.

Looking back to that same childhood from the perspective of the 30- or 40-year-old, or 80-year-old, you may place less emphasis on the individual experience and more on the social patterns of family and community: 'Where did I belong in the greater scheme of things?' With that may come a softening of judgement and a willingness to see the contradictions in all human relationships.

To become an adult, it's necessary to move into an unblinking realisation of the complexity of your parents, and *your own complexity along with that*. The father you loathed as a teenager might be seen quite differently when you understand how he was overlooked as a child, starved of opportunity during the Depression, or exposed to inhuman cruelty in a prison camp. Or how sad he felt that his life failed to meet his modest dreams of accomplishment.

With age, we also see how we are influenced by many people and experiences. The influence of our parents and siblings will continue to reverberate throughout our lives. But the effects of that are not inevitable.

We do not need to become our parents. Nor do we need to live in opposition to them. We have our own choices to make. And it's our choices – the awareness with which we make them and the values and principles that underpin them – that eventually determine who we are and what we make of ourselves.

WHY THE PRETTIEST GIRL GETS THE HUNK

Nevertheless, we enter few relationships without emotional clutter. All kinds of assumptions and attributions – and the feelings that go with them – are present in at least the early stages of the relationships that significantly stir us.

In my 16-year-old son's age group, for example, there is a high degree of appreciation for the television character Buffy the Vampire Slayer. The scriptwritten Buffy manages to be simultaneously brilliant, brave, witty and beautiful, yet not in the least bit intimidating. This combination is difficult to pull off in real life, I fear. When a young man of my son's age meets someone who is somewhat Buffy-like (maybe in 'feel', rather than in appearance or brilliance), he may project onto this girl some of his romantic idealisations of Buffy. And project his own idealisation of how cool he will appear and how appreciatively he will be seen! It may turn out that no problems follow. More likely, though, as the real girl gradually emerges from behind the projection (a little less brilliant, a little more intimidating) things may go flat. They may also end fast if he quickly meets someone else who fits his unconscious projections even more neatly. Or if the original girl was projecting *her* Ricky Martin or Matt Damon onto him, and he turns out to be more like the boy next door and not the larger-than-life creation of a young woman's fantasies!

Projections are everything during the hormone-flooded years. That's why the hunk gets the prettiest girl – and the prettiest girl gets the hunk – while some of the funniest or most interesting people must wait their turn for romance glory.

Even as people get older, there are still complicated projections going back and forth in all kinds of situations. These arise out of idealisations that may be more sophisticated than the assumption that the best-looking people have most fun. But not always.

We shape people in our minds according to our own needs, just as a child might shape two figures out of Plasticine and tell us with confidence that Mr Red is very, very bad, so we should watch out, and that Mr Pink is very, very kind, so he'll take good care of us. Of course we are also reacting to the people themselves and to what they bring to the situation. Some of what happens between people is highly conscious. And can become increasingly so. But for all that, what's going on in our unconscious mind at any time remains extremely powerful.

TRANSFERENCE: LIVING OUT AN UNCONSCIOUS SCRIPT

Transference is another psychological term that is useful in thinking about catching the tail of our own shadow. The term itself is an attempt to make sense of a process whereby we unknowingly transfer part of our unconscious and incomplete inner story to an outer situation. This transference might have its origins in a larger-than-life or archetypal situation that stirs our imagination: like the longing to be a 'good wife', or to find a 'dark, mysterious lover' or the guru or therapist who can understand us 'perfectly'. It might also arise from an unfinished story from our own childhood. Transferred feelings are not memories as such. Memories are conscious and easier to deal with! They are more like repetitions, some of which may be experienced as so automatic that we can hardly believe we need to pay them any attention – until they begin to cause us problems.

Grief, jealousy, envy, frustrated longings, feelings of rejection: these are part of all family relationships, however outwardly benign a family may appear. Yet they are often not identified, and are rarely resolved through explicit understanding and acceptance. Because of this lack of resolution, as well as the compelling familiarity of certain kinds of situations, a type of magnetism is set up in the child, which may steer them towards similar kinds of emotional connections as an adult, perhaps in an attempt to find a better outcome than the original interactions with their parents or siblings could allow. Inherent in this dynamic is the powerlessness and frustration of the child who cannot make it better, get it right or find the unconditional love they believe they need and seek.

We don't 'transfer' haphazardly. Nor do we do it consciously. Something in a current situation unconsciously reels us in. But not always to our advantage.

We might, for example, return like a homing pigeon to cruel, unpredictable circumstances that frighten us *even when what we consciously want is absolutely the opposite.* Or we might find ourselves in yet another relationship with someone who is outwardly generous but privately cold and withdrawn – even though we had fully resolved 'Never again!' This is not because we are foolish. Or because we are undermining ourselves. On the contrary, it is often because we unconsciously yearn for a happier ending to a longstanding story and *want the healing that would come with that.* Also, because we don't know that's what we are seeking (consciously we may want no part of that story), it's easy to look for clues in the wrong direction.

You could, for example, marry a quiet, self-effacing man. You congratulate yourself on how unlike your bullying father he is. Two years into the relationship, however, as life becomes more complicated, you begin to experience the power of your spouse's covert hostility. This mainly expresses itself through his disowned acts of passive aggression. There is nothing here that you could say is just like your father's behaviour. And when you challenge your husband with it, he denies any ill intention. But you are chilled by *how familiar your own anxious, placatory behaviours are.* It is *this reaction of yours* that, most of all, prompts you to look at the situation more closely and perhaps take action.

Recognising a familiar response in yourself – even when you don't understand it – doesn't mean that you are doomed to replay what has already been difficult or dangerous. It may only mean that you must make an extra effort to locate and assert your own *conscious* needs and desires ('I am not prepared to put up with these sulking and controlling behaviours – I don't want to see myself crawling around trying to make things all right').

Clarity of that kind may be slow to come. In the swirl of a transference situation, you might, for example, feel uncharacteristically lost or uncertain ('I don't have a clue what's going on').You might find it more difficult than usual to act on your own behalf. You might even feel stripped of your usual inner resources.

In any situation where that's happening, or where you are suffering from the anxiety or depression that may accompany an experience of confusion or powerlessness, it can be useful to work with a therapist to disentangle your actual situation from the transference issues that are clouding it. Of course it *is* possible to work your way out of a transference unease or idealisation without the help of therapy. A loving and constant friendship, or a devoted relationship, can itself be tremendously liberating and healing. Often, though, in 'catching' these elusive patterns and in *moving beyond their reach* (just by seeing them for what they are), we need the 'eye' and experience of an intelligent, experienced observer, at least for a short while.

The repetitions or difficulties that trip us up in adult life do not arise from dark or troubled childhoods only. Eric's story showed that.A perfect childhood is no guarantee against negative transference experiences in adulthood. Transferences can be archetypal. They can also come from earlier adult relationships. And even when the transference does actually seem to have its origins in our personal past, it's useful to know that we are not talking about predictable cause and effect here. Those childhood experiences pushing you into difficult transference situations as an adult may not have been bad or ill intentioned. In fact, the very reason these situations catch us out is that they may have little outward resemblance to the inward patterns of call and response that our unconscious mind has recognised and hooked into.

You might, for example, be afraid to approach your amiable boss with suggestions about improving conditions in the work-place. You have great ideas, but through many meetings you sit in silence. You are not timid. On the contrary, you are known for your extroverted good humour. Yet you don't speak up.

Then one Saturday afternoon when you are lying around talk-ing to an old school friend, you suddenly remember how deeply you once admired the headmistress of your school. She had seemed to you like a perfect career woman, devoted to the stu-dents and admired by the staff. But – once only – you witnessed her behaving in a completely unreasonable manner, totally 'losing it' in correcting a girl who was particularly shy and vulnerable. In a moment you lost the woman you so admired, and saw instead someone whose human fallibilities were all too obvious.

It's been years since you thought about that incident, but without struggling you now see your situation with your own boss a little differently. You admire her too. Perhaps you don't want to risk seeing her in a less favourable light should she not appreciate your contributions. Your boss and your former head-mistress are quite different people. And you are now a different and less perfectionist person than you once were. Yet that old sit-uation has continued to affect you.

Recognising where your inhibition has come from, at the next opportunity you risk putting forward a couple of good ideas. They are received well, without much fuss. You move on.

YOU BE DADDY, I'LL BE SWEETIE

In some cases transference needs dovetail nicely. That's partly why transference feels so magnetic, almost literally 'drawing' us into sit-uations that might, in more conscious moments or different circumstances, seem banal or unattractive.

Authoritative doctors, who rarely take off their white coat even in the privacy of their own mind, may prefer and even attract docile and adoring patients, for instance. Patients who don't play the part expected of them might shake the doctors' view of themselves in uncomfortable ways. Similarly, a docile patient who wants to believe that 'Doctor always knows best' may be thrown when a less dogmatic doctor asks them to participate actively in their treatment programme.

In personal relationships too, people may comfortably and quite unconsciously slip into the roles on offer (mother/boy-child; victim/rescuer; creative/sensible; boss/helpless; rich older man/ young beauty). They may even do so with a very nice sense of a 'good fit' – at least until one or other of them unconsciously moves beyond the transference and wants to relate in a way that is less restrictive and more complex.

In relationships of a rather different kind, people may have crossed agendas almost from the start. Both may want to be 'baby', with neither interested in paying the bills or bringing in the washing. Both may want to conquer Everest. Or both may bring a level of anger and emotional hunger to the relationship that neither is psychologically free to appease.

Awareness may dawn that a transference issue is in the way when people begin to see they are ending up with the same feelings they have had many times before, even in a new situation. Or when they are having the same fight repeatedly, often 'about nothing'. Or when they confess to feeling unsatisfied and restless – no matter what's on offer. Or when they are able to glimpse that the reassurance they are demanding is too extreme. Or when a moment of insight shows them that their anxieties about money, safety or fidelity really do bear little resemblance to reality.

In all deep relationships, there is some transference. Where this is a positive transference, we may be inspired to 'rise' to become the person our lover, partner or boss believes we are. And where there are difficulties? An instant solution does not arrive the moment you recognise a difficult pattern. But that recognition does give you a chance to think more openly about your way of relating. It also allows you to take charge of your own reactions and feel less 'dangled on the hook' by the other person. And because transference issues are often present for two people simultaneously, even a tentative realisation of what's going on gives you a chance to consider what transference might be coming from your lover or partner towards you.

Does your anxious lover see you as wounded and vulnerable? Does that slob lying in front of the television unconsciously believe you are grateful and delighted to be running the household on your own? Is your apparently compliant husband actually experiencing you as a suffocating mother?

Even partial answers to these relationship conundrums can be almost absurdly helpful. After all, if his suffocating-mother transference is buzzing and your inner anxious child is pleading with him to say that he will never leave, the outcome for your relationship could be fatal.

Unravelling these loaded messages from the past, it is supremely helpful to realise that you may not have 'caused' the other person's extreme reaction. Nor are they (or you) inevitably to blame for a disproportionate response to what might have seemed a neutral situation to either of you. Taking for granted that your relationships will sometimes tell you surprising things *about yourself* (as well as whoever else is involved) makes it easier to be tolerant when these often passionate or painful confusions occur.

What also helps is to make every effort to communicate what is being felt and experienced: 'This sounds crazy, I know, but sometimes I feel it's as though my father is here in the room with us', or 'When I hear that edge in your voice I feel as though nothing I do will ever be right.'

The magnetic power of the transference – that compelling sense of inevitability – *depends on its being unconscious*. When each person can make a concerted effort to see beyond those reactions to who the other is now, and to be real about what's 'on offer' now, it becomes possible to move into a more conscious and much more mature and sustaining way of relating.

'HIDDEN ISSUES' MAY CONFUSE FRIENDSHIPS

Claudia offers a most useful account of how friendships can also be vulnerable to transference confusions. She is a rehabilitation counsellor, a single woman with close friendships and wide interests who has had several years of intensive therapy. Talking about transference she says, 'When I look at many of my major relationships in life I see transference issues being extremely active in them. The few that have been relatively free of transference have a clean feel to them, a lack of complication. This is my beacon for the rest of my relating.'

At the age of 42, Claudia can see clearly where transference has played a part in her close friendships. Because this depends to a degree on recognising certain patterns of relating, often over quite long periods of time, she can do this in a way that would not have been possible in her twenties or even her thirties.

Claudia confirms this. 'One of the most powerful transferences in my relating has derived from my relationship with my mother where there was a lack of primary bonding, probably due to postnatal depression. Having an emotionally unavailable, depressed and often ill mother as a child, I formed the unconscious belief that to win mother love, with all of its resonances of belonging and the right to exist, I had to successfully care for and heal the depression and pains of others.

'As an adult, much of my primary focus on relating has revolved around a drive to nurture/heal. As a young adult my usual mode of forming any kind of relationship was to hone in on the pain in a person and to encourage them to share that with me. I unconsciously felt this to be the path of love, and the more pain there was in a person the more I felt the hope of possible love and bonding. My strongest friendships were often with older women who carried a lot of emotional pain, and I would feel a great charge every time they affirmed how valuable or helpful I was to them. My unconsciousness meant that I couldn't recognise how one-sided or ultimately draining this form of relating was to me.'

Becoming aware of this over several years, Claudia consciously made changes to how she relates. This allowed her to have more equal relationships. More valuably, her recognition of those unconscious responses removed their 'charge' from them. She is still vulnerable to old patterns. But they can't draw her in with the same sense of inevitability they once did.

Claudia explains: 'My awareness resulted in me putting a conscious set of checks and balances into my relating. I look now for shared interests, laughs, an energy boost in potential new friends and lovers. I check that I don't encourage friends to talk on about themselves without participating in my own sharing. I remind myself that I am not responsible for friends' pain and do not have the answers. I know now that being appreciated for being sensitive and caring is not the same as feeling loved for myself.'

And the benefits for Claudia?

'I feel far less anxious and driven to take care of friends' welfare and to "make them happy". I feel far less dependent on them and their approval. I no longer equate this approval with their love. I am more able to see them for themselves in their own unique personalities and situations rather than overlay them with my transference of "suffering mother" who requires every last ounce of my effort to feel better. I imagine that in turn they feel far less burdened, either consciously or unconsciously, by my need for them to be happy.'

MAKING THE DARKNESS CONSCIOUS

Your view of the world may always be skewed by your hidden self, or rather by the fears, longing and needs that it pushes you to express. Recognising that, and also that other people will see you through the prism of *their* unconscious issues, may seem at first glance to complicate the whole relationship story quite unbearably. Yet, as incomplete and mysterious as this unravelling may ever be, there are also key ways it can bring significant relief.

I very much appreciate the way that publisher and writer Anne French talks about this. Anne is now 43, which she says is 'much like being 23 but with twenty years' experience to fall back on, or trip over'.

In recognising shadow issues – or simply that things are not always as they first appear – those extra years do count for something (if we let them). Anne says, 'Perhaps the thing that benefits me is an understanding (I mean that in a relative sense, as in a better understanding, not a perfect one) of my own weaknesses and shortcomings. That is, I can now begin to see how much we project ourselves and our unconscious needs and desires on those around us. I have therefore learned caution, not exactly wariness, but I have learned to temper my natural enthusiasm and optimism with a little caution.

'I know that the way I see a person or a situation *now* may not be the way I see it later, with the benefit of hindsight. The initial flush of enthusiasm can be blinding; the true nature of a situation will take a while to emerge. If this is a kind of patience, then it is a remarkable thing for someone as impetuous as me to have begun to learn and value. So I am more aware of the psychological complexities we each bring to our relationships, and more respectful of the dark shadows that we cast.

'None of this did I learn at home, growing up, where the world was a simpler matter, and no one reflected on the hidden underground streams flowing through our relationships, power-fully but out of sight.

'Having said that, I also want to make a different point, about courage. I've had some searingly painful experiences – things that I never expected to be able to recover from – yet I now believe that the only way to live one's life is to engage with it fully. Approach life with a spirit of optimism, and with an open and loving heart. Greet new people as though they will turn into friends – and so often they do. Most of the time such an attitude will repay one a thousandfold. Sometimes it's very risky indeed – and as soon as it looks like a bad idea, one must take steps to protect oneself. So I am wholehearted until such time as it looks as though it could turn out to be damag-ing, and then I take evasive action as speedily as I may. (All of this takes energy and effort of course, so I am inclined not to practise it when I am tired or stressed, and just retreat into a more passive state.)'

In difficult situations our own strengths and weaknesses *are* more fully revealed to us. This can leave us questioning or even not trusting ourselves. Anne reflects on this too: 'The last big disap-pointment has taken several years to get over. I never gave up hope – I knew I would survive it, and come out stronger – but it involved the loss of certain beliefs about myself. For instance, not only did I lose the dream of being a family, and somehow "com-plete", I also lost all sense of my ability to judge wisely and to choose a partner wisely. It was a terrible shock to my rationality to discover that I could get things so disastrously wrong when I was trying so hard to do the best thing.

'I think I am beginning to regain some sense of my fitness to judge, but it has taken four years of being careful and letting myself recuperate emotionally. That may sound very precious, but I simply banned myself from having any kind of new intimate rela-tionship until I had regained a little confidence in my ability to choose well – and of course opening myself up again took a great deal of courage. I may not be fully back to openness, but I'm well on the way.'

You may recognise yourself in Anne's story. I know that I do. Again it is helpful to see how everything that's happening in a relationship is not conscious or wilful. It may be more useful to hesitate than to blame. Acknowledging that the most emotionally loaded issues in your relationships (power, control, boundaries, an insufficiency of loving) are only somewhat to do with what's happening right now, it becomes easier to remain open and inquiring when a relationship turns a corner you would never have expected.

There is a brief demonstration of this in Piero Ferrucci's book *The Gifts of Parenting*. In this passage Piero, himself a writer and psychotherapist, talks in his own tender and honest way about how difficult it is, when two people have young children, to maintain time for each other, as well as a little for themselves. Piero describes how, when his children were very young, he got up earlier and earlier each morning to try to get some time for writing. He knew he would go crazy if he had no opportunity for the reflection and utterly concentrated attention that writing demands, yet as his children also woke earlier and earlier, and his rising time wound back to four in the morning, he finally realised that his wife was sitting with a 'ghost' in the evenings, and that he would have to give up his writing time in order to 'give back to my wife a husband who is no longer a ghost'.

Piero rediscovered, inevitably, that 'The people in our life are much more precious than any interest or activity.' He also found that once he had shifted his priorities, his writing flowed and he could get up early without being exhausted.

That was valuable, but better still, something shifted in the family dynamic. Piero writes: 'The relationship between Emilio [his older child] and Vivien [his wife] suddenly improves. It was not bad, but I didn't like the way he was often rude to her, or sometimes spoke with me as if Vivien did not exist. He would ignore her, as you might expect from some callous chauvinist. I strongly disapproved, but did not know what to do about it, other than preaching.'

This point of 'preaching' may be where many of us would get stuck. Piero went further: 'Then I realised, without knowing it, Emilio was showing me my own attitude towards Vivien. It was I, not he, *who was treating her like a shadow* [my italics]. Fortunately I found out. Every time I change my inner attitude toward Vivien, Emilio's outward ways with her also change.'

What a vivid example this is: that it was Piero's shadow that was treating Vivien 'like a shadow'; that his own previously unrecognised behaviour was revealed to him not through observing his own behaviour directly, but through perceiving the effects of his behaviour on his little boy.

A truthful life, a passionate and fully lived life, is not made up of one up-beat affirmation after another. Reflecting on your actions, checking out your intentions, soothing some of your fears, acting with awareness: these are invaluable tools for living. But they can't make everything in our human garden all right, all of the time.

Accepting that *there is always more to know*, and trusting that what there is to know has value, is vital in maintaining the freshness of any living relationship. It is also humbling. When we allow life to move more freely through all our relationships, it will shatter our illusions of omniscience. It will keep us, quite properly, surprised.

It's precious to realise this and to welcome the moments when we literally wake up to something that we hadn't understood before, just as Claudia did, and as Piero did when his son's behaviour showed him what he had been blind to.

The terms that surround these wake-up calls – shadow, projection, acting out, transference – should not be overvalued. They are simply props for us to think about something that can be troublesome and mysterious in equal measure but can unfold as we listen and look more closely, watching to see what we are attracting towards ourselves or are resisting. As we notice with interest the patterns of our inner commentaries and hasty judgements, and connect with what arouses deep feeling in us. As we look back on our past with curiosity and interest rather than regret or shame. And as we look inward for insight and explanations – rather than too quickly assuming that it's time to switch our attention and move on.

Light up Your Shadow

This is the chapter that could have been called *Stop going from one relationship to another without a clue about what went wrong!*

You may believe that dealing with what you can see in front of your nose is quite hard enough. But whether or not you want to bring your hidden, shadowy self into more conscious awareness, it will certainly make itself known to you – often through those 'worst' moments, the things you vowed you would never do or think, or even through the pain of desperately envying or longing for what someone else has.

The more conscious your life is, the greater and more real your sense of choice will be. So it is encouraging to know that the restrictions your 'disowned self' can cause, or the difficult situations it can return you to repeatedly, will ease rapidly once you begin to pay attention to what your shadow may be trying to tell you and see things freshly.

You live out the shadow in several key ways: idealisation, projection, transference and acting out.

Idealisation is what can lead you into romance or a dream job or any highly idealised situation. You create the idealisation through what you hope for. It depends much less on the other person – that perfect person! – than on what dreams or fantasies they unconsciously evoke in you. Idealisations are not all to be avoided. They can move us into beneficial situations. But we need to temper our expectations just a little, and certainly curb our rage when our royal person turns out to be only a sweet green frog.

A *projection* is when you put 'out there' what you are actually feeling 'in here': when you assume someone else is thinking the thoughts that describe or focus on what you fear most ('You think I'm hopeless') or, less often, what you most hope for.

This is a convoluted attempt to take good care of yourself, but the pity of it is that you can't deal with the feelings effectively when you have disowned them. And you may also sometimes respond to Dr Grim when actually it is just plain old Dad or your rather ordinary boss or partner standing there in front of you attempting to communicate with someone who is filled with angry or defensive feelings (meant for Dr Grim).

A *transference* situation has strong elements of projection. But think of it as broader in its sweep. Here you bring into an everyday situation strong feelings either from your childhood, an earlier part of your adult life or from an archetypal, larger-than-life situation. These feelings can confuse you about your current situation.

A transference situation can be positive. Especially when there is an opportunity gradually to incorporate the complexity of the 'real' situation.

You might, for example, initially believe that your spiritual teacher is as kind as the Dalai Lama and as beautiful as Madonna. Gradually this transference disappears as a real-life relationship takes its place. When there is a sudden burst into reality, that can be painful. But when you realise that the wisdom and beauty you longed to see in someone else is *yours to claim*, the transference has taken you in a healing direction.

You may be the person who is idealised or is the 'hook' for someone else's positive transference. Treat that with respect. Don't take it on, feel aggrandised by it or much affected at all. But also don't mock the person or take advantage of them. Absolute respect is crucial here.

The feelings that arise in a transference situation can be mesmerising and absolutely convincing – and may also have nothing much to do with the circumstances in which they are being *acted out*. This is how people come to have terrible fights 'about nothing' when really what's activated is fierce unfinished business – sometimes on both sides. Or why someone's subjective reality can flood their capacity to see what's actually going on. Or why someone may feel strangely drawn to and at home in situations that are not rationally attractive.

The initial warning signals of negative projections and transference are frequently intense. Here are the clues.

- You feel emotionally charged or aroused and often defensive.
- You feel compelled to yell, defend yourself, accuse or attack.
- You feel puffed up and self-righteous or withdrawn and defensive (inflated or collapsed).
- You experience the situation itself as compelling. *You are at home here – even if you hate it.*
- Your inner commentary is narrow in focus, persistent, heated, attacking or self-attacking.
- Your physical symptoms reflect your agitation: dry mouth, hot cheeks, churning stomach, clammy hands. You have a felt sense that this is 'the only thing happening in the entire universe'.

When any of those elements come into play you can help yourself.

- Walk away from the situation. No matter how difficult it is, pull yourself away. Do something rigorous and demanding – such as running or walking fast.
- Return to the situation only when you know that your inner monologue and your physical self are no longer agitated. When you are caught up, it is not the time to find insight or solutions.
- Refuse to be sucked back in no matter how compelling that feels.

Shadow issues are, by their nature, 'in the dark'. They emerge when you look at:

- the things you didn't mean to say or do (your 'Freudian slips')
- the disjunctures between what you claim to want and how you are actually living
- the larger patterns emerging from your relationships ('It seems like I always end up with someone who is angry/unable to make decisions/can't commit/can't love me. What's going on here that I am not noticing?').

It is possible to deal with your own shadow.

- Observe what arouses strong negative reactions in you such as fear ('Everyone will think I'm an idiot'), condemnation ('Young people think about nothing but sex'), envy ('What's he done to deserve . . .') or bitterness ('I could have been a success if I hadn't had you kids'). Follow those clues about what you've not yet claimed for yourself or given yourself permission to understand.
- Listen in to your own inner monologue. Write down what you tell yourself in those mesmerising times. Ask your strong feelings, 'What are you trying to tell me? How could we handle this differently? Show me your opposite face.' Write down your questions and answers. This *is* effective.
- Be aware that many people are too afraid to dive in and think about their unconscious processes. Take heart from that.
- Find the patterns in the monotonous repetitive things you tell yourself ('I felt like this in my last job – maybe it *is* something to do with me').
- Observe when you attribute your feelings or beliefs to someone else ('I know you don't like me') or hand over to them the power to judge you. Give the person 'the benefit of the doubt'.

- Use the patterns in your reactions to become more conscious. When you *recognise them as patterns* you are free to react differently; to know genuinely that 'This time it will be different.'

- Recall the heated, defensive moments in your workplace, family and personal relationships (the ones you never wanted to think about again). Step back from them imaginatively. *Look at the bigger picture.* Find the *trigger* that tipped you over. (Perhaps you feel 'unreasonably' enraged if someone calls you lazy, lucky, hot tempered.) The trigger will be much less powerful once you recognise it as a 'button'.

- Remember not just what the other person did or said, but what *you told yourself about their behaviour* ('She thinks that I can't do anything right').

- Understand how your own moods will also affect the way you see others, and interpret their responses. This insight alone lets you deal with many difficulties without defensiveness.

- In ambiguous situations ask yourself, 'What feelings am I conscious of here? What's my own state of mind? Is this situation familiar? *Are my own thoughts making this worse?*'

- Know you will be influenced by the core belief or 'story' that's running through your mind ('Nothing I do is any good', 'He'll want to leave me any day now').

- Save yourself from grief. Check out: 'How realistic is this story? How often do I replay it? Does it conflict with what this person is trying to tell me? What do I need to *disentangle* here?'

- If someone else is involved, ask them to state clearly how they see things. Try to get some of that written down. You may be shocked at how different it is from what you believe you are hearing or dread hearing.

- Learn to discern when an uncomfortable situation is *not* confused by shadow issues. If someone is attacking or undermining you directly, *assert your authority*.

It is possible to deal with someone else's shadowy confusions.

- If a difficult situation is ambiguous, give the other person the benefit of the doubt: 'He's in a bad mood again. It may not have anything to do with me.' Check it out: 'Is something troubling you?'
- Know your partner, friend, colleague or child may be in a foul temper for reasons that have nothing to do with you, but they may nevertheless react defensively ('What's it to you? I felt fine until you asked me that stupid question').
- Value the boundaries that awareness and explicit self-responsibility bring ('Actually I feel depressed and hopeless but I don't have a clue why. It's got nothing to do with you'). They save you from feeling powerless.
- Without those boundaries, accusation, self-accusation and blaming can run wild. Talk and think about self-responsibility when you are *not* under stress.
- Know that two people can be suffering equally from the illusion that the other person is 'causing' their unhappiness. Review that possibility when you are not stressed. If that seems likely, it can be useful to enlist the help of an experienced therapist.
- As you listen to someone else 'going off', being unreasonable or acting out their own misery, *pay attention to your inner monologue.* Keep your commentary as impersonal as you possibly can.
- In the face of an attack, *back off.*
- The very nature of shadowy distress means that 'reason' can be deeply unhelpful, even insulting. Remain calm, rather than attempting to 'put the person right'.
- Recognise that when people are caught in a transference battle, a difficult moment can escalate rapidly. When it's safe, ask the other person to consider a process of self-exploration

similar to your own: 'What were you telling yourself while all that was going on?'

- Without accusing, let them know what feelings *their behaviour aroused in you*. This may give you both useful clues.
- Value these discussions. Treat what you discover with respect. Making this process more conscious prevents you from believing another person is ruining your life and may also prevent them from accusing you. In a largely positive relationship, *swap stories*. You might be amazed to discover how differently you perceive the same situation. Or what sadness lies behind an attacking response.
- Use your instincts to know if you are in danger. If you are, remove yourself immediately.
- Never expose yourself to someone else's rage or abuse.
- Never subject someone else to your rage and abuse.
- If your shadowy outbursts cause you distress, consciously cultivate a belief in the innate goodness of all that you are. Your defensive behaviours originated in an attempt to save yourself from hurt or from other people's disapproval or contempt. It is possible to transform the energy of those behaviours not through despising them or shaming yourself, but through using insight and kindness to discover what you fear, hope for and most want. Hiding less from yourself, you give your shadow its best chance to come into the light. And you give yourself your finest chance to become fully conscious.

Transform

Aggression

Our path is to heal. To create the circumstances

where healing can begin.

A COURSE IN MIRACLES

*I*f love is what connects us; if love gives us the space to think curiously and courteously about other people; if love salves our loneliness; if love lights up and delights our lives; if love makes it easy to seek and find the good in other people, to give up something for the sake of someone else, and to put ourselves second without feeling the least bit denied – then is it possible to say that aggression is the antithesis of love?

Please know this: I am not talking about high-voltage displays of emotion. I am not talking about caring passionately and expressing yourself so loudly that 'the rafters of heaven ring'; nor about standing up for yourself; nor about the harnessing of the energy necessary to do something that takes you to the edge of your abilities, and to do it well.

What I am talking about is that same high, fierce, wonderful energy soured, curdled, polluted into personal and social expressions of hatred, violence, self-righteousness, denigration, withdrawal, sulking, contempt and abuse of all kinds that undo love, defame it, or even banish it.

Feel the heat of aggression – coming from you, coming towards you – and know how different that is from the heat of enthusiasm or passion. Enthusiasm draws us towards things; it invites us to participate, to engage, to feel alive and open. Passion pulls us in, closer, closer, while it also remains sensitive, asking 'What does the other person want?' Aggression is not like that. Aggression stirs our body-mind. It reminds us keenly of earlier hurts, other insults. Aggression pushes us to cross lines of decency, consideration, care; of personal or social space; of awareness of other people's rights and integrity; between adults and children, lovers, people in neighbourhoods, cultures, religions, nations.

Packing bags of groceries into the boot of my car, at six o'clock on a balmy spring evening, I hear 'Get in the car, you arsehole!' My daughter ignores what she is hearing and packs faster. She hates a fuss. I look around. A woman, my own age I would guess but a harder life is written across her face, is fixing her young adult daughter with a gaze she must have learned from the Gorgons. Yet there's pain in that too. Pain for her as well as pain for her daughter.

AGGRESSION BLIGHTS OUR LIVES

Aggression separates people but it also binds them: in agonies of betrayal, disappointment, contempt and humiliation. Caught up in the whirlwind of aggression, the expression of our own feelings becomes all that matters. Like the danger that lifts and fills cats' fur, aggression puffs us up also – although not with wisdom.

Thinking about aggression, we may first imagine shouting, hitting, pushing, bullying, biting, bashing, raping, tormenting. Those things are happening every moment of every day, in all kinds of situations and with devastating results. They generally arise from and express high levels of frustration, a need for power over others, as well as an inability to see one's needs alongside the needs and integrity of other people.

Love cannot coexist with the desire to hurt someone else. What's more, the divided awareness that allows someone to hurt one person while loving and being kind to others is also internally dangerous. In a healthy life we aim to be more or less 'of a piece'. This doesn't mean that we don't sometimes act out of character;

we do. But when we attempt to persuade ourselves that the actions in one area of our lives do not affect the rest of our lives, we are gravely deceiving ourselves.

It is not our personal lives only that are profoundly affected by the agonies and divisions caused by aggression. Our planet, cities, countries, cultures, even some of our neighbourhoods are all deeply scarred and shaped by the perverse claims for power that aggression drives, and the fears that arise in response to that.

Psychologist Alfred Adler believed the aggressive drive for power in human beings is as potent as the drive for sex. Given the glorification and worshipping of violence that pervades contemporary Western culture, and the abject fear of sensuality and sexuality that sits alongside it – or even thinking about the fiercely sustained public denigration of the notion that all our lives are of equal value – it is possible to suggest that Adler was wrong. The aggressive drive may be stronger than that for sex. And the costs are immeasurable.

Self-assertion is the positive face of this drive. It's expressed through creativity, cooperation, enthusiasm, passion, idealism and inspiration. Self-assertion lets you take your place in the world; discover what kind of world you are living in; make plans, make changes; live at the very centre of your own life while valuing actively the lives of other people.

Assertiveness is far less volcanic than aggression. Assertiveness wants to win; but doesn't have to win. Assertiveness wants to get its point across; but won't risk death in the attempt. Assertiveness can say, 'I won't stand for this' or 'I've had enough.' But also: 'This is worth trying. This is worth my while.'

I like this father's story from Bobby, now in his mid-forties. 'I'm not naturally an easy-going person,' he says. 'But I've realised, particularly with my children, that nothing works like dignified consistency. When I would shriek at them over something, it became obvious that they were transfixed by my bulging veins, my popping eyes and verbal decibels. What I was saying was lost!

'Anger frightens children and I would like my children not to be afraid of anything. They have been my greatest teachers in respectful relations. I always apologise to my children if I lose it and, if it's appropriate, I talk about what the issue was for me. Often it has nothing to do with them. The fact that there were clothes on the floor again didn't warrant my reaction.'

In everyday life the line between self-assertion and aggression is easy to cross. Restraint helps us most. It provides that essential split-second's pause that lets us choose, let's us remember that some issues are worth fighting for – but some are not. That sometimes it's appropriate to 'hold your ground' and sometimes it's futile. That sometimes the costs of being 'right' are far too high. Or that there are more effective ways to deal with your weariness or tension or inability to move mountains than to dump your rage on others.

Few strong-minded people move through adulthood without some serious regrets about crossing that line; about being over-insistent when it was patently unnecessary; scoring points that are actually worthless; forcing a point of view at the loss of goodwill or friendship; making someone else wrong because of their own limitations or frustration; or maintaining a position of self-righteousness at the cost of other people.

The question of self-value is crucial here. Bobby's desire not to expose his children unnecessarily to anger beautifully expresses that.

In Adler's view the person who believes they are superior – or who believes they must be seen to be superior – is as unfortunate as the person who acts from an unconscious belief that they are inferior. Either way that person's drive for power and unease about whether or not their life has value has painfully negative effects on themselves and other people.

We see this clearly with those people who must always have the last word in any argument; who have to win points, even in petty matters; who take life's setbacks as personal affronts; who over-identify with the success or failure of family members; who are obsessively controlling or critical, rarely delegating or conceding to others; or for whom no level of success, fame or fortune can ever be enough. All of those characteristics – and many like them – speak of a lack of trust and ease within the person.

Adler's view was that we function most healthily when we feel valued by others *and can also value ourselves.* That's easy to agree with. And that's certainly what most readily supports the development of loving and respectful relationships.

It's good to know that valuing ourselves is something that can be learned, not least through living the kind of life that consciously supports the integrity and development of other people. Empathy teaches us how much we have in common with others. It also shows us how, leaning in a little closer to other people's lives, we can see them in their complexity and not simply as an ugly obstruction on our path to glory.

Learning what we share with others, really taking that in, we no longer need to puff ourselves up by making other people wrong, stupid or contemptible. Nor do we need to fall into masochism or martyrdom, falsely valuing other people's lives but not our own.

Balancing our personal *and* social awareness, we see much more realistically how we are affected by other people, and also how we affect them. Awareness of that interdependence can literally be our saving grace.

'It is the individual who is not interested in his fellow human beings who has the greatest difficulties in life and causes the greatest difficulties to others,' Adler wrote. 'It is from among such individuals that all human failures spring.'

Those ugly externalised acts of aggression need our attention urgently. What we may know less about, or may less consciously recognise as dangerous, are the more covert, indirect or passive forms of aggression.

'Passive' is a deceptive word here. Passive aggression is sly, certainly, and easily denied, but it is also so nasty and disrespectful, so wounding and harmful that it too kills good intentions – and ends love.

Passive aggression includes the deliberate withholding of encouragement or kindness; flooding someone with contempt; punishing with silence or sarcasm; blaming people, though not directly; being 'just too late' for appointments that really matter to someone else; smugness; teasing; belittling; humiliating; breaking promises; divulging secrets; spoiling someone's pleasure; saying the wrong thing 'by accident'; turning inward, denying that anything is awry while nourishing a private and potent sense of woundedness.

THE COURAGE TO CHANGE

If you love but are also aggressive, then the intention to stop is not enough. Action is needed as well as the courage not to be distracted by your own excuses, least of all that you are acting out of helplessness or as a victim of your own past or because someone else has 'made you'.

Honesty is also needed: this behaviour cannot continue. What you might see first is that it cannot continue *for the sake of someone else*. That's a fine place to start. Soon you will see it cannot continue for your own sake either. What you think about someone goes some way to determine how you will treat them. Just as crucial, though, is the way that you think about yourself.

We hurt the people who involuntarily hold our own powerful feelings of self-disgust. Into them we project our own feelings of intolerance, helplessness, abandonment, rage. We hate them for their inferiority. We hate them for their superiority. Whether they actually feel inferior or superior is irrelevant. We believe it. That's what counts. This doesn't mean that we hate them all the time or think of them with disgust all the time. On the contrary, these may be the very same people whom we sometimes think of as gorgeous, precious and to be treasured.

It is good to know that we can take back those feelings of self-disgust. Few people are terminal victims of their own aggression. *Abusive or denigrating responses can be unlearned.* Stress management, insight, a less gruelling or empty schedule, the will to change can all contribute to greater impulse control and equilibrium. Psychotherapeutic or counselling help for anger management can also be found. The impulse to hurt – actively or passively – can undoubtedly be transformed.

AGGRESSION MARKS TERRITORY

We need no invitation to understand how aggression affects us. Willingly or not, we all know how aggression looks, feels, smells. We know the fear and prejudice it creates. We know how it walks all over people, mows them down, and leaves disaster in its wake.

When aggression rules it is not possible to do what love asks – to consider others' wellbeing alongside our own. *Do unto others as you would want them to do unto you. Do no harm. Do good. Hate is not conquered by hate: hate is conquered by love. This is a law eternal.*

Aggression marks territory and invades it. It does for humans what also works for animals. Aggression seeks to dominate others, to control others – and to punish them for their refusal to be controlled. Aggression pushes in where it does not belong. Aggression walks away from those it injures without looking back. Aggression believes its own myths, glories in its self-justification. Aggression ignores the wellbeing of others. It causes suffering and often enjoys it.

Self-respect and respect for others depend on our capacity to contain our aggressive impulses: to redirect the fire or ice of aggression into creative passions and idealism; into benign and healing expressions of love; into an awareness of nature and our need for it; into a consciousness of other people's integrity and their right to that.

Meanwhile, many people (and my perception is that their numbers are increasing) relish their moments of aggression. This comes as no surprise in a culture where most people rarely dance or sing out loud; where we have the chance to roar only if we are keen sports fans; where we almost never run or jump or leap or glide for the sheer joy of it, or throw ourselves onto sand or into a freezing lake, or ride impossibly high waves when we are no longer a young surfie; where we no longer sit together telling wild or tender stories; where we look at other people's paintings and don't hold paints in our own hands; where we buy food that has no earth left on it; where we wash the sweet-smelling vernix off newborn babies moments after they are born; where we may do a small part of a whole job, but rarely witness anything completed; where our sacred sense of ritual may be reduced to a plastic tree at Christmas time; where community may be only what we see on a small screen; where the whole world is available to many of us but we complain that we have nothing to do and nowhere to go.

In the face of this, the sheer intensity of aggression can feel compelling and exciting. A year or so ago, at a dinner function with twenty people I didn't know, a widely esteemed man said to me with no prompting, 'I know it's wrong, but I am addicted to rage every bit as much as I am addicted to working inhuman hours and running from one meeting to another. It gets me going and I like that.'

Standing over someone else, in reality or in our mind's eye, we do indeed grow larger. What's more, we grow in intensity. We feel alive, powerful, *certain*.

LACK OF SELF-CONTROL IS A MYTH

Few adults are aggressive to those they perceive as having more power than they do. That simple fact is itself instructive. While young children will throw tantrums with almost anyone, few adults throw tantrums or are directly aggressive to those they perceive as having more power than they do. Or rather they are rarely directly aggressive on their own. Gangs, groups, armies, militias: all are capable of acts of aggression that would be virtually impossible to imagine, much less accomplish, if each person acted alone.

People are of course individually capable of hideous, dehumanising acts of aggression, but far from these expressing a lack of control or failure of self-restraint, it is chilling to note how routinely they are 'saved' for those who are perceived by the aggressor to be weaker or more vulnerable. Or saved for situations where the aggressor believes they have a 'right' to their aggression through a misguided sense of ownership of another human being.

Such acts of aggression take place every day, not least in many workplaces. My urbane dinner companion gave me no explicit examples of how he expresses his aggression. I don't know whether his speciality is yelling at someone in front of other people; 'tearing strips off' someone in private; making fun of someone vulnerable who can't answer back; trivialising someone's efforts; waiting until someone has let their guard down before he 'puts the boot in'; firing someone abruptly and disrespectfully; leaving someone in a state of uncertainty for weeks or months; loading people with impossible levels of work; setting people up in unnerving competition against each other; using others as shields or to do the dirtiest of the dirty work for him.

To our shared shame, all those behaviours pass as normal in many upstanding, high-flying workplaces.

DOMINATION AND CONTROL

Potent issues around domination and control are present in any situation marred by aggression. Sometimes the aggression arises because someone refuses to be controlled ('You do things the way I tell you or else . . . '). Sometimes it arises because the aggressive person feels unsure, weakened, caught out or confused, and dislikes this feeling so intensely that they mask it with an aggressive outburst, making someone else 'wrong' rather than momentarily feeling wrong or uncomfortable themselves.

Fear drives this situation. Fear of loss of face and ego strength. Because men are generally encouraged to be more concerned about face and ego than women are, this particular expression of fear is still more common with men than women, especially in situations where the man feels he *ought* to know what's happening, or *ought* to be able to meet a problem with an adequate solution – but cannot. He could possibly admit to that, but sometimes his feelings of insecurity will translate so rapidly and automatically into feelings of rage that the question of choice becomes irrelevant.

The parent who is unable to get the washer off a tap may yell at the child who brings the wrong set of pliers. The boss who is unable to get a report prepared adequately may scream at the assistant who is attempting to key in from an illegible draft. The driver whose car won't start may kick it and curse it.

Each of these people is taking this setback as a personal insult. Their behaviour screams, 'This shouldn't be happening to me!'

With a little awareness it becomes clear how human it is to take the most absurd setbacks personally, often experiencing them as direct affronts ('It rains every time I go camping'). Yet, quite illogically, we don't also see ourselves as personally responsible for the *attitude* we bring to these troubling events.

By the time someone has reached their workplace on any normal morning they may have found a whole string of people to blame or think of as a nuisance: those who have failed to deliver their newspaper onto the porch; those who made noises at the breakfast table; those who were not ready on time; those who were waiting first in line at the bus stop; those who should have been driving the buses that didn't arrive; those who were driving the cars that got in the way of the bus; those who closed the only ATM on the route to work; those who moved their chair or touched their desk, computer or machinery . . . And all this, before the 'real' day has even started.

SEE LIFE AS A SERIES OF IMPERFECT FACTS

In both women and men aggression depends for its energy on a fundamental sense of injustice, a sense of grievance: things should be other than they are. If someone is 'in your face', or is threatening someone or something you care about, a fierce retaliatory response may not always be useful but it is certainly understandable.

Many great and small expressions of aggression, however, arise from something far less provocative. They arise from a failure to see or accept things as they are – *and to work with those facts.* The parent who is unable to face their own inability to fix the dripping tap blames their child for making a mistake. The boss who doesn't know how to get the report done on time makes their assistant wrong. The driver who doesn't know what's wrong with the car blames (and hates) an inert object.

Those small events can be seen as symptomatic of a general outrage about how wrong life often is. And a much more specific outrage that *my* life is wrong. But does that make sense?

In her invaluable book *Anger: The Misunderstood Emotion,* social psychologist Carol Tavris points out that people who experience emotions intensely personalise events. (And I would say vice versa: that people who personalise events *then* experience the intense emotions of affront and self-pity.) Not only that, Tavris says, 'they *pay selective attention* to the emotion-provoking aspects of events ("I focused on the worst part of the situation"); and they *overgeneralize*, taking a single event as a sign of a general state of the world. They exaggerate, in positive as well as negative directions.'

In other words, as frustrating and as tormenting as the world is 'out there', your reactions to it are largely determined by what's going on in your *inner* world of thought and feelings. One day the bus sails by and you chew your nails, feel your stomach clench, grow red of face and hot in temper. Another day the bus sails by. You worry ('Will I be late for work?') but you also relish the pause. Between one place and another, you breathe. You may even smile. This moment, you realise, will not come again.

Aggression is nothing more than one possible response to a situation you don't like. It is not inevitable. Even in the face of not knowing, feeling wrong, feeling insecure, trespassed upon, lost or abandoned – all potent catalysts for aggression – and even if we are struggling with a hot temper or cultural idealisations of aggressive outbursts (for men), *there are other choices*.

Recognising any common triggers for the feelings of helplessness, shame or frustration that translate into aggression is vital. So is an awareness of the territories or boundaries you feel most sensitive about. And equally useful is an awareness of the hunger, weariness or feelings of being overwhelmed that can also rapidly cause people to lose their inner sense of balance.

Even highly impulsive or anxiously reactive people can learn to hesitate in most situations for just that vital split second to ask, 'Is this worth it?' And then a second longer, 'Does this reaction help?' And perhaps: 'What am I actually expressing here? What would be a more useful response?'

It's in that millisecond's pause that we can remind ourselves of what elevates human nature: *that we do have choices*.

Those choices shape all our relationships. They create them. Carol Tavris points out: 'The ultimate purpose of thinking twice about anger is to enhance the long-term benefit of the relationship . . . But both the individual and the relationship benefit.'

It is also possible to move with the humour of the universe: to learn to *see life as a series of imperfect facts*. This is not a cynical choice;

nor is it defeatist. We may not consciously admit to expecting perfection, yet the odd thing is how many of us collapse or go into a frenzy when things are *not* perfect! So what is it that we were expecting?

Once we consciously accept that most things will not go entirely our way, we will be far less thrown when that inevitably happens. We'll know for sure that we can survive that. What's more, we can then be delighted when things are exceptionally good (noticing this now where we didn't previously). And we are likely to become more sanguine still once things become facts in our view of them rather than personal insults ('I need to call a computer repair person', rather than 'Every computer I've had goes and dies on me'; 'The plane has been cancelled', rather than 'I might have known it would be the plane I'm on that would be cancelled').

This weird and very human form of egocentricity veers from amusing and harmless in its effects, to chilling and dangerous.

A man lifts his eyes from his newspaper in a subway and is shot because the gunman believes 'He was looking at me funny.'

A stranger in a big city pulls up to check her map. A truck driver yells, 'Out of the way, bitch. D'ya think I've got all day?'

When the facts get untangled from the personal insult and the personal insult has been set aside, it again becomes possible to ask: 'What's going on? Do I need help with this? What outcome do I want here? How can I ask for that? Which bit of it actually matters?'

PERSONAL POWER DEPENDS ON SELF-CONTROL

Aggression gnaws away at the tender heart of our relationships.

Here is 34-year-old Anna: 'Sometimes I am shocked when I suddenly hear myself speaking to my husband in a sharp, curt manner. I don't hear it enough. It has become almost my regular demeanour at home. It's ugly. We have some friends who recently separated. The wife did this a lot – she would speak to her husband in an ugly way, and in front of everyone. I am sure that she had no idea how she sounded. Somehow she had lost her sensitivity to this. I think about her a lot now. I am so close to becoming like her at times that it scares me.'

Personal power – and the confidence that comes with it – evolves through a lifetime of gradually increasing awareness of the effects of your behaviour on others. And a gradually increasing sense of choice *that can only come with awareness.*

You may assume you have little self-control – because you don't practise it.

You may assume you have a limited emotional range – because you've so far made no effort to extend it.

You may also assume that expressing your aggression you will be rid of it. Yet, curiously, the opposite is true. The more you practise being aggressive, the more accomplished at it you inevitably become. The more you practise being angry, the more angry you become, and *more will make you angry.*

What's needed, then?

Again it's that invaluable moment of restraint, that split second that reminds you that you can think *and then act.* Standing back mentally for just that moment, assessing the facts, accepting them as imperfect, asking, 'What needs to be done?'

Or perhaps not going that far. Simply noting, even in a fairly incoherent way, 'I won't react out of anger only' or 'This isn't the moment to act, I'm too angry', can rapidly increase your sense of choice – and the spaciousness and relief that accompany it.

Defensiveness can also lead us rapidly into battle, sometimes clearly against our own best interests. Martine's account of her pattern of behaviour strikes a familiar chord. She is an architect in her early forties, the mother of two young adult daughters and currently not in a sexual relationship after two decades of moving from one long relationship to the next.

'I punish other people (more specifically men with whom I am having an intimate relationship) with criticism,' Martine says. 'This starts when they have hurt, betrayed or disappointed me in some way. I think it's a way of distancing myself from them. I endeavour to convince myself that they are unworthy and not valuable to me. I push this quite a long way, which often ultimately results in rejection – either way. This is the way I defend myself against feeling vulnerable *and it is very unsustaining*.

'On the rare occasions when I can say what I want, and listen to what the other person wants, and we can both negotiate from that point of being heard and accepted, there is a feeling of solidity there that oddly enough allows me to be vulnerable – but not feel weak.'

CURB YOUR 'RIGHT' TO MAKE OTHERS WRONG

That thin line between assertiveness and aggression continues to haunt us. Sometimes different cultural styles can lead to misunderstandings ('What do you mean I was shouting?'). And sometimes it's a more personal question of perception.

Bella is a refreshingly outspoken mature-age student who grew up in a noisy, expressive family, but now in her mid-thirties she lives with a very different kind of man. She says, 'I find it difficult to talk about aggression. It doesn't interest me. I think people would say I'm aggressive and maybe I am. I think I'm just assertive. Certainly I don't shut up. If someone stands on my toes, I tell them loudly to get off.'

Is she right to do that? Do we have a right to tell other people to get off our toes? Most of us would say yes. And indeed there are many people who need to learn just that skill: to say, 'Get off my toes – please', without falling into a heap for doing so.

Bella continues: 'I think my assertiveness can get a tad heated when I am frustrated and haven't thought it through. Perhaps I am not clear about what is bothering me. Then my aggression becomes emotional and less effective. The other day I got a disappointing mark for a university assignment, which pissed me off because I am always getting disappointing marks even though

I take the work seriously. Anyway, I made loud complaining noises in a class. The lecturer asked why I didn't take up the matter if I was so offended, and I blurted out that I couldn't be bothered. In fact, I was extremely hot and bothered and the whole class knew it. But after ten minutes I was over it.'

PASSIVE AGGRESSION ALSO HURTS

The hot, quick flame of Bella's aggression seems relatively harmless, although it could certainly burn someone who was in the way at the wrong moment. Nevertheless, Bella believes her aggressive style is at least clean. What bothers her – because of its extra dimension of denial – is passive aggression in any of its pervasive modes. Bella says, 'With me there is absolutely no manipulation, sarcasm, withdrawals, refusal to say what the matter is. With me, what you see is what you get. If I am pissed off, I will say so in no uncertain terms and try to explain why.'

Interestingly, Bella's live-in boyfriend has a very different style of expressing his dissatisfaction. Bella describes this: 'When we first started living together, his passive aggressive behaviour wore me down. But I started getting wise to it and began to relentlessly mow him down with confronting attacks. "There you go again, like a bloody martyr. Why don't you just hang yourself on the cross and get it over with . . . " That sort of thing.

'I would point out time and again when he was doing it: sucking in his lips like he'd just sipped citric acid, shaking his head in despair, the comments that would come out supposedly as humorous, but were actually depressing put-downs. I freaked out big time, shouted my head off about how unattractive it was and why didn't he just grow up and deal with things straight, et cetera, et cetera!'

I haven't met a single person who finds overt forms of aggression easy to deal with; neither their own aggression, nor other people's.

And I don't suppose you have either. Nor have I ever met a single person who did not eventually feel driven to despair by covert, passive forms of aggression such as sulking, injuring with silence, refusing to say what's wrong, freezing them out, sarcasm, put-downs. In some ways, these can be more difficult to bear because the person behaving in this way won't take responsibility either for their part in the situation that caused the upset – or their part in prolonging it.

Bella's mother was a 'sulker', and when Bella had conflict with her mother Bella's father would invariably ask Bella to apologise, no matter who had been in the wrong, because only an apology would appease her mother. It was not until she was a mature woman that Bella felt able to refuse to do this and to confront her mother about a pattern of blaming and belittlement that she found false and humiliating.

In her relationship with her mother, Bella has been able to achieve relatively little change. Her mother seems fairly stuck and her father is always anxious to placate her, hoping that she will relent and move on to bring him the peace he badly wants.

Within her own intimate relationship, however, Bella has recovered much more ground.

'It has worked! I *never* have to say anything like that any more. And all praise to the darling man who listened, ingested, noted and improved. He thinks I'm a chaotic nutter but he does admire my emotional honesty, so he's picked that up from me while I have learned other things from him. I would add, though, that I know now never to seek love or reassurance when he is "chilly". It's just not on.'

The passive aggressor uses their body language – a tight face, a melancholy air or literally 'the cold shoulder' – to tell someone that they are wrong or have done something wrong. But the passive aggressor generally doesn't say what, precisely, that wrongdoing is.

They are shoring up their own sense of injury while accusing the other person of an unnamed crime – without giving them a chance to clear the air.

From their perspective, they are fending off yet another insult or terminal disappointment. To name this may feel difficult or impossible, not least because they have fallen into one of the worst traps of magical thinking: 'If this person really loved me/cared about me, they would know what's wrong and *I wouldn't have to mention it.*'

This kind of thinking is painful – and foolish. All it can do is add self-injury to an already heightened sense of woundedness. Moreover, in failing to state what's wrong or finding the courage to speak up, the person increases their sense of helplessness, perhaps without realising that it is their helplessness above all that is already driving and fuelling their passive aggression.

Thirty-year-old Jason describes this dynamic in his relationship with his 22-year-old girlfriend, Tessa. They have been together for a little over a year. The chances of the relationship surviving do not look good. Jason says, 'If I'm on the receiving end and am being driven crazy by Tessa's silence and withdrawn, glowering behaviour, it's difficult not to dislike her and feel enraged by her as well as by what's she doing. I find it really hard to keep those two things separate. And I find it impossible not to take it personally.'

What does Jason do when Tessa appears to be stuck in her own dark feelings? 'I've tried everything,' he says. 'I try to talk her out of it. I try to coax her. If that doesn't succeed, then I avoid her until things seem a bit better. I have to say to you, though, my patience is wearing thin.'

The sad thing is, Tessa probably does feel powerless. She may even feel inferior. The most common unconscious defence against this is to make someone else 'bad'. However, as her punishing behaviour threatens to drive Jason away, and as Tessa is juggling her feelings of contempt for Jason with her equally powerful desire for a good relationship, this defence offers Tessa little comfort or salvation.

Making it difficult for someone else to love you is one of the saddest chapters in the passive aggression story. We all share a longing to be loved, accepted, cherished and cared for. The passive aggressive person is no different in this. What is different, though, is that often they will powerfully push away the love that is on offer, as Tessa seemed to be doing. They may do this by belittling the person trying to love them. Or perhaps by constantly challenging them ('You don't really love me . . . '), setting tests for them that no human being could pass, or becoming so demanding that their partner legitimately feels exploited or even abused.

They may also push love away by talking about their partner, friend or lover in a disrespectful way, diminishing that person in their own eyes and in the view of others. Or, perhaps less consciously, they may through their behaviour act out their inability to feel lovable: disrupting intimate times; running several relationships simultaneously; letting someone down constantly; breaking promises; behaving in highly critical, sullen or self-absorbed ways that push the other person away even when that person's intentions are, like Jason's, genuinely well intentioned.

Someone who has difficulties accepting love frequently feels hollow, bitter, empty; perhaps shamed by past events; and, driving that, unlovable. There is real agony in not finding it possible to accept good feelings, hold onto them, trust them, internalise them, make them your own, especially when that may be what you want most in all the world.

Once again, becoming even tentatively aware of a pattern of responses can be exceptionally helpful here. It moves the person away from thinking someone else is at fault or that all situations are disappointing, to realising: 'I am playing a part in these difficulties. I can also play a part in improving an unsatisfactory situation.'

Perhaps over a period of some years, for example, the person may become more consciously aware that it's not only in love affairs that they are undermined or even tormented by feelings of self-doubt, disbelief or resistance to what others can offer. Perhaps at work too or in their studies or leisure activities, or simply making a meal or setting a table beautifully, they can perceive how difficult it is to accept other people's appreciation, concern and affection; how easy it is to rush past that to diminish or disown a compliment or kindness, and in doing that refusing for themselves any meaningful experience of satisfaction.

CLAIM YOUR POWER TO MOVE ON

Passive aggressive impulses severely restrict the ease and flow of rewarding relationships. They stunt the glorious freedom we have to express love for others; to heal rather than to judge; to connect rather than to divide – and to accept and enjoy what others can give us.

Because passive aggressors generally see themselves as the victim, as hurt, diminished and hard done by, their emotional story is often a stuck one. If it moves at all it does so at a deadly pace. There are people who can keep their shoulders cold or keep up their embittered, self-pitying behaviours for weeks, months, even decades. It is a way of wielding power, of breaking other people, of wrecking all kinds of relationships between lovers, family members, neighbours, workmates. The essential tragedy of it is that love remains, from this perspective, always highly conditional: something that must be 'won' rather than given – and received.

Patterns of response always do emerge from this constricted view. Yet sadly the passive aggressor may, like Tessa, turn away from these clues, deny them, look outside themselves for someone to blame; take no conscious responsibility for what's happening, even while noting the most subtle shifts of reaction in other people.

The 'stuckness' or unconscious lack of self-responsibility is also neatly caught in Rodney's story. He's a late-twenties, open-faced, delightful man who spent two and a half years in a company with only two employees (he was one of them) and a famous boss. Rodney actually shared an office space with the other employee but was never able to breach her defences or her determination to freeze him out.

Rodney says, 'I really tried very hard at being *extremely* generous with my colleague. I went into my job fully prepared to be close colleagues and to give her as much support as she needed. And I needed her support too. It just didn't work. She decided before I ever stepped in the door of that office that she was not going to cooperate with me. She only wanted to work with Nicholas [their employer]. She stuck firmly to her resolve. She resented me in an extreme way and showed it! In more than two years we never went out for a cup of coffee together, let alone lunch! Very sad in an office of three.

'I felt powerless to turn the situation around. And it became too tarnished. I thought that once I left the job, I would never encounter her again. We are very different personalities and in spite of a lot of effort on my part, and I believe I can say honestly none on hers, we never found any common ground.'

Did Rodney learn anything of value from this difficult and really rather sad situation? 'Yes. I thought about it a lot. Now I am much more able to let things ride than I used to be. I don't have to make them all right. I couldn't with that colleague! Sometimes you just have to back off from situations. I tended to want to make things better. Tie up loose ends. This is not always possible. It was a hard lesson to learn.'

POWERFUL PEOPLE *CAN* MAKE MISTAKES

People who are convinced that they never make mistakes, or whose inferiority complex is so strong that they cannot dare ever to see themselves as being in the wrong, are truly in the most dreadful bind. For them even quite small affronts stick and fester. And as their self-disgust deepens, it emerges as disgust and disillusionment with others.

This is a truly pitiful way to feel. It is also dangerous. Passive aggressive people put themselves in real danger because their lack of reality will be felt keenly by others suffering along with them, who cannot read their minds and may not know precisely where their own errors lie.

Passive aggressive people believe others should know why they are suffering, *even when they won't or can't speak up*. Because these others will generally fail to do so, they become more angry still, and their anger often becomes increasingly global ('You can't help me. No one can help me', 'You hurt me. People always hurt me').

Driving passive aggressive people is often the sensibility of a hurt child who believes others should be able to read their mind or that everyone should see the world the way that they do; the child who believes that their injuries alone matter and who will not or cannot pause to consider how they, in turn, might be injuring others.

Faced with the pain and confusion caused by passive aggression, most people would believe they have three choices: to walk away in search of a more rewarding workplace, as Rodney did; to draw attention loudly and firmly to what the passive aggressor is doing, as Bella did remarkably successfully with her boyfriend; or to treat the person as an invalid or child and cajole them back into a more reasonable frame of mind, as Jason tried to do and as Bella's father has done for decades with his wife, without ever confronting her or requiring her to grow up.

They may also respond with their own aggression, almost invariably establishing a pattern of mutual bitterness and disappointment that leaves all too little room for the demonstration and experience of love.

TRUST YOUR CAPACITY TO CHANGE

The unravelling of unhelpful passive aggressive responses is rarely achieved simply by having new relationships with different people. Or by changing job, country or religion. All those calls to change can be extremely tempting. Yet they keep the idea of a possible solution 'outside' the person, rather than within where it belongs.

What matters most in this situation – and indeed in other blocked or harmful patterns of relating – is the recovery or establishment of a secure foundation of self-love. The presence of self-love, as much as the capacity to express and give love, offers relationships of all kinds their greatest chance of success. But how on earth can this be achieved if the feelings you have about yourself in your worst or darkest moments are curdled, disparaging, full of helplessness and rage or even despair?

It is wonderful to know that countless people do learn to love themselves through being loved consistently or simply treated kindly and respectfully by someone else. This need not be a partner. It could be a true friend, a patient aunt, a mentor or a spiritual teacher. But the people who can be healed in this way are usually able – for a variety of reasons – to accept the love that's on offer and let it soothe them, even if this is not consistently or easily achieved.

Those reasons might include a mixed view of themselves rather than one that is largely negative; or a more balanced temperament; or a gift for insight and an active willingness to make change. It may also be that they have suffered through someone else's aggression, either passive or active, and are highly motivated to create the change that will bring them and others greater harmony and wellbeing.

For those who find change more difficult, or who defensively (and understandably) deny and disown the pain they are causing, self-love may be discovered or rediscovered most effectively through a period of fairly intense psychotherapy. The vulnerability of the person can be looked at safely when trust has been established between the therapist and the client. That trust can also be pushed and tested in a way that will hurt the experienced therapist a great deal less than it might a friend or lover. Gradually different responses can be aired and tried out. Habits of defensiveness can give way to different and more trusting patterns as new possibilities are rehearsed and discussed – and as the feeling of safety within the person becomes more reliable and stronger.

Self-love is also learned through acting lovingly, thoughtfully and respectfully. Sometimes this means acting 'as if' you felt loving already, even if this experience is relatively foreign. Such a straightforward remedy seems almost too simple. Yet a deeply positive *response* from others is always healing. We long to be loved; to be accepted; to do good for others. To recognise, and beyond that to demonstrate, a capacity for kindness takes us home, opens us up to our deepest nature. The relief of arriving there, of recognising that power for good, can be profound. *Perfect comes from Perfect*, the Hindu scriptures, the *Upanishads*, tell us. Love, acceptance, delight: this is what reflects the essential good in all of us – no more in one human being than in any other.

If you recognise that some of your responses are hurtful, undermining or attacking, then it's fiercely empowering to know that the most effective changes will always be made by you. That requires insight, self-awareness and determination. It requires you to think deeply about love and your capacity to make change for the sake of love. Not love for others only; for yourself also. The rewards of making such a change are dramatic and gratifying.

Speaking openly about what drives your defensive reactions and responses releases the other person from their sense of helplessness or guilt and makes a wonderful beginning ('When I am frozen and unresponsive like that, I'm actually trying not to cry or scream'). However, it is not enough to speak up only during those lovely calm times when insight is available. You need also to short-circuit the process *while it's happening* – even if this can only be done between clenched teeth and in shorthand ('Feel vile. Off to walk the dog. See you in the morning').

Just a few words can bring to an end the manipulative, dead-end requirement that someone else should read your mind *before* you can begin to feel better.

Here's a fine example of how to *operate from a frame of mind that deliberately chooses to be open, accepting and loving*, even when old habits of self-pity and feelings of insufficiency tug at your coat-tails.

Thirty-year-old Benedict grew up in what he calls 'the holy tribe of silent martyrs'. His 27-year-old partner, Kurt, grew up in a family where 'Every door was open. Nothing was left unsaid. Most things were said more than once. And real dramas were accompanied with brass bands and trumpet solos.'

When Benedict and Kurt got together, despite their mutual delight and love, their different styles of expression caused them both misery. But, unlike many couples or families who take years to find the help that could support them, these two recognised fast that they would have to respond in new and less provocative ways if their relationship were to thrive.

Kurt was willing to tone down and cut short his florid outbursts. Benedict was equally willing to call a halt to his cold-shouldering, withdrawn and sulky behaviour (not least because he had suffered from it in his family). As an expression of his commitment to a global change in attitude, he drew up the following list of what he could do on a daily basis to train himself to be more 'out there':

Never miss an opportunity to help someone else. Too bad if they've done nothing for me.

Never walk past someone at home or work without acknowledging their existence. Nod. Smile. Kiss.

Never walk past someone else's cup or plate or dirty washing without picking it up. Who cares whose turn it is.

Never brood on injustices. Speak up. Check them out. Or shut up.
Never set tests that the other person doesn't even know they are
failing.
Never, never punish.
Never agree to do something that I'm sure to resent or that
feeds self-pity.

You will see that this list includes *doing things* that support love, as well as *not doing things* that undermine it.

Just weeks later – then once again, a year later – Kurt reported with pride that Benedict had kept to his resolve and found a way of relating that was straightforward and respectful of Kurt. Just as significantly, it was much better for Benedict.

CREATE NO OPPORTUNITIES FOR REGRET

Love is not only a feeling, it is also an energy, the finest, fiercest energy of all.

When we close down to love, or shut down our memory of our own essential loving nature, we experience ourselves quite differently from the way we feel when love flows freely through us. These are not abstract ideas only. Love literally lives in our cells; moves through us with our breath; heals us; wakes us up. In *The Broken Heart: The Medical Consequences of Loneliness* Dr James Lynch writes: 'The mandate to "Love your neighbour as you love yourself" is not just a moral mandate. It's a physiological mandate. Caring is biological. One thing you get from caring for others is you're not lonely. And the more connected you are to life, the healthier you are.'

Aggression can certainly feel exhilarating. But repeated experiences of the loss of control that comes with aggression will disturb you as much in your body as in your mind and emotions. Aggression can be pushy, demanding, intrusive, insistent. It floods the person feeling it and floods the person at the receiving end also. Faces go red; hearts race; breathing is short and intense; focus narrows.

Passive aggression is different, but no healthier. The energy here turns inwards; people hunch in over themselves, hoarding their self-pity, injuries or righteousness.

What's to be done?

Few of us enjoy admitting mistakes or raising difficult issues with our colleagues or loved ones. Few of us want to say aloud what sounds petty even in our own minds. Few of us want to move off the mountain top of our own self-righteousness. Yet there are occasions when this must happen. If life is to move on as it should, we must move first. Forming the intention to respond differently, and then *seeing yourself responding differently*, is crucial. For your own sake. For the sake of someone else. For love's sake. Once the impossible has been said, raised or done, your entire physical being will flee the prison of those constricted feelings. *You will feel like yourself again.* And the world outside yourself will also be experienced quite differently.

Remaining stuck, the aggressive person risks regret. They may grow to regret their own behaviour. More tragically, they may also grow to regret the chances they missed to show the gratitude or devotion that their aggression effectively masked.

Regret is one of the most painful issues that people bring to psychotherapy: the things that weren't said; the forgiveness that was not offered in time; the care or thoughtfulness that was withheld until it was too late. Caught up in their own inner dramas, many people forget the events unfolding outside themselves. They act as if they have all the time in the world to re-establish closeness and love. As though they alone are determining the timetable of events, despite their agonising feelings of insufficiency or self-pity.

Yet in that too they are mistaken.

Polly is not the least bit aggressive. Rather like Kurt, she is inclined to the celebratory sounds of brass bands and trumpet solos. She is generous in her appreciation. She's also absolutely confident that she can and will spend much of her time 'in the creation of happiness' and as little time as possible 'wrecking it'.

Perhaps Polly is lucky. Certainly her partner, adult daughter and her many friends would speak readily of their good fortune in knowing her. But what makes sense here is that she learned a striking lesson about our power to encourage and support others quite early in her adult life and has not forgotten it.

'I always remember my mother, after suffering what in fact was a cerebral haemorrhage, holding her head in hospital and saying how it ached. I told her I thought she was being so brave and the look of gratitude from her eyes was so moving. It was the last time I was able to speak to her before she went into a coma and then died. I was twenty-five. Ever since then I have never held back from reaching out to another and saying, "I think you are being very brave . . . " I gladly give and receive praise and gratitude and do make a point of holding back the criticism.'

Questions of personal power, choice and the will to express love once again rise to the surface. Yet in the face of our own misery or confusion, the desire to change almost anything but our fundamental attitudes seems almost universal. A new job, house, wife, child, country, holiday destination – all of that can appear more enticing than looking at ourselves, reflecting on what drives us and observing dispassionately the life we are creating.

Do we fear that the changes we can make will always be too limited? Or is the problem more challenging than that? Does it seem too devastating to acknowledge the part we are playing in creating our own difficulties?

In the great Indian text the *Mahabharata* appear these lines:
Six kinds of people suffer misery:
those who envy others,
those who hate others,
those who are continually dissatisfied,

those who lean on others' wealth,
those who are suspicious of others,
those who are angry.

Commenting on this verse, Siddha Yoga teacher Swami Chid-vilasananda says, 'In reality, it is anger that produces the other five conditions.' And she adds: 'Basically, anger is a trick you play on yourself and others, to get your own way. Think about it. In your own life . . . when have you gotten angry? Why did you get angry? What did you use the anger for? How did it bear fruit? . . . *No one wants to change his own actions . . . They want the world to change instead* [my italics].'

BEWARE OF DEFENSIVENESS

Bethany and David's relationship tells a familiar, painful story.

Bethany is a community nurse. She is 29 and has been married for less than a year to David, who's a year younger and works in the IT industry. David's lack of self-awareness, coupled with lethally high levels of defensiveness, have led him by the nose into a particularly nasty version of aggression.

If you were to ask David if he is capable of doing wrong he would say that of course he is. Yet when David is told how his behaviour has been hurtful to Bethany, his aggressively defensive response exhibits a serious disbelief that he could make any errors of judgement or have anything in the world to apologise for.

'Dave has to be right,' Bethany says. 'I liked that when I met him. I thought he was decisive. The dark side, though, is getting shoved aside in the wake of it. And being made "wrong" if I try to raise anything that he doesn't want to hear.'

Bethany gave this example. They had planned a weekend at her brother's beach house. It had been in their diaries for weeks. Bethany had made the arrangements, finished work early and bought wine and food to take with them. They had planned to leave home on Friday evening by half past six.

At 7.30 David called to say he was still at his office. He was sorry but he was not going to be able to leave until ten. What's more he'd probably have to go back to the office on Saturday, so they couldn't go away until late Saturday afternoon. If at all.

All of that was said quite kindly. But when he heard the disappointment in Bethany's voice, David's defensiveness pushed him straight into attack mode. Didn't Bethany know how important his work was? How would it look if everyone else stayed back but he didn't? Shouldn't he be able to expect support from her? Here he was, working in a cut-throat industry, and she could do nothing but worry about a couple of days' lazing around her brother's beach house . . .

As Bethany listened she noticed David was sorry for only a few seconds about spoiling their plans. Then suddenly, as soon as he heard disappointment in her voice or what he took to be a reproach, *he* had every reason to be angry.

From the outside it's obvious that David's need to protect himself from being wrong is painfully self-defeating. Faced with the necessity to make last-minute changes, David could with just a dash of insight have taken an entirely different tack. He could have acknowledged Bethany's disappointment and promised her that they would make up for this soon. Then as long as his promise was sincere, the disappointment need not have harmed them. On the contrary, negotiating such a setback together would have pleased them both and shored up their relationship.

Instead, when Bethany did try to speak to David a week later about how she was feeling, David's renewed anger made things much worse. Bethany wanted to explain that she believed David had shown no interest in her feelings and had actually manipulated the situation so that he could then blame her for her own disappointment.

When Bethany tried to say this, however, David again attacked. (Not because he is a terrible or a stupid person – he isn't – but because he wasn't able to see beyond himself or move beyond this habitual self-defensive reaction.) He again belittled Bethany, telling her he couldn't believe that she was still fretting over a couple of nights away and that he was surprised to discover what a trivial person she was.

Bethany withdrew, wounded. And quite significantly angry.

Seeing this scenario written out in black and white, it is impossible not to marvel at how blind human beings can be about their own behaviour. Our jaws drop at stories like these because they are so familiar. And why? In part because in many people a core belief exists that life is a battle and that in most situations, and certainly where there is any conflict, someone has to be right – and someone else must be wrong. In that mind-set being 'right' is associated with having power, with being 'someone'. Being 'wrong' is associated with powerlessness – to be avoided at all cost.

Beliefs like that make the external world dangerous: a place populated by victors and losers. They also make a person's internal world deeply uncomfortable because while this belief remains unchallenged, they will do everything they can to avoid being simultaneously wrong and a self-styled loser.

Projecting one's own sense of wrongness onto someone else is a painfully common defence of a shaky ego. When David made Bethany 'wrong' – accusing her of trying to drag him away from his important work, then 'harping on about it' – he was reacting as though he had been injured. And in his subjective view of things, this was true!

People like David, who seek to protect a fragile view of themselves by making someone else wrong whenever a crisis looms, are ignoring the complexity and fascination of their own human nature. *Being wrong need not be a problem*. It becomes a problem only when it is unconsciously associated with what Adler called an inferiority complex – when someone's self-love is so fragile or conditional that they feel devastated or even unlovable because they are not entirely 'right'.

LOOK FOR THE OTHER PERSON'S POINT OF VIEW

Defensiveness *is* understandable. We all want others to think well of us. We want to be able to think well of ourselves. But thinking well of ourselves – or trusting our emotional responses – becomes likely only when we can see the bigger picture, look at a complex situation from someone else's point of view, accept ambiguity and difference; when we can pause, wait, listen, reflect.

A defensive mind-set often pushes people to score points and keep emotional ledgers, even within their own households. It sees them ruthlessly sacrificing colleagues or friends for the sake of winning what they perceive to be a battle or competition. It can lead to grudges sustained over years; to ending a relationship because a wrong cannot be admitted and forgiveness offered; to hiding a fault or error with increasing fear of 'being found out'. It leads to an atmosphere of mistrust as well as calculation, to talking to former loved ones through the mouths of lawyers, or in extreme cases even to hitting, bashing, maiming or killing, rather than listening, talking, sharing, asking for and offering forgiveness, then healing and moving on.

Blaming others, making them wrong, sliding away from the role you have played in complex events, undermines self-trust as well as your commitment to love and care for other people.

In some instances this pattern of defensiveness extends beyond a personal version of blindness to whole families who foster a rigid refusal to accept the idea that any family member could be in the wrong or have more to learn. This pattern may coexist with a fairly punitive attitude towards wrongdoing within the family; but to outsiders the castle walls are secured and there is no moat.

Rowena came up against this problem when she married Hugh, the youngest of four sons (all lawyers) in a fundamentalist Christian family. Hugh's mother, Gillian, is a competent specialist nurse, an intelligent woman who is nevertheless convinced that Hugh has made a terrible error in marrying someone who does not share the family's faith. Her God is judgemental, harsh and divisive, and, sadly, in her life Gillian mirrors him.

Gillian cannot accept that Hugh practises his Christianity differently from his family and had done so for years before he met Rowena. She ignores those facts because they don't match her inner picture of how things are. Instead she complains bitterly to whoever will listen about Rowena's malign influence and the version of hell it will lead to. She also complains bitterly about rarely seeing Hugh, again apparently without grasping how torn and uneasy he feels in his parents' presence, even if he visits them without Rowena.

The scenario here is of someone who believes rigidly in the rightness of the actions of her own family members. In Gillian's view the family can't be wrong. Years after they have left home, her sons still can't be wrong. Whatever they do, it's right because they are doing it. Any unhappiness or difficulty has to have been caused by outsiders. In this case the culprit is Rowena.

Gillian's attitude to life takes a great deal of emotional energy to maintain. (It is also horribly uncomfortable for Rowena and Hugh.) And it leads inevitably to a high degree of denial and defensiveness.

The truth of our relationships is much richer than the narrow version Gillian is seeing. There are many valid ways to exist and coexist. If our values are based on love, if we believe that love can heal us and express our respect and delight in other people, then this gives us every reason to hesitate before judging others and exempting them or ourselves from the complexity of life.

We become truly part of the world only when we can see how

its contradictions also live in us. This is the absolute foundation for tolerance, inclusiveness, generosity and forgiveness.

In our interactions with each other, *none of us is blameless*. No family or group or nation is blameless. We all cause some unfortunate things to happen. We all need to take responsibility for those experiences. We all need to learn from them. Some events will be beyond our control to influence directly. But even there, hasty condemnation is rarely helpful.

MOVING FROM FEAR TO LOVE

Our trust in life becomes virtually unshakeable when, like Benedict, we can look at our behaviour and create the changes that are needed. For love's sake. Or when, like Polly, we can allow the tragedy of loss and grief to draw our attention back to what's sustaining and healing. Our path is to heal, *A Course in Miracles* teaches: *to create the circumstances where healing can begin.*

But, I would add, not at the expense of ourselves.

In the face of aggression many of us will fall into behaviours that are timid, anxious or placatory. Wanting to 'make things right' we may even make ourselves 'wrong'. I hear echoes of this when Bethany tells me, 'Even when I'm not wrong, and actually no one's wrong, I can feel disturbed. I can take the situation far too personally. I rush around trying to make everything right. That's not really about taking responsibility either because, unless I catch myself, I can quickly spin right down into a kind of global self-blame. Of course that makes me feel hopeless, and then depressed. In some ways what I'm doing to myself is almost as uncomfortable and self-defeating as David's outrageous manoeuvrings that blame me for my own disappointment!'

Bethany's experience suggests that for her a lack of harmony is barely tolerable. Her reaction is totally different from David's or Gillian's, yet curiously they are all acting out of fear. Again 'rightness' and 'wrongness' seem over-emphasised. *Think of life as a series of imperfect facts.*

Bethany needs the courage to find and assert her own point of view. And to create boundaries in her mind between the events she can influence and those she can't. She also needs to find a way to look at a difficult situation as a shared responsibility and not as her problem only. *And so do those of us who are like her.*

And David? He could discover through experience and observation how 'being wrong' and owning up to the reality of things is far less dangerous and upsetting than making other people wrong. He could also discover what 'being wrong' means to him. What is he telling himself? What story gets acted out when the 'wrong' button gets pressed? Doing that he may never entirely lose that painful sense of life as a series of battles, but at least he'll be able to recognise his patterns and switch tactics fast when that's called for. *And so could those of us who are like him.*

That extra note of insight, self-control and self-assurance would give David his best chance in his relationship with Bethany. Just as crucially, it would also give him advantages in the world of work.

People who are afraid of personal failure or of being seen to be wrong are severely limited. Successful people have high standards, but also know that *they can afford to take risks.* Being wrong is unpleasant and undesirable for them, but it is not terrifying. They know that they can recognise and learn from their mistakes, keep them in proportion and move on. They can also be much more relaxed and open with colleagues, seeing them as people whom they can cooperate with and learn from and enjoy, rather than solely (and fearfully) as judges or competitors.

In relieving tension and finding our way back to a sense of rewarding connection with other people, there may be no greater asset available to us than a sense of humour.

Michael is a teacher in his early thirties. He loves teaching and devotes himself to it. Michael is also quite flamboyantly gay and gorgeous looking and regards his sexuality as God-given, like any of his other gifts.

At the end of a recent school day, as his 8-year-old pupils milled around him and parents gathered to take them home, one disgruntled young girl turned to him suddenly and said, in a voice that could carry for twenty blocks, 'You are a fat old poofter, Mr Blank!'

Michael could have met her remark with anger, a sense of affront, or outrage. Instead, with a totally enviable sense of self-possession, he put his hands on his hips, looked her in the eye and said, 'How can you say that? I have worked so hard to lose 5 kilos – and you call me fat!'

There are few journeys more worthwhile taking than the one that moves us beyond the grip and limitations of aggression. Our relationships need that. Our planet and societies desperately need it. And for our own peace of mind, each one of us needs it also.

Routinely expressing anger and aggression cannot free us. It is a tragic illusion to believe that through our acts of aggression towards others or ourselves we rid ourselves of psychological injury. Healing lies in another direction altogether.

When you can turn your attention away from hurt or outrage and discover what a difficult situation can teach you, or how you can help someone else get through it, aggression loosens its hold.

When you experience the power of choice that even the briefest moment of restraint gives you, aggression loosens its hold.

When you perceive how inevitably self-respect and self-esteem follow your positive demonstrations of care for others, aggression loosens its hold.

When you dare to state clearly what you need or want, without demanding that your needs are met, aggression loosens its hold.

When you can raise your energy through what delights, exhilarates and pleases you, aggression loosens its hold.

Change speeds up too when a sense of mortality is added. Our time on this earth is fleeting. *Is this the way you want to spend it?*

Fear drives most acts of aggression. But fear is not a static state. The Indian Jesuit Anthony de Mello tells this story:

The student asks the Master, 'What is love?'

'The total absence of fear,' the Master replies.

'What is it we fear?' the student asks.

'Love,' says the Master.

HOW TO

Transform Aggression

Value the energy of your aggression – but know that you can put it to finer use. The key factor in the transformation of anger and aggression is empathy. Caring about other people's feelings, learning to see things from another person's point of view, acknowledging their integrity, valuing their welfare: all of this supports the transformation of aggressive, self-pitying or angry impulses.

There are many ways to be aggressive. The aggressor often wants to pass on to someone else their own discomfort. But the results may be disastrous. This is never a one-way process only. *What you do to others, you do to yourself also.*

In any relationship where aggression is routinely expressed, or where the threat of aggression hovers, it becomes difficult to work through the conflicts of interest and viewpoint that are part of everyday life. Aggression pushes people to take sides, to strike extreme positions. It cuts short discussion. It narrows people's view of events. It limits choice.

Aggressive habits can be unlearned. True power arises from self-control, restraint, choice about how you respond. All of this can coexist with spontaneity, exuberance and raw delight.

It is possible to help yourself if you are the person who is angry or aggressive.

- Avoid alcohol and drugs. They decrease self-control, increase irritability. If you are often angry, cut them out altogether.
- Take care not to become overtired, hungry or overwrought.

Each markedly affects the way you see the world and reduces your capacity to cope with tension.

- Check your life for stress. Do less of what stresses you; more of what invigorates you. Do this for your physical health as well as psychological balance.

- Check out whether you are depressed or anxious. That can translate into anger or irritability. Medication can help. So can psychotherapy, stress management or meditation – also recognising what's going on and *making the changes needed*.

- Discover whether you believe there is a hierarchy of aggression – and that your outbursts are 'not too bad'. If they hurt another person – physically or emotionally – they are 'too bad'.

- Identify the triggers that 'drive you crazy' or 'make you mad'. Maybe you can't bear to be wrong? Or you feel enraged when you don't know what you're doing? Or when you have to make a decision fast? Or when you feel rejected or laughed at? Or you are too tired and overwhelmed to hear one more demand? *Look for the patterns.* They will give you the best clues about the situations where you need to be vigilant and tender with yourself as well as other people.

- Once you know your patterns of response, you can recognise the signals for your frustration early and *can respond differently*.

- Notice what your body is telling you: heart beating fast; hands sweating; feeling icy. *Take care.*

- Remember that a habitual response can feel inevitable: as though you are being sucked into a vortex and there's nowhere else to go. The better your mental preparation and clarity, the more effectively you can resist that.

- Wherever you are in your cycle of aggression, as soon as consciousness dawns that you are sucked in again, *stop*.

- In a heated or dangerous moment, *remove yourself physically*.

- If you can't leave the situation, *remove yourself mentally and pay attention only to your breathing*. Force yourself to do this. It's extraordinarily effective.

- Know what you routinely tell yourself when things go wrong. Listen to your inner monologue. Often that affects you more than the event itself.

- In the heat of the moment, *talk yourself down* ('This is the kind of situation that throws me. I can get through this' or 'I am overreacting because I'm behind at work' or 'She probably snapped at me because she's exhausted').

- Know it's possible to be 'insulted', yet see this much less personally ('That delivery guy's always rude').

- Create supportive inner messages ('Life is a series of imperfect facts', 'I can meet this stuff-up with a sense of humour', 'This is a nuisance – not a tragedy').

- Be open about your vulnerabilities. That builds courage and honesty as well as awareness. It's also much fairer to the people around you.

- Do not rehearse injustices. Look for closure. Move on.

- Don't blame. It weakens you.

- Look for the bigger picture. Talk to yourself about that ('I love this person', 'I can let this go', 'I need something to eat and some rest before we get into this').

- If the issue still matters when your rage has gone, *then deal with it.*

- Notice if you are bringing the frustrations from one situation (work?) and dumping them in another (home?). Recognise the unfairness of that. Take a few minutes at the end of one situation imaginatively to draw the day to a close. *Envisage yourself* literally shutting the door on the day's issues; putting unfinished work into a drawer; leaving behind the pressures as you look forward to a time of reconnection and intimacy with friends, family or your own self.

- When discussing a difficult issue, speak in the first person and 'own' your opinions ('When things go wrong I feel . . . ', not 'You make me . . . ').

- Know that love gives you no 'rights' to control or dominate other people. Think about this deeply. Review the possibility of unconscious assumptions or prejudices that tell you, 'It's really all right to . . . '

- Practise empathy. Remind yourself what you know about the person, or look at the world through their eyes ('She's also tired', 'That old bastard of a boss must be desperate to be so insistent', 'My brother's always been afraid of new situations').

- *Acknowledge the other person's feelings* rather than overriding them or berating them ('Having so many people waiting in line must be stressful', 'Being without a job can feel terrifying', 'It *is* difficult to go against the tide of what other kids are doing', 'I understand you need to call me, but I also need time to work uninterrupted'). Acknowledging is a neutral activity. It doesn't 'approve' but doesn't humiliate or belittle either.

- Consider whether your expectations are reasonable.

- Know that when something major is troubling you, you will be thrown by smaller issues. *Talk openly about the big issue –* even if it's unresolved. Let people know what's going on. Work your way towards solutions, insight or acceptance.

- If competitiveness drives you, practise gratitude both for what you have and for what you have achieved. This makes you feel far less assaulted and vulnerable.

- Know what your prejudices are. It's easy but no more acceptable to be especially aggressive to or about people you either envy or despise.

- Discover if someone who teases, belittles or provokes you *needs your violent response*. Be aware that you don't need to satisfy this.

- If you believe someone is inciting your anger or 'driving you to it', talk to that person about the dynamic, seek help together or end the relationship.

- Value problem solving. Increase your skills (ask, 'How can we improve this?', not 'Who's to blame here?').

- Learn the skills of conflict resolution from books or courses. It's an invaluable skill for work and home.

- Censor what you expose yourself to. Avoid violent movies, books, computer games. Choose what's inspiring.

- Increase your physical activities. Lift your energy levels to the roof – but pleasurably.

- Know what relaxes your mind fully: meditation, a game of chess or squash, ten minutes in the bath listening to music. Do what delights you.

- Read Carol Tavris's excellent book *Anger: The Misunderstood Emotion*. It is insightful, intelligent, supportive.

Transform Passive Aggression

Passive aggression is also a demand to get your own way or a negative reaction against not getting your own way. Because it's less overt, it may be easier to deny that you are being angry, punishing or manipulative. But those denials only prolong a response that keeps you feeling powerless, yet powerfully harms other people.

Passive aggression includes controlling other people with your bad moods, sulking, injuring with silence, refusing to say what's wrong, freezing someone out, sarcasm, put-downs; expecting other people to read your mind and punishing them when they can't; spoiling other people's pleasures; becoming ill or weeping when anything is demanded of you; talking to or about other people disrespectfully.

You may see yourself as a victim. Yet passive aggressive behaviours are extremely controlling. The 'stronger' person in the relationship may be surprised to see how frequently the 'weaker' person gets their own way. Empathy is vital here too. It creates the way out to behaviour that is self-respectful – and open and loving to others.

It is possible to help yourself if you are the person who sulks, blames, punishes with silence or frequently feels injured.

- Recognise the ways in which you are affected by other people's behaviour. Now use that knowledge to *see the effect of your negative responses on other people.*
- Notice how hurt, bewildered, placatory, anxious or angry

other people feel in response to your passive aggressive behaviours. When you are feeling good, talk to the people around you about how they feel at these times. Take what they tell you seriously. *Ask them what would help.*

- Put into practice what other people tell you would be helpful. Then talk about the results with them. Keep communicating.

- Face the reality that passive aggression wrecks relationships, spoils people's lives, promotes depression and helplessness – *and can be unlearned.*

- Wherever you are in the cycle of aggression, as soon as you recognise what you are doing, *stop.*

- Develop self-love. *Do this by acting lovingly, thoughtfully and respectfully towards other people as well as yourself.* Do it 'as if' you felt loving already, even if this experience is relatively foreign.

- Treasure the positive response you get from others.

- Take responsibility for the emotional atmosphere in your home or workplace. *See yourself as influential.* Do what encourages others. This will increase your sense of power, decrease your sense of injury.

- Discover what you tell yourself when you are feeling injured. Write it down. Recognise how *you influence yourself* through what you think.

- Dispute undermining thoughts ('No one's ever done anything for me. Well, actually, only yesterday . . . ', 'My parents loved the boys more than me. And drove them crazy interfering in their lives').

- Forgive other people for their shortcomings. *Life is a series of imperfect facts.* Move on by focusing on what has been done for you and what you are capable of doing for other people.

- Never blame others for your misery. It keeps you powerless. Move on.

- Discard the myth that other people can read your mind. They can't.

- Free others from helplessness or guilt. Tell them what's going on ('When I'm frozen like that I'm actually trying not to cry or scream', 'When I lash out sarcastically I am usually feeling quite desperate myself').
- Don't use those reasons as excuses. Deal with the issues that make you want to scream. Find out what increases your wellbeing – and not only what makes you feel desperate.
- Short-circuit the process *while it's happening* ('Off to walk the dog. See you in an hour').
- Let your body support you. When your mood is plummeting, your body will also sag. *Move.* It's hard to feel helpless when you are breathing deeply, walking fast, talking honestly.
- Practise speaking openly about your *positive* feelings. This may seem awkward at first. Keep going. Write in your diary only about what is possible, enjoyable, positive. You can already 'do misery' well; now's the time to discover pleasure, power, delight, enthusiasm, encouragement, optimism.
- See complex situations from someone else's point of view ('Tell me what's going on for you when . . . ', 'What would help you most right now?').
- Cultivate interests that are stimulating and challenging. Talk about them. Give your mind plenty of nourishment.
- Avoid people who are stuck in a poor-me mentality. Ask them, 'How could you help yourself to move on?'
- Develop a sense of humour. Learn clowning, drumming, singing, dance. Let your inner stand-up comic come to life. Get 'out there'.
- Find the courage to love your life, including its imperfections.

Deal or Live with an Angry or Aggressive Person

- If you are afraid of the person or for them, *seek professional help immediately*. No one should live in fear.
- Be frank about the effects this behaviour is having on you. Avoid making accusations. Talk about *your* experience, *your* feelings.
- Respect your own wellbeing. Care for your own welfare. If you feel confused about your right to a more peaceful life, discuss that with a professional.
- Ask the person for their cooperation in creating change. Look for solutions. Talk about possibilities ('Do we both need to find more free time?', 'Could we make courtesy an open value in this relationship/organisation/company?').
- Ask the person what would help them. Perhaps they see the situation differently from you. The more you understand each other's point of view the more effectively you can work together through problems.
- Think about the patterns of the person's anger or aggression. Is it over in ten minutes? Staying out of the way may be enough. Or listening as they explode and ventilate their way out of a bad mood may be helpful. Does it last for hours and exhaust everyone? *Changes must be made.*
- Set limits ('When you start yelling, I am not going to hang around and listen. I'll listen when you've calmed down' or 'I can stand your injured silence for an hour but no longer').
- Does the person have a problem with drugs or alcohol?

Taboos can be strong. Confront those taboos. Seek professional help from a drug and alcohol counselling service if needed (for your support).

- Does the person feel misunderstood, unloved, depressed, fearful? Find ways to help them air those feelings without blaming. A simple invitation to talk may be enough. If that's too confronting, seek help.

- Be vigilant that you are not provocative (by teasing, undermining, mocking, sarcasm, belittling). If someone has a short fuse, help them through their difficulties with that. *Never* use it as a means to undermine them.

- *Value and respect other people's experiences* (say, 'That must be hard', not 'I can't see why that's a problem'; or 'How can I help?', not 'You ought to be able to manage'). Many people routinely deny other people their reality without even noticing what they are doing. *It is upsetting and can be enraging.* (I tell you I feel unwell. You tell me I look perfectly fine. I tell you I am worried about my job. You tell me there is nothing to worry about. I tell you I feel unloved. You say, 'What do you expect me to do about it?') Break that habit by pausing, allowing yourself to take in what the person has said and *to move with that*, rather than deflecting it ('Have you felt sick for long?', 'What worries you most?', 'If you feel unloved we must look at how we're spending our time together'). Simple acknowledgement of that person's reality eases tension immediately.

- Create an atmosphere where people feel accepted; where feelings can be talked about openly; where different viewpoints and experiences are respected; where common values are honoured; where love is openly expressed.

Fight Clean and Recover Fast

- Be clear that whatever you are fighting about is worth the heat.
- Never fight when you are tired, ill, drunk or hungry.
- When someone challenges you, *agree with what's true or acceptable*. When you hear 'You didn't get the cat food', instead of getting into a defensive or attacking mode say, 'I'm sorry. I'll buy some in the morning.' Do not confuse your honour with the absence of cat food.
- Avoid whining ('You always . . . ', 'I never . . . ').
- Use language collaboratively ('Let's look at this together').
- Do not raise inflammatory matters while your own blood is boiling. That may seem the most appropriate or inevitable time to fight; it's also the worst.
- If you are very angry, take a shower, put headphones on and play loud music, go running, dig the garden. Move your way through it and out of it.
- State your position clearly and succinctly. Don't lecture.
- Do not re-run old grievances.
- Do not review old injuries.
- Do not assume that only one person can be right. Aim for win–win.
- Monitor your internal monologue constantly. *You will be urged on by what you are telling yourself at least as much by the other person.*
- Agreeing to disagree does not undermine intimacy. On the contrary, it confirms the reality: intimacy does not depend on sameness.

- Avoid self-pity. It weakens you and infuriates the other person.
- *Never* attack someone personally. When you hear an ugly remark come out of your mouth ('Who'd want to have sex with you, anyway?'), *apologise.*
- Don't tell yourself you didn't know what you were saying. It won't be true.
- If the other person cries, wait patiently or walk away. Don't shout or blame.
- If you are the 'cryer', think about what's not getting said. Be more direct.
- Know the character of the person you are fighting with. Hostile people often have low self-esteem. You can make them crazy with a few remarks. Is it worth it? Someone who's generally calm may be legitimately angry: *pay attention.*
- Keep to the topic. When accusations become global, end the argument. Make a time to talk about more general concerns or dissatisfactions.
- Check how frequently you fight. In calm moments, talk about the function fighting serves. Is there a more harmonious way to get those same needs met?
- Be aware of gender styles. Men may (in general) find that aggression releases their tension. Women may (in general) find friendliness releases theirs. Explore how the world looks from the other person's perspective.
- Be prepared to give up scoring a point for the sake of love.
- *Never* go to bed or leave the house without making peace.

Relate as an

Adult

Friend, it's time to make an effort,

So you become a grown human being,

And go out picking jewels

Of feeling for others.

ANSARI

*I*t's a tough business, growing up. We long for it in childhood, imagining that when it's our turn to be an adult
we'll have the power to choose exactly the kind of life we
want to live. Then, when we do become adults, we discover
that our power to choose unfolds slowly. What's more, with
adulthood comes responsibility for who we are and what we
do. Taking that seriously may be unwelcome.

It's true that assuming responsibility for ourselves offers us
exquisite freedoms. But it also takes away some treasured illusions:
that we are the person who matters most in the whole wide
world, and that only when our own desires are satisfied should we
begin to look after someone other than ourselves.

Our biological programming tends us towards a high degree of
selfishness. Some people never grow out of this. If we are to go
beyond it – and there are good social as well as personal reasons
why we should – then we will learn to do so through our interactions with other people.

It may not be all that noble to learn how to be self-sacrificing
on behalf of people you love and whose love you want in return.
Nobility (or plain kindness) may really click in only when you can
treat everyone equally well, regardless of your need for them or of
their proximity to you.

Expanding that theory (rather tentatively actually) to an American physician, I was a little surprised when she jumped down my

throat. It simply isn't possible, she asserted, for human beings to regard everyone with the same level of concern. She brought lots of biology into her arguments, and some heated theories about the human compulsion to defend one's own family, tribe, race, and so on.

Perhaps the truth encompasses both our points of view.

Many inspirational figures have shown us that it *is* possible to reach a point of equanimity and compassion where notions of separateness fall right away: when the suffering of any person affects you deeply and you could no more turn away from a stranger or rip the reputation of a former friend to shreds than you could neglect or disparage a vulnerable member of your own family.

Those are the absolute expressions of universal love. They are the basis of all religious teachings (however poorly they are often lived out). And they transcend religion. In the Gospel of John we hear Christ saying, 'This is my commandment, that you love one another as I have loved you.' And in the *Sutta Nipata* we hear the Buddha say, 'Just as a mother would protect her only child at the risk of her own life, even so, cultivate a boundless heart towards all beings. Let your thoughts of boundless love pervade the whole world.'

For most of us, struggling with issues of self-love and self-acceptance, those words create an invitation to think deeply, to reflect on how vitally love matters to us, and to learn little by little how to put those words into practice. First, perhaps, through learning how to bring to the people we already know increased levels of gratitude and delight. And experiencing those feelings within ourselves. Then, gradually, making *all* our encounters with other people respectful of their integrity, whether or not those people are useful to us; whether or not they will ever know how we are learning to value their lives as much as our own.

COMBINE THE WONDER OF CHILDHOOD
WITH THE WISDOM OF MATURITY

It's a marvellous thing to be a child, especially when you are fortunate enough to grow up in a family that can offer you love,
safety and a sense of how wondrous life is, how magnificent our
universe is, while also owning up to how testing and sometimes
extremely hard living can be.

Some adults do sustain childhood's sense of spontaneity and
delight, which even many children have lost by adolescence. In
fact, the adult who can encompass the gifts of childhood and the
rewards of maturity is the luckiest of all beings.

Those precious gifts of childhood are truly something we could
all benefit from retrieving. But what more often stays with people
into adulthood are not those gifts, but rather the self-absorption,
low frustration levels, incapacity to postpone gratification, inability to enter someone else's reality and take it seriously, and the
restricted capacity to set their interests aside that is acceptable in
childhood, but limiting and disabling in adulthood.

Quite recently I had a leisurely Sunday lunch with a couple of
friends who are senior public servants. We got onto talking about
people behaving cruelly and unfairly in the workplace. With some
glee they told me one anecdote after another about highly paid,
highly educated and supposedly highly intelligent people who
scream down their telephones at staff who are junior to them; who
get up and walk out of meetings, slamming doors; who pollute the
atmosphere of their large open-plan offices with their sour irritability and bad temper; who make arbitrary and ill-considered
decisions – and who then loudly and publicly blame other people
if those decisions prove inept.

As my friends talked, it was impossible not to notice that the
behaviour they were describing is like the worst you'd expect from
an angry adolescent. But adolescents at least have the excuse that

they are in a period of intense transition. They are awash with uncertainty and inexperience as well as hormones. Those elite public servants (and their counterparts in the private sector) have no such excuse. Yet when I asked my friends how these people might explain their own behaviour to themselves, one said, 'They are under such intense pressure. They work inhuman hours. They'd probably see this as a legitimate way to let off steam.'

But is it?

Those anonymous public servants have not, it would seem, learned one of the most vital lessons of emotional intelligence. In the face of their own distress or anxiety, *they do not know how to soothe themselves*. They cannot calm their emotions down in order to assess the situation realistically and make a cool decision about what needs to be done. Responding to their own feelings of frustration rather than to the needs of the moment, they show how distanced they are not only from caring about other people, but even from their own wellbeing.

This is no surprise. People can suffer for years from tension and stress-related diseases without seriously considering how their own regressed emotional responses are harming them, as well as making other people's lives tense and ugly.

Reading a complex situation, assessing what's urgent and knowing how to respond appropriately, are intellectual and psychological processes that are crucial not only to the smooth running of a professional life but also to emotional maturity. It's these interdependent processes that actually develop and deepen feelings of wellbeing and self-control – and the personal power that comes with that.

These same processes are crucial to the development of what used to be called 'character', that vital expression of integrity and maturity that reassures you that you could face most situations with equanimity. And that reassures other people that they can rely on you also for your cool head and warm heart.

It is tempting – and easy – to make slick moral judgements about employers or senior staff who treat more junior staff or their colleagues with contempt. And over that lunch we certainly did so. Yet the problem demands that we go further.

It would seem almost incredible that in the twenty-first century senior management in any large organisation could continue to be unaware of the negative effects of this kind of tyrannical, hysterical behaviour. And could have failed to measure its costs financially and creatively, as well as psychologically and socially. But clearly the culture in many workplaces remains profoundly *un*intelligent.

Through their behaviour, those women and men demonstrate that they really have not grasped the effect of their behaviour on themselves, other people or even their revered 'bottom line'. For all their worshipping of power, they appear not to have grasped that the most authentic power that maturity offers is the power to choose to behave well – in ways that are reasonable, respectful, self-respecting and, ironically, far more productive.

There are many reasons why they may not be doing this.

Their capacity for self-awareness may be limited, however sophisticated, privileged or well educated they are. People may rank far lower in their value system than 'ideas'. And certainly their behaviour suggests that. More crucially, however, in a world where emotions are not understood, valued or respected – where 'reason' is king – it's no surprise that *emotional* outbursts drive the atmosphere. And drive out reason. That particular contradiction may be one of life's finer ironies. What you despise, and particularly what you disown, has a strange way of insistently making itself known to you.

Those outward behaviours can be seen as some kind of measure of what's happening 'on the inside'. People who feel good about themselves and who want to be in control of their own lives, or at least their own responses, do not behave cruelly towards other people. They may have a temper tantrum. They may certainly be rude, offhand or inconsiderate. But they would not be so routinely, nor without *recognising what's going on*, and offering to make amends.

It is possible, therefore, to predict that the perpetrators of this office mischief are likely themselves to feel hollow and unauthentic, inwardly depleted; that they are 'running on empty', living a life they do not fully 'own' – spitting out contempt for that life through their behaviour towards others, even while they strive for more power and control within it. Where there is no inner balance, there can't be much outer balance either. The two are absolutely united. (Try holding a yoga balance posture if your mind is agitated!)

To seek to understand where these outbursts come from is not to excuse the attitudes that drive them, nor to feel any less concern for those who work in emotionally polluted workplaces. It is only to wonder how *everyone* – including vile employers and bad-tempered public servants – could become more emotionally aware, more tuned in and awake to the reality of other people's lives and wellbeing. And much more understanding of how *their own wellbeing depends on the way they behave.*

In this situation, as in all others, a 'story' is being expressed through specific behaviours. It's worth asking: how could this story be a little different?

A life built on love – and self-respect – demands that you remain constantly aware of the impact of your responses on other people. In your workplace as much as in your home self-awareness can develop only when you do everything possible to avoid causing others hurt or embarrassment. This is especially vital when those people have less status or overt power than you do – or have no matching opportunity to complain about your behaviour.

And if you do recognise that you have hurt someone or accused them unfairly? The process is easy: correct the situation, apologise, make amends, move on.

To lay any claim to maturity we need to understand how our behaviour affects other people. And we need to perceive how it affects us also.

Sometimes we will behave badly almost without knowing what we are doing. Sometimes we will have planned what we are doing down to the last detail. Either way, we help no one when we don't look hard at the *effects* of our behaviour. And that's not all. Where we see we have done wrong, we need to get some insight into why we have behaved that way *and* do something active with our feelings of shame and guilt.

We should feel shame when we have done wrong. Shame, though, is not enough. We need to use the discomfort that shame causes us to move to a higher level of self-responsibility. We need to see our shadow or disowned side more clearly. We need to know more truthfully what we are capable of. And, where it's called for, to make amends as best we can.

Small daily expressions of consideration not only express who we are, they create who we are becoming. From Shantideva's classic eighth-century Buddhist text *The Way of the Bodhisattva*, these exquisite lines encourage us:

All the joy the world contains
Has come through wishing happiness for others.
All the misery the world contains
Has come through thinking only of oneself.

KNOW YOUR PLACE IN THE UNIVERSE

We come to adulthood willingly and also reluctantly. We certainly come to adulthood unevenly. Some aspects of who we are take much longer to mature than others. Some vital bits may never reach maturity at all. However young or old we may feel, living an adult's life does not begin to get real when we have a licence to drive a car, have our first serious sexual relationship or find our first job. Those markers may give us the status of adulthood, but psychological maturity begins when we truly comprehend that we are only one person among many: no less important than others, certainly, but no more important either.

This knowledge needn't crush us. On the contrary, this is what sets us free from the limiting delusion that the sun rises and sets for our sake only, or that the world begins and ends with our concerns. It lays the ground too for our moral concerns – our conscious wish to avoid harm and to do good – without which we can also make no claim whatsoever to adulthood.

There are many ways to get a realistic sense of proportion about where our life fits alongside the lives of others. Watching constantly to see how we affect other people is the central way: empathy, intimacy, curiosity and delight flow from that.

And what about our place in the universe? I was inspired to learn that every evening in the later part of his life, the wise (and supremely good-humoured) founder of psychosynthesis, Roberto Assagioli, would meditate on the vastness of our universe and his own tiny place within this vastness. This did not make him feel insignificant. In fact the opposite was true. It made him feel part of something that was and remains magnificent, mysterious, wondrous and eternal. During that evening hour Assagioli found that many of the difficulties of the day would shrink in importance or simply slip away.

That sense of proportion, and the discernment that comes with it, is one of the finest gifts of adulthood. If Tommy takes my red truck when I am 2, I will open my mouth wide and I will scream. If Thomas bumps into my red truck with his blue Mercedes when I am 22 or 52, it is certainly a nuisance and could be a real financial setback. *It is not, however, a tragedy.* I will probably fume. I have no right to scream.

Assagioli's meditation practice helps to keep an invaluable sense of proportion and connection between your life and all of life, but there are other ways.

I am incurably a city person. I love living in the heart of Sydney, a sprawling city that is tremendously varied in its subcultures and styles of living. Yet I notice too how easy it is in a city to become lost in one's own concerns: to mistake them for the universe while forgetting the healing that the true universe offers. Whenever I can be dragged or persuaded to take some time in the bush or by the ocean, and when I can really *be there* in my mind as well as my body, I am cured of some of my worries almost magically.

We human beings lose something essential in our own natures when we lose touch with earth, sky, sand, water, trees, leaves, grass. I am not suggesting that everyone who lives in the country or by an ocean leads an idyllic life, because that's not so. It is possible to live in a place of great physical beauty and not ever actually register how the earth or sand or damp grass feels beneath your feet, or how brilliantly the stars shine on cloudless nights, and allow yourself to be soothed by that.

This inner 'clearing of space' has a function that goes beyond whether you or I personally feel better or can practise what it takes to lower our blood pressure. While our minds are crowded with our own concerns, it is impossible for us to think clearly about other people. And perhaps quite impossible for us to think communally. Still, that is what adulthood asks of us. Or that's what life asks of us if we want to make any serious claim to finally being grown up.

THE VISTA OF ADULTHOOD IS UNLIMITED

Is it so hard to leave childhood behind? It was, without doubt, the most extraordinary adventure. You moved in not much more than a dozen years from the limitations of lying on the ground cooing and dribbling, to crawling, standing, finding a voice, and then to the vast freedoms of standing, striding, declaiming, reflecting, choosing. But adulthood too offers each day as a new possibility and each year and decade as experiences through which you have never gone before. There is still time for freshness. The trick is to have that freshness while also holding onto a conscious sense of where you've come from and where you want to be going.

As you take your place in the wider community and look out to a world beyond your immediate concerns, the vista of adulthood becomes unlimited. This insight, however, comes alive only when you can take a sustained interest in other people's lives; when you can be self-sacrificing, yet not a martyr; when you can evaluate situations not to see what you can get out of them, but to find out what you can do or bring or give.

The young woman who is barely out of childhood herself, but can get up uncomplainingly, night after night, for the sake of her baby, is experiencing something precious: that her capacity for love extends way beyond herself. Recognising that she can do this, *her sense of herself changes*. The infant gives her a new sense of herself, just as much as she gives the baby his sense of comfort, emotional nourishment and that vital experience that *someone is there*.

Perhaps this is only a start on the road to adulthood. After all, many people are able to be fiercely protective of their own family while remaining apparently indifferent to the fate of others. What's called for here may be a conscious stirring of memory about how much it matters to be cared for. And then the leap of imagination and empathy: *This is how it is for others also.*

Sophie is a devoted mother. She speaks with particular gratitude about what she has been given by her little daughter, Rafaella. Sophie is not such a young mother – although she is no less vulnerable for that. She was in her late thirties when Rafaella was born three years ago, and she is raising her daughter under difficult circumstances, with relatively little money and only occasional support from Rafaella's father, who left to live in another city soon after their daughter was born. Despite those considerable disappointments and struggles, Sophie can say, 'I experience the most wonderful warmth, joy, light and happiness that well up in me when I'm with or thinking about my daughter. The experience is so pure and spiritual, overwhelming at times, that I want to laugh and cry all at once. Before she came into my life I only experienced moments of this rare quality. Now I have been and am lucky enough to have this constantly in my daily life. I guess I could call this unconditional love because it's the closest I've come to experiencing that phenomenon. It's the most wonderful thing to be able to look into the eyes of another human being and feel humbled and so grateful to have such "richness". All other more material, physical expressions such as flowers, hugs, being listened to and heard, gifts, et cetera, seem often to have something else attached to the offering. They are not so simple, pure and wonder filled, although of course they are much appreciated and important too.'

Rafaella is fortunate that Sophie's difficult circumstances increased her sense of joy in her daughter and didn't shake it. Whatever else has happened, Sophie is able to be present emotionally in the way Rafaella most needs it.

For any infant it's the essential experience of moving away through sleep or inattention, then waking up or looking around and *discovering that mother or their close caretaker is still there*, that allows them to feel safe. And it's through continually experiencing those precious moments of reconnection and relief from tension that the young child learns that they 'belong'.

WHY ABANDONMENT IS DEVASTATING

The need to belong is one of the most fundamental yearnings we human beings share. To know that we matter to others, and that we in turn can offer love and support freely, creates the foundation of human existence. Our capacity to live civilly and cooperatively depends on it.

So powerful is this yearning that, in the face of an experience of not belonging or of not feeling safe, even the most mature adult is likely to regress: to feel once again as a child might who has not yet developed trust in their powers of resilience. This will be especially true in situations that echo the child's agony in the face of abandonment. A young child cannot survive abandonment. Their instincts warn them that they must be rescued fast. And the child in the adult can feel just like that.

It's common, for example, for someone who has been abruptly sacked from work or has been forced from their home through poverty, social disruption or war, or who has a long or disabling illness or who is in grief, to feel almost literally that 'the ground has gone from beneath my feet'. They may feel they can no longer easily recognise themselves; that all their familiar reference points both inward and outward have deserted them.

Experiencing such profound loss, many people feel ashamed. An experience of helplessness may challenge our underground longings for immortality, foresight, omniscience ('If only I had known . . . ', 'I didn't see it coming . . . ', 'It just doesn't seem possible . . .'). Faced with circumstances way beyond our personal control, many of us berate ourselves for the absence of qualities that we never had.

Something simpler also deeply affects us.

In adulthood, just as in childhood, we need rhythms and routines to hold our lives in place. We may chafe against them, but they provide the essential borders for our lives that unconsciously tell us – as the continuity of our mother's presence once did – that we are safe. With those familiar boundaries in place, we can trust our outer environment and our inner one.

It's quite different when we take a voluntary break. Then the power to choose has not been taken from us, and anyway our thoughts will have already moved us forward, sensing out and alighting on other points of reference: the itinerary, the familiar airline, the baggage, the route, the phone calls home.

When loss of safety, wellbeing or familiarity is involuntary, or it affects what we most rely on, many of us literally break down, expressing this inner collapse of reality through severe depression or psychosis, or a loss of physical immunity against disease.

END ANY RELATIONSHIP WITH CARE

Those chaotic feelings of loss – and the desolation that comes with them – can also engulf the person who involuntarily loses a close, sexually intimate relationship. This was certainly true for 30-year-old Nathan. He had been married for only eight months when his 32-year-old wife, Matty, told him that the whole thing had been an absurd mistake and that she was leaving that same day.

Nathan's grief was horrible for him to experience. But on top of that he was also experiencing shock and shame. His first reaction was to wage war against this new reality. 'I couldn't believe it,' he told me several months later. 'She'd gone to stay with a woman we both knew and for the first couple of weeks I went there whenever I could, leaning on the bell of the apartment and begging our friend to let me in so that I could talk to Matty. I told myself that if I could talk to her she would realise how wrong she'd been and would pack up her things and come home.'

Nathan had been a genuinely easygoing and composed person before this happened. He likes his work as a sports journalist. He has good friends, a wide range of sporting interests and a supportive extended family. But, like many people whose relationship is ended by the other person, he became convinced that without Matty he wasn't safe or whole. He began to say (and mean) things such as 'I can't live without her. She's my whole world. If she doesn't come home I can't go on.'

The depth and intensity of Nathan's responses stunned Matty.

When I saw them together to help disentangle the last strands of their marriage, Matty told me that she had been appalled by Nathan's response, partly because she saw him as resilient, but also because she had never felt particularly important to him. 'Of course I knew Nathan loved me,' she said, 'but I was one part of his rich tapestry, not the whole of it. And, in fact, there were many ways in which we were not close. That was partly why I got out. Closeness matters to me and, from my point of view anyway, we didn't have that.'

With time it was easier for them both to accept that Nathan's responses had not come from his rational mind. Abandonment and the fear of losing one's safety (or the person or job that has come to represent one's safety) can easily overwhelm rational thinking. Any sane person may, with those kinds of triggers, become pleading, obsessive, physically ill, sleepless, depressed and deeply fixated: unrecognisable even to themselves.

This is always painful. And it was sobering for Nathan, who had, until that point in his fairly charmed and well-protected life, never experienced even a serious disappointment.

It's also true that Matty handled her departure badly. The child in her ran away from an uncomfortable situation and did so impulsively. The child in her also recoiled from confrontation and attempted to persuade her that she had no real responsibility to Nathan because her own need to escape felt so pressing.

The adult in Matty would have done much better to talk openly with Nathan *before* leaving. And to have seen a counsellor or therapist with him – not necessarily to keep the marriage going if that was not appropriate, but to ensure that what they had shared could continue to be respected.

Matty did have the grace and courage to begin that process a year later. By that time Nathan had worked through his initial shock. The child – or powerless self – in him was no longer attempting to persuade Matty to return. Nor was Nathan any longer convinced that he couldn't live without her. He continued to miss Matty. And he was obviously hesitant about beginning anything new with someone else. But he could speak about his loss with sorrow rather than total desperation.

Several strands in Nathan and Matty's story are particularly familiar.

Someone in a couple or friendship is restless or angry but doesn't talk about it. Then a hasty decision to end the relationship is made unilaterally. In the wake of that, the person who is left becomes agitated and demanding. And the person who is leaving now begins to justify their decision through exaggerated claims about how unhappy they were, how impossible the situation was, how intolerable it would have been to continue. *Those mix-and-match processes of demanding and self-justifying cause massive additional suffering.* They also make it difficult for either person to see clearly what the actual shortcomings might have been in the relationship; how they could learn from them; what they could continue to value about their lost intimacy; and what could be retrieved or healed.

Careful, respectful communication will minimise hurt. Finding the courage to speak openly to each other or with each other in the presence of a counsellor; having the courage and patience to *listen* to what may feel hurtful or even horrifying; taking time to respond with the least defensiveness; looking at the difficulties as *mutual* and not as something one person is 'doing' to the other: all of that may not lead to a conclusion that both people can welcome, but the respect underlying that effort will maximise each person's opportunity to grow in awareness – even through upheaval and sadness.

HURT OTHERS AND YOU INJURE YOURSELF

Listening to people cry out in anguish in the safety of my therapy room, I am repeatedly reminded that regression in the face of shock and loss is a real and agonising response to the world not being the way we believe we need it to be. We are not talking about the mixed comforts of tolerable self-pity here. Usually the person feeling lost and powerless will complain bitterly: 'I hate feeling like this. I am out of control in my own life. I can't make even small decisions. Nothing's making sense. I hardly know who I am.'

The adult in us can recognise this pain, even if we have not experienced it. Something in us stirs – perhaps only to recoil: *Thank heaven it's you and not me.*

It's that instinctive knowledge of how dangerous and unsettling abandonment or loss is that makes it essential we avoid treating other people like robots in our personal or professional lives. And that we avoid treating ourselves like robots in relation to them: deceiving ourselves that we can go in and 'sort them out' or offer them empty gestures of support, without this also affecting us at the deepest (and perhaps most hidden) levels of our own existence.

To imagine that we can hurt others without also damaging ourselves is a common delusion. Given the violence of the world we live in, it is also a terrifying one. A particularly fine example of what I'm describing comes from an anecdote told by Dr Dean Ornish, the author of *Love and Survival* and widely known for his pioneering work shifting the attitudes and lifting the health of patients suffering from serious heart disease.

Twenty-five years ago Dr Ornish was running a group that included two men who instantly hated each other. One was a man who hated homosexuals; the other man was gay. So intense were their negative feelings that they exploded when they met, insulting each other and calling the other one names. 'As the tension rose,' says Dr Ornish, 'I actually had to stand between them to keep them from hitting each other. One got severe chest pains, cursed, left the room and slammed the door, and the other got severe chest pains requiring Demerol and nitroglycerine to relieve them. I thought that that was the end of my very short research career.'

Here is a very clear demonstration that you don't get rid of your negative feelings by spitting them out. Rage that fuels negativity is highly toxic for the person expressing it, as well as for whoever is receiving it. You may feel pumped up, self-righteous or highly excited. But this can be literally suicidal. As Dr Ornish said to his patients all those years ago, ' "You're giving the power to give you chest pain and maybe even cause you to die to a person you hate. Does that make sense? You have different choices that may help and empower you." '

It must have taken a great deal of courage for a young doctor to speak so frankly to two much older men, however foolish their behaviour was. What's more, long before the self-evident connections between spiritual, psychological and physical good health were widely recognised, Dr Ornish made a practical suggestion for healing that brought those elements into unity. Each day he required the two to do some small thing or make some small effort that would specifically help the other one. The point of this was less to help the other person than to help them free themselves from anger and the pain and threat of death that accompanied it. And the result? 'They never became best friends, but they both became free of chest pain. Their tests showed that their heart disease began to reverse after just one month.'

LIVE WELL IN AN IMPERFECT WORLD

The consistency of care we are able to give other people has a significance that goes way beyond our personal maturity or comfort. Our communities absolutely depend for their health and stability on the trust and safety we can give one another. *It becomes socially as well as personally dangerous when large numbers of people care about no one but themselves.* Or when large numbers of people feel so marginalised or bereft that they shut themselves off from connecting with and supporting others.

It is not just the socially disenfranchised who can feel like this, although any experience of disenfranchisement makes people extremely vulnerable to depression and social isolation. But even in the midst of a successful professional life, someone can come up against an experience of isolation that leaches their social concern, heightens their self-concern and throws them dangerously off balance.

Hilary described a situation like this to me. She is a psychotherapist, professionally trained to be open and helpful to other people. But still a combination of circumstances threw her into a state she describes as 'terror'. She was in her late thirties at the time and working in a busy city practice with two other psychotherapists, each of whom was married with children and had many other commitments.

From the outside Hilary appeared, as always, calm, attentive and professional. But inside she was screaming. 'I was very anxious about my financial situation,' she told me. 'I was anxious about my client numbers, the weight of running a private practice and, being single, the feeling of "aloneness" in the world and wondering would I ever be able to provide for myself when I can't work. This translated into not taking time off when I wasn't well and not taking much-needed leave.'

For any of us, our problems will magnify when we believe we are alone with them. A familiar phrase expresses this: 'A trouble shared is a trouble halved.' Unsurprisingly, this situation improved only when Hilary was able to name her fear and reach out for help.

'On one particular occasion when my business partners and I were discussing the practice finances, I brought up my concerns. Olivia simply responded, "Well, if anything ever happens to Hilary, she's just another person to take care of."

'The answer was so simple,' Hilary explained, 'yet provided that fundamentally essential sense of connectedness that has really freed me now to get on with my life and not feel so scared. In this one simple sentence I experienced unconditionality, connectedness, continuity, caring, generosity of spirit – simply what it means to be in relationship with another. Now I am very conscious of practising this in my life with those close to me.'

Our lives are linked to the lives of others through inevitable and indispensable ties. Our sense of personal autonomy and freedom need not be threatened by this. In fact, the opposite is true. Moving beyond the egocentricity of childhood and early adulthood, we have the chance to recognise how much we owe to others for the very facts of our existence.

It's clear from Hilary's story that it was Olivia's frank, uncluttered concern for her that released Hilary from fear and renewed her capacity to care for others. It is impossible to overestimate the importance of this dynamic, emerging from and reinforcing a social interdependence that extends way beyond our most personal relationships and concerns. We *need* to be available to care about other people. We need to regard that as an urgent priority and not as something that can wait until that elusive day when we have more time. And in those draining moments when we feel lonely and adrift, we need also to cultivate the trust that other people can and will care about us.

None of our intimate or dependent relationships will be or even could be continually easy. We are always in conscious and unconscious processes of change. Our lives reflect that. Catching up with those rhythms – accepting that as tough as the tough times are, they give way to good times, and as good as the good times are, they give way to tough times – the treacherous moments feel less engulfing. And much less dangerous.

Looking backwards as well as forwards, we see how life is mysterious as well as ever changing. We discover that we can't immediately judge which situations will be beneficial, or even in the slightly longer term most enjoyable. We become less entangled in the futile quest for perfect relationships. We become more content.

In human relationships imperfection is what we are going to get. But there's nothing to be frightened of in that. That's how we are already living. That's what we already know. That's what's already bringing us much delight and comfort, spiritual nourishment and intellectual stimulation and, as we dare to get more deeply engaged in all our connections, could bring us much more.

When we cease measuring our relationships against some illusory model of constant satisfaction, and give up comparing our real-life relationships with those portrayed in fiction or movies, we give ourselves and more especially other people the chance to be real, fallible, foolish, misguided, contradictory – anything but a stereotype that is perfect only because it is one-dimensional.

This doesn't mean that we won't do our best or expect the best of ourselves. It certainly doesn't mean that we won't be learning all the time. The art of relating is subtle. We learn it little by little, mainly by turning the volume down on our complaints. Pausing. Waking up. And growing more conscious of what we are capable of giving.

LOVING WELL MAKES YOUR WORLD SAFER

Our personal relationships give us our best chance to grow up, and they have their best chance to survive and flourish when we can constrain our demands, look around us and extend our capacity to care.

For Caroline this chance did not really arrive until she had been married for eighteen years and Matthew, the husband who adored her and cared for her, suddenly became extremely vulnerable and quickly suicidal. During her marriage Caroline had trained as a social worker and had two children. She is an assertive woman, capable and inspiring in her work life. Nevertheless, the dynamic of care between Caroline and Matthew had in some key ways kept her childlike. It was only when Matthew himself collapsed that she took the chance, as she expressed it, to 'finally find my heart'.

Caroline's earliest experiences of life were not easy. Her parents divorced when she was ten. At 12 she was declared uncontrollable by the children's court and was handed over to the care of her father. She felt abandoned by her mother, and after a year of living with her father she was homeless. 'My mission in those days,' she says, 'was a search for love.'

When Caroline was only 15, 19-year-old Matthew offered to drive her home after an evening in a local hotel. 'I accepted the lift,' Caroline explains, 'even though I had no home to go to. I slept in his car for two nights. I was "promoted" to his bedroom and we have been together ever since – now twenty-five years.'

By the time of Matthew's crisis Caroline says she had come to take for granted that he 'would always dote on me on a daily basis. Nothing could have prepared me for the sudden and unexpected emotional breakdown that he had, which has changed our life and our relationship irrevocably.

'He became a different person and I became a different person too. It shook the foundations of my life, of our life as we had known it. It threatened my safety and security, which had become so comfortable. I had this obnoxious and demanding presence, a self-centredness that would make the most self-absorbed person look like Mother Teresa.'

In the period immediately after Matthew's breakdown, Caroline had no idea each day if he would survive or not. 'When my husband left for work, or to take the children to school or to go shopping, his state of mind was such that I never really knew if I would see him again. He would drive around the beach road with the narrow and winding road tempting him, luring him to let go and head for the edge.'

In the face of this, Caroline had no choice but, in her words, 'to grow up'.

'Not only did I grow up, but I also finally took on my role as wife and mother as never before. I ran my husband's bath and made his coffee, instead of the other way around. His withdrawal and suicidal ideation were the new powerful force to be reckoned with, instead of my restless, overbearing needs and wants.

'My husband had worn out, I think. He had come to a cross-road in his life. I had to open myself to real thoughts and possibilities that were so painful and confronting. The vulnerability of our relationship and our future at times seemed too tentative for words. I learned how fragile and tentative life really is and that there is a fine line between life and death.'

The cause of Matthew's breakdown arose in large part from unresolved grief and guilt from an event in his childhood that he'd actually had no way of avoiding. His little sister of 6 had run onto a road and been killed when Matthew was only thirteen. When Matthew and Caroline's own daughter was 6, this early tragedy precipitated the breakdown that was to turn their relationship upside down.

'From the age of 13,' Caroline explains, 'until his lifesaving therapy, my husband had denied himself. So much so that he would ignore a toothache until it became an abscess, and even then he would need strong encouragement to go.'

Matthew's grief was exacerbated by the loss of their first son, his own father's sudden death and the death of Caroline's father, who had become his closest friend. Despite the tremendous love he had shown to Caroline, Matthew felt 'undeserving, unworthy and worthless'.

Seven years on from that period of utter crisis Caroline can say with relief, 'Out of the pitiful and unhealthy reality of our life together, I have learned to share, to give unconditionally, and to love and appreciate this beautiful, generous, honourable man. Survivor guilt can be an emotionally crippling phenomenon. So can marrying a needy, insatiable, desperate little girl. I thank heaven that I finally found my heart.'

SELF-LOVE IS NOT SELF-ABSORPTION

The roles that other people play in our relationships fascinate us. They are frequently the focus of our conversations with third parties. And even when we are alone, our minds may be bursting with stories about what the people closest to us are doing or failing to do for us. We become highly skilled at those assessments. We practise them constantly.

What's often harder to work out – as it was for Caroline and perhaps for Matthew also – is what we ourselves are contributing to those dynamics, especially when things have slipped from the ideal state where we'd like them to be. With our minds fixed on the other person's shortcomings, or on their perceived power to make us happy or send us into a spiral of despair, we may not ask: 'How am *I* contributing to those difficulties? What am *I* looking for from this person? Is it appropriate? Is it realistic? Is this what I am also willing to give?'

Asking this, you might discover how easily you could give more, or that you are giving too much and are feeling empty. Self-love and self-care *must* coexist with love and care for others. It's rarely possible to be loving and generous from a place of depletion.

Writer and monk Father Laurence Freeman refers to this when he comments on the traditional Christian teaching that we should love God first, then our neighbour(s), then if there is anything left of love, it can go to ourselves. That's the wrong way around says Father Freeman: 'First, love yourself, and there's no quicker way to do that than to meditate. You will find how much you don't love yourself, how much you are in self-rejection and self-alienation, so battle away, be still, and learn to love yourself. One of the immediate fruits of that in your life will be the quality of your relationships; the diminishing of fear ("perfect love casts out fear," said Saint John), increased capacity for relationship with others, for honesty and truthfulness, tolerance, compassion and non-possessiveness, and in that dynamic the love of God becomes conscious.'

A lack of self-love keeps many people stuck in unloving relationships that echo the way that they feel about themselves.

Thirty-three-year-old Tolly, a school teacher and new father, speaks of this when he says, 'I had constant migraines in my first marriage. If you had asked me if I was happy in my marriage I would have said yes. But when it collapsed and Eve left me, I was shocked at how relieved I was. I had allowed myself to become a kind of servant to her. She was a fairly determined kind of woman, I guess. I'd also say that she exploited my kindness and I let that happen. I wanted her to see me as a good guy. I wanted her to lean on me and *need* me. That was my idea of a good husband, which I desperately wanted to be. How ironic: I wanted her to think I was a good guy when I thought so little of myself. The contradiction there was awful!'

A lack of self-love is never terminal. It is always possible to move from an unloving relationship to insight about what's been going on. And from that to increased self-acceptance, self-trust and a more satisfying way of being close to someone else. This has been true for countless people who have recognised and transcended unhelpful patterns – and grown in self-assurance as they did so.

It was also true for Tolly.

He describes this with great pleasure: 'In my relationship with Katrine I am much kinder to myself. I can say no to something or have time out without getting sick. I am not less kind to her either. Well, it's quite different. I feel real – and certainly much more loved. It's not even a conscious question of "being kind". I can't tell you how different this is.'

It is also possible that looking with fresh insight at your closest relationships, you might discover that you are the one who is overly self-absorbed; that you are more accomplished at taking than at giving. To recognise this in the way that Caroline did, and *to do something about it*, isn't easy. It involves wading through layers of self-protection, guilt, neediness. But the rewards are tremendous. As Caroline said, 'I finally found my heart.'

BE REAL IN YOUR EXPECTATIONS OF OTHERS

We move through adulthood constantly adjusting and readjusting our expectations of ourselves and others. We do this unconsciously for many years (sometimes for a lifetime). Our most painful personal tragedies may arise when we misjudge a situation and our expectations are lifted, then dashed. But as with so many things our capacity to be more 'realistic' about what others can or should give us, or what we can and should do for others, ripens with age and experience.

Where only one person wants a committed relationship or friendship, there can be no commitment. Where only one person wants an exclusive sexual partnership, there can be no exclusivity. Where only one person is genuinely interested in taking the relationship forward, there can be no real progress. Where only one person sees the personal relationship as a place to celebrate and express divine love, there can be great loneliness.

In any situation where intimacy is longed for, it will be painful to recognise that the way you see the relationship is not how the other person sees it. Or that what you want from the relationship is not what the other person wants. It is the uneven sexual relationships that may come first to mind. But this lack of reciprocity can be agonising also between family members when one person longs for a level of closeness that the other rejects or where there is a breach of trust or difference in values that seems almost impossible to overcome.

Tolerance, patience, the curbing of demands, matched by a constancy of love, can more often than not restore the giving and receiving of love to a greater equilibrium. The timetable of that, however, is rarely predictable. And often trust as well as love is called for.

A sexual relationship may also make you especially vulnerable. It can be terribly painful if you hoped that with this person you might have a child or raise together the children one of you already has – and that longing is not reflected in the dreams of the other person. Often our deepest and most tender longings are for the sharing of a life and the raising of a family. Around those issues even the most mature and reasonable among us may yearn for a life that's more golden, more fulfilling, than the life we presently have. In that frame of mind it can be easy to envy others; to min-imise their difficulties; inflate their joys. To do that, though, is to abandon what you have. It can take immense strength of mind to withdraw those envies, own them and move on, perhaps not to the life you wished for but to the fullest possible expression of the life you have.

Or perhaps you are almost there in the relationship you want – but not quite. Something is a little false or disappointing. It could be that the values you share need to be articulated. Or maybe your commitment is not explicit. It may also be that you are taking what you have for granted, treating it carelessly and not bringing to it your delight, creativity, energy and consideration.

It may also be that there is a covert tug of war going on, a struggle for power or supremacy that can sneak in and injure even those people who would publicly declare themselves to be the best of friends or the most devoted of partners.

YOUR PARTNER IS NOT YOUR PARENT

One of the hardest tasks of adulthood is truly to accept that our friends and partners are not our parents and *may not give us every-thing we want.*

Naturally we would say we don't want our adult companions to be our parents (sometimes we want them to be anything but

our parents!).Yet we may consciously or unconsciously be requiring them to be as self-sacrificing as our parents were; to meet our
needs with the same devotion and speed that our parents did; to
'put the kids first' as automatically as we became used to through
those wildly undervalued years of childhood; to admire everything
that we do, however bumbling ('Look, Mum!', 'Watch me, Dad!').

The problem is of course that in many relationships there are
only kids: two adult-sized kids pushing to get their needs met or
fighting for supremacy. This can feel awful if our idea of what we
should be getting from our relationship differs dramatically from
the way the other person sees it. We may believe the other person
is holding out on us deliberately. We may feel outrage as well as
rage that the person who we believe could give us what we want
is not doing that. (A tantrum or two may be the least we consider
the other person deserves!)

Or maybe the pain is even greater than that. Perhaps it is the
universe, which we trusted and had appeased through our excellent behaviour, that hasn't brought us what we deserve. We don't
have a partner, a child or the career success, physical strength or
health we had always envisaged. Or we have a partner, a child and
a fine job, but little joy.

Growing up we discover how even great differences in point of
view can be successfully negotiated. We also discover that disappointments are an inevitable part of life; not just our life, all
lives. *We are not there*, said the writer Joseph Campbell, *until we
can say 'yea' to it all*. You may not welcome that knowledge, but
you discover how your own disappointments have distracted
you. You might have overlooked major losses in other people's
lives. Or overlooked the good things you do have.

Ironically, life feels safer after we have experienced a major
upheaval and have moved beyond it. Knowing that we can
surrender ourselves to the unexpected, that we can survive

disappointment and negotiate difference, it becomes possible to risk more. Resilience flourishes in experiences of recovery, compromise, surprise. We discover how much we can do without. The tension of grasping and neediness subsides. And life is richer.

ACT ON YOUR OWN BEHALF

Whatever your age, there is also growing up needed if you must leave a relationship that is injuring you, yet are reluctant to do so. You may feel overwhelmed by failure. You may be terrified about the consequences of your decision on other people's lives. Or perhaps you never knew how to be without a partner or lover. You may be unused to acting on your own behalf and have forgotten where your centre is.

Years might go by with a crushing sense that you are neither in a relationship nor out of it. But it's here that observing the relationships of other people can teach you something of great value. *Self-love and self-respect should live in all your relationships.* And especially those where you are most intimate and vulnerable.

In a situation where mutual interest and respect have died, or where self-love and self-respect are at risk, it is usually necessary to gather up your courage and move on.

Still you may linger, persuading yourself that you can rescue the person who is harming you . . . Or telling yourself how that person is about to change . . . Or that this difficult or even abusive situation is all that you deserve or will ever get.

Where you feel unable to act on your own behalf, it can be powerfully instructive to ask, 'Would I want my child or best friend to be in a situation like this one? Is this how I would have wanted my mother or father to live? Is this what my ideal loving parent would want for me?'

If the answer is clearly no, the adult in you needs to act decisively to rescue that paralysed child or that anxious do-gooder within you, encouraged perhaps by the frank words of the

Indian master Swami Sri Sathya Sai Baba: 'Association with the evil minded is like companionship with a poisonous snake.'

Of course the relationship that drains your energy, your vitality and your hopes may be with someone who is not in the least bit evil minded. Perhaps the person you think constantly of leaving is an angel, but somehow your clash of interests, concerns or values remains debilitating. Life is tasteless. Sex is distressing, mechanical or non-existent. Therapy has been tried. Your feet and heart are carved from stone.

In those less clear-cut situations, it can be particularly difficult to act. Many people feel guilty about considering their own emotional wellbeing at someone else's 'expense'. Or they question the other person's capacity to cope without them. Their guilt may lead them to feel depressed. Their depression may sap their capacity to make decisions. In those grey situations, do they too have a right to act on their own behalf?

I believe so. I believe that we have the right to act compassionately and decisively on our own behalf, *but not to blame others*. Swami again: 'No one has the authority to hate another or condemn him. You have the chance to love him, serve him; or to keep yourself free of him. That's all.'

OWN YOUR PART IN ALL YOUR RELATIONSHIPS

Leaving a relationship behind, we need to take something vital with us: strength to avoid mindlessly blaming the other person; strength not to see ourselves as a victim; grace as well as strength to identify our part in what was lost as well as what was gained; a willingness to act with care for others, and self-love.

To achieve this we need a clear sense of the part that we have played in the creation of our own relationships. We must see what needs drive us; what values we set aside or cultivate; what desires push us in one direction rather than another.

What a sad irony it is that in this information-rich age, literally millions of people move from one relationship to the next without any useful understanding of how or why their relationships are breaking down. And without having any sense of how to move into new relationships with greater wisdom and confidence.

At the same time, the pressure of too much work – or the absence of satisfying work – also means that many people are demanding more and more from their intimate relationships: consciously or unconsciously requiring those relationships to make up to them for a brutal or indifferent outer world. Yet they have increasingly less time available for their relationships or to give to those people they want so much to be able to love and depend upon.

When time for thought and reflection is not available, the temptation to create external change will be overwhelming. But unfortunately this may not change our capacity to relate lovingly and well. It may not change the way we feel about ourselves either.

Thinking about this, I listened with sadness but not too much surprise to Virginia, a thoughtful woman in her mid-forties who works in pharmaceutical research and is the single mother of two sons. Virginia told me: 'I am at the end of my second long, intimate relationship, if I don't count the defining relationship with my father. As I reflect on this succession of relationships, I conclude that although they may be better or worse, relationships do not provide escapes, or anyway not for long.

'I acted as though they did; at first it felt like it too. As I moved into each relationship I am sure I felt that I was leaving behind all the painful, unsatisfactory things that were happening to me and making me unhappy in the previous one. Now I see that there were painful, unsatisfactory things about me and my way of relating in each relationship. Some of those patterns of behaviour and attitude that I most dislike in myself are not expressed when, as now, I am not relating intimately with another adult. But that is a regretful resolution indeed.'

Does this mean that Virginia might have been better off sticking with her first relationship and making changes within it, rather than making the change of leaving it?

'There are times when I think so. When I am reminded that I have more in common with that person, and that those things we had in common matter increasingly to me as I get older, and not less. And truly I didn't think about that when we were breaking up. I focused on what was wrong, not on what we had in common or still appreciated about each other.

'Yet I am irritated sometimes with the view, often expressed by people in apparently successful relationships, that the hardest and best course, the most noble kind of loving, is to stick it out. Yes, I think. That's what I should have done. But then, could I have? I might have stuck it out with bitterness and resignation. Or did I need to leave in order to learn this obvious lesson, that I go along with myself into each and every relationship? I take my patterns and projections with me.

'And now, with this insight, might I be in a better position to persevere in a relationship with self-awareness? I hope so.'

Seeing ourselves through the idealising eyes of a new lover, we may feel reborn. And certainly it is true that in each relationship the dynamics are different and different aspects of ourselves are free to retreat or advance. A new relationship can be utterly unlike the old.

But the truth of what Virginia is saying is also unavoidable: *I go along with myself into each and every relationship.* We may feel reborn. We may grow in wisdom. We may be vastly more fortunate with one partner than with another. But we are not remade.

PRACTISE THE CARE THAT EXPRESSES INTIMACY

Recognising *how you influence your relationships*, and are not in any simple way just acted upon, clears the way for you to understand that you don't need to look for someone to blame at the first sign of trouble. You don't need to run if things become heated. You don't need to judge real-life people harshly against the ideal fantasies living in your mind; or yourself.

Growing up, growing wiser, a workable balance between idealism and reality must always be found. Personal growth must develop alongside increasing social awareness. Work must at least sometimes give way to creativity, spiritual inquiry, a lively interest in the concerns of the people you love. The ego must have its day – but so must the spirit.

And such balance is not just 'found' either, once and for all. It must continue to be reflected upon, negotiated and trusted through the inevitable cycles of closeness and harmony, difference and dissension that not only mark the seasons of all our relationships, but can also move through us within the course of a single day.

The most simple gestures of love need to be made often: kind words, small courtesies, thoughtful encouragement; a beautifully presented meal; a candle lit by the bath; a smiling welcome; a hug held for several moments; a flower on a pillow; criticisms swallowed back and forgotten; fewer demands; delight in someone else's pleasure.

Questions need to be asked sometimes ('What's on your mind?', 'What's interesting you most right now?', 'Do you need help with anything?', 'Am I taking enough interest in your concerns?', 'Would you like more time alone?', 'Would you like us to spend some of our time together a little differently?'). And the most straightforward answers need to be given.

In our closest relationships, more than in any others, we take too much for granted. We need too much; we give too little. We rush by the precious details of our lives. We ignore both the omens of pain and the signs of love. We force our relationships into shapes and sizes that are of other people's making. We risk and dishonour other people's devotion by carelessly ignoring it.

Intimacy offers us our best chance to grow up. Not only because we love, but in order to learn what love is. Yet in our hands, and out of our impatience, intimacy can be blinding as much as freeing.

A sexual relationship may end because someone feels unable to say they want occasionally to sleep alone. A marriage may end because two people don't understand how differently each is experiencing and expressing grief. A relationship between a parent and an adult child may sour because one of them is unable to explain how much it would mean to be sometimes listened to without any interruption. An adult sibling relationship may take years to recover after someone was unable to ask for the help they needed in a time of personal crisis.

However intimate we are with other human beings, however compatible we feel, we live in a world of mind and heart that is our own. In opening our hearts and minds to others we do not become wholly transparent. Misunderstandings can happen over the slightest things ('You hear me say . . . although actually I said . . . ', 'I assumed that you would also want . . . ', 'You know that I have asked you a hundred times . . . ').

Accepting the reality that our intentions are not inevitably transparent, we can risk speaking more openly and honestly about what is in our minds and hearts while still maintaining those vital capacities to care for ourselves and limit our demands.

Lauris Edmond has been a friend and inspiration to me for years now. She is passionate, intense, talented, humorous and fascinating.

But that's my experience of her.

Her adult children, each one of them, may see her differently. Differently from me and all her other many friends; and just as likely differently from each other. Lauris's life as a poet, writer, social commentator, mother of six children, wife and lover seems to me to be unusually open and consistent. Yet she warns against too much presumption of common experience, making it exceptionally clear that even the closest bonds of love do not guarantee a shared vision or experience.

'I have occasionally been sharply rejected by several of my children,' Lauris says, 'who felt my interest in them was too close, too demanding, too strong a reflection of the parental power they evidently felt I was still trying to wield. The fact that I *didn't* think so alarmed me; it suggested a much deeper division between us than merely a kind of style, or a casual continuation of old habits. I had to rethink, slowly and painfully, my ways of behaving with them, as it were naturally, once I knew that they required, for the time being anyway, a muted version of my usual personality. To put it simply, they wanted my support, interest, enthusiasm, indeed admiration, for their activities; they did not expect to give the same to me. I now think this is entirely natural and am amazed that I didn't understand it earlier. If I need support and encouragement these days I tend to look to my friends, not my adult children.

'And the lesson has a broader application. It has underscored for me the need to understand how each different person establishes and defines separateness. I know far more than I once did how various are the ways one can best meet each loved (or liked) person's needs, while achieving satisfaction of one's own, and without the loss of intimacy I once feared. My children have sharpened the question, they didn't create it. I think as a younger woman I craved closeness and took it for granted that mutual affection proved there was an identical – or at least similar – need felt by the other person.

'A long-standing sexual relationship has taught me most about this. I met the other person more than twenty years ago, when both of us were emerging from hurtful and unhappy marriages. The intensity of our response to each other told me – wrongly, as it turned out – that we needed from each other the same kind of detailed and constant involvement. We did not. Our encounters were mutually exhilarating – still are – but the "space between" is vastly different.

'I wanted continuing affirmation of our closeness; he, a natural solitary I think, wanted to recover a lost equilibrium. The only way for this relationship to survive and grow has been through a high degree of separateness. We spend important time together, but live in separate houses, conducting separate relationships with our adult families, and to some extent with work and friends. I didn't want this, not at all; now I know it has been the price of our happiness.'

Maturity depends in great part on our capacity to accept difference within a relationship or even to recognise it. That doesn't make difference easy. We want what we want, and we want others to want what we want. We see the world in one way and may be jolted when we discover how others we care for deeply can and do see it differently.

Yet, just as Lauris did, in stretching ourselves beyond the limited cocoon of our own concerns, or our own vision of how things 'ought' to be, we enhance our experience of connection. Our world becomes psychologically safer as it grows larger.

Do we, then, also want to know that our relationships will sometimes be limiting and disappointing – almost simultaneously with them being fruitful and enriching?

Do we want to accept how divergent even the most compatible individuals' needs will sometimes be?

Do we dare face that, as wonderful as a long relationship may be, it will only ever be wonderful in parts? And will be wonderful in those parts only as long as the people creating it through their constant everyday interactions can be at least as flexible as they are resilient; at least as willing to welcome difference as to point with pleasure to similarity; and at least as able to encompass periods of boredom or even isolation as they are periods of charm, discovery and mutual delight?

Forget what others want, for a moment. Our own inner needs are frequently in conflict if not at war. We want time to ourselves yet feel bored to death on our weekend away alone. We feel driven crazy by the partner we also adore. We want a safe job *and* a high level of excitement. We want more friends but don't want to try new experiences. We are innovative at work but stuck in our personal relationships. Into that muddied picture comes the clash of needs between ourselves and other people, as well as collisions of temperament, age, gender, culture.

Staring those difficulties down, however, I find no reason in the world to avoid relationships. In fact for me, and most other people too, quite the opposite is true. The older I get, the more I value relationships. How could I not?

We learn many things during the intense years of childhood. Above all else, we learn to survive someone else not always meeting our needs, or not always meeting our needs in the way that we might want (perfectly and immediately!).

As adults, coming into new relationships or renewing those from the past, we can build on that confidence and take it further. We can discover how to be our own selves, responsible for who we are and everything we do, while at the same time becoming increasingly sensitive to other people, open to how they see the world, and aware they will do so through the lens of their own unique experiences.

Doing that we shatter the mad illusion that a worthwhile relationship is built on sameness or that people who really love each other move in harmony at all times.

Difference, even conflict, is fundamental to human experience. In its ugly forms conflict can cut us down, certainly, but difference doesn't always need to lead to conflict. And even conflict, when it is managed with a measure of intelligence, can stimulate us, invite us into more engagement with the world, expand our horizons and enhance our visions of what life – and happiness – might be.

It's true that we long for harmony – and need it much of the time. Many of our most treasured memories will be of times when harmony was most perfectly realised within our families or friendships, or when our workforce or community pulled together, sharing a sense of purpose.

Perhaps it's those unifying, stabilising experiences that people mourn when they speak of the loss of extended families; the loss of close communities within large cities; the loss of small, safe towns; or the loss of confidence that people are looking out for each other. As much as we long for harmony, however, we are also brilliant at disrupting it.

EMBRACE YOUR LIFE WHOLEHEARTEDLY

Several years ago my second novel, *Tasting Salt*, was published. This was a book I had written during a long period of unhappiness and uncertainty. Yet I believe that the novel exhibits none of this. In fact, writing it during that hard time gave me welcome relief from difficulties I had little or no way of controlling.

The questions raised in *Tasting Salt* resemble those in the rest of my writing: how do we continue to renew ourselves throughout life? How do we learn from what we have lived through? How do we deepen our appreciation of others and of life itself? How do we find our way inward to the source of spirit and of love?

Let me assure you that the answers to these questions are not easy to convey in the single catchy phrases loved by the media! So you can imagine how amused I was on the day after the book was launched to find a small news story in the *Sydney Morning Herald* ingeniously captioned 'Dowrick reveals secret of happiness'.

The article that followed had little to do with what I had

attempted to say my novel was 'about'. And it certainly did not convey to *Herald* readers what the secret of happiness might be. Nevertheless, in a muddled way it did draw attention to my belief that the experience of happiness – or contentment – lies in our own hands. It cannot be given to us; it cannot be entirely taken away.

This is a difficult idea for most of us to accept. Experience shows us that when someone we love is returning our love, or when our friends and family are well and in good spirits, our own sense of wellbeing soars. Conversely, if we have been ejected from a job we enjoyed and needed, if we have a seriously ill family member or if we ourselves are ill, homeless or impoverished, then life will feel hard, even agonising, and happiness can seem totally elusive.

And both those perceptions are true.

We *can* be most generous when we ourselves feel 'filled up' with the kindness of others. We *can* be most thoughtful when we ourselves feel valued. We *can* be kind or even gracious most easily to people whose way of life we respect.

It is a challenge of quite a different kind to reach beyond the limitations of our own weariness or emptiness, or our knowledge that there will be no reward for what we have to offer, and to remain loving and respectful even when nothing in a person's life is comprehensible to us or gives us hope.

Is this possible? Is this wise?

In finding and maintaining inner peace, spaciousness and balance, it would seem so. The teachings of all the great wisdom traditions agree that it is precisely when giving is *not* easy, when kindness is most difficult to locate, or when there will be no obvious reward for what we are doing, that we have our best chance not simply to be generous, loving, kind, *but to know what love is*.

This may make no sense to your logical mind. After all, we live in a culture that is ruled by potent myths of scarcity and the equally powerful idea that love, respect or even kindness should be given only if the other person deserves it.

Yet, the truth is, it is in the moments of totally unencumbered giving that our real freedom lies.

As long as we are kind only because someone is going to smile and say thank you, we remain dependent on that other person to trigger those impulses of kindness in us. As long as we are respectful only when we can 'look up' to someone, we remain dependent on a sense of inequality that will probably cause us also to 'look down'. As long as we are generous only because this will elevate us in the eyes of other people, we remain dependent on those people to notice what we are doing and to approve of it.

Another way is possible.

We can give kindness, respect, attention, forgiveness, support *for no other reason on earth except that we have the capacity to do so.* And if we take remotely seriously the idea that our lives offer us the chance to learn something more profound than how to run our computer, DVD or cappuccino machine, then developing this capacity to care and give freely becomes the psychological and spiritual practice upon which our call to wholeness and freedom entirely depends.

Habits of self-absorption diminish reluctantly. Living lovingly will continue to need our conscious attention. That will deepen our sense of freedom, certainly. It will liberate us from the idea that love should be conditional. It will disentangle our ideas of love from our ideas about approval. It will bring questions of choice into focus in new ways. But even as we glimpse these exhilarating freedoms, we may also be hearing the familiar sound of our own resistances ('Why should I be the one who . . . ?', 'He's never . . . ', 'She's always . . . ', 'They won't . . . ', 'They don't . . . ', 'They can't . . . ', 'Why should I . . . ?').

During a hot, sticky January some years ago I went to a Tibetan Buddhist retreat. It was a memorable retreat in many ways, but one of the best things for me personally was that I was helped by a woman called Barbara who recognised that I was finding it hard to be comfortable after a recent illness and who not only made me physically comfortable, but also put me at my ease in new surroundings in a way that allowed me to be much more alive to what the retreat was offering.

Talking to that same Barbara recently about the freedoms that love allows, she told me a story to show how possible it is to go beyond our self-concern without really giving up very much. Or perhaps giving it up, but not caring as much as we might have expected.

Barbara lives in a cliff-top house overlooking the ocean. It has a gorgeous panoramic view that has brought her great pleasure for all the time she has lived in that house. (And for the sake of that view she has driven long distances to work for many years.)

One of her two sons has recently been living there with her again, along with his partner and their infant child. Barbara says, 'I have been sharing with them for four months. I turned my house into two apartments in order to give them support because their relationship was faltering. This period was very harrowing. I gave them half my house – including the ocean view! It was difficult to do this as my view of the ocean has been a great source of inspiration and nurture for me for the last fourteen years. But I decided that their need was greater than mine, and I continue to focus on that angle while at the same time making myself as cosy and comfortable as possible in my new situation.'

Barbara is not a Pollyanna. She freely admits to difficulties she sometimes has dealing with people. Yet she is also able to say, with confidence won not just from her meditation practice but also from maturity, 'Generally, the more we are focused on benefitting others, and not being preoccupied with ourselves, the easier and more joyous life is, *even when there are difficulties.*'

Buddhism explicitly asks its students to find out for themselves
what life's 'secret of happiness' may be. Certainly it offers inspirational teachings to support this discovery. Teachings alone,
however, are not enough. For those teachings to come alive, their
meaning must be discovered through personal experience – and
reflection on that experience.

In the Judaic and Christian traditions explicit invitations also
exist to work things out for ourselves; to find the source of
happiness; to set dogma and authoritarianism aside; to value freshly
the wisdom gathered from our own lives. And to take the chance
to come fully alive.

From 3000 years ago we can relish this bold invitation to living, recorded in *Pirke Avot*:

No matter how famous the mouth,
check the words against experience . . .
We are here to do.
And through learning to know;
and through knowing to experience wonder;
and through wonder to attain wisdom;
and through wisdom to find simplicity;
and through simplicity to give attention;
and through attention
to see what needs to be done . . .

Relate as an Adult

Watch little children at play. Notice how enchanting they are, how touching their behaviour is – until something goes wrong. If they are frustrated, if someone has what they want or they want what someone else has, or if they are simply too tired or hungry to go on 'playing nicely', they are likely to roar or scream, stamp or kick, hit or punch. They may lie down on the ground and refuse to be moved. Their behaviour tells us that their whole world of happiness has come to a halt. They can't remember the pleasure they felt five minutes earlier. They can't anticipate the joy they may feel five minutes from now. They can't negotiate their way out of their difficulties. They can't soothe themselves. And they certainly can't take into account the effect their actions and mood are having on anyone else. The world has failed them – and they're answering back!

Wholly or in part, many adults behave in much the same way: charming when they want something or when things are going well; 2-year-olds when they are not.

Relating as an adult requires you to be a grown-up person all the time. And to discover that while you undoubtedly lose the satisfactions of yelling or stamping and insisting on having your own way, you gain more crucial satisfactions: insight, wisdom, choice, restraint, inner balance, self-control. You also gain the humility to see how much you depend on other people. And sufficient empathy to see how crucially you affect them also.

It is possible to have the spontaneity and creativity of childhood and the range and choice of response that an adult perspective gives. That combination is exactly what your relationships need. It is also what will give you a rewarding and deeply satisfying life.

- Take responsibility for the *quality of presence* you bring to every situation and encounter. Let this reflect the best of who you are.
- Visualise yourself as fully grown up. Is this different from how you are?
- See yourself taking on the mantle of adulthood not as a burden but as a way to know real freedom.
- Take responsibility for your own happiness.
- Take responsibility for the pain you cause others, even inadvertently. Responsibility is the key to maturity.
- Forgive your parents. Look at them through adult eyes.
- Forgive the child you were: doing your best with limited experience and insight.
- Know where you have come from and how it has affected you. Salvage what you can. Don't allow yourself to be a victim of the past.
- Let past hurts encourage you to be a loving presence now.
- Find out for yourself what your adult values are. Commit to them. Let them inspire you.
- Give up the need to score points, keep tabs or play any other power games. Real power comes when you recognise how free you are to enhance the lives of other people.
- Reach out to others. It's the greatest cure for loneliness.
- Know or discover what makes you happy. Do more and more of that.
- Find out what lifts the spirits of the people you care about. Do more and more of that.
- Accept the differences between you and other people. Set fear aside. Welcome them.

- Create an active sense of what you want to achieve in all areas of your life. Visualise yourself not only doing these things, *but also enjoying them.*
- Set yourself challenges that stimulate you.
- Identify your goals – goals help you work out what's important. Talk about those goals. That will help you to realise them.
- Listen to other people's views. Align them with your intentions and values. Enjoy them.
- Allow yourself to be deeply interested in a wide range of concerns. Think about issues, read widely, share opinions. Engaging with life in this way lifts your spirits and supports all your relationships.
- Distinguish between doing what's impressive and doing what you love. One serves the ego; the other, the spirit. Find a balance.
- Accept loss and failure as part of life. Move on.
- Move through times of suffering with determination to continue valuing your own life and life itself. Don't ask, 'Why me?' Ask, 'What can I learn from this?'
- In difficult situations ask yourself, 'How would a really wise person respond here?' *Be* that person.
- Ask for what you want openly and directly. Know that you can cope if you don't get it.
- Notice how intimately your wellbeing is tied up with the wellbeing of the people you care about. Do everything you can for them as an expression of love.
- Expand your capacity to care. Offer strangers your respect and concern.
- Know that the most altruistic people are also the happiest. And that the happiest people are also the most altruistic. Give because you can.
- See yourself as able to 'give ground' without loss or shame.

Visualise the balance that a martial arts practitioner has. Contrast that with the rigidity of someone who is stuck, defensive or frightened. Find your inner balance and move from that place.

- Develop a collaborative approach not just to problems, but to life.
- Think deeply about what you are responsible for. Extend that to include the welfare of your community, the environment, the planet.
- Decide what your relationship legacy will be. *Plan for that.*
- Take on the joy and responsibility of inspiring and encouraging others. It will profoundly influence your own life.
- Let your need for certainty fall away. Life is mysterious. Go with it.
- Never let a day go by without expressing gratitude – if only for life itself.

Remember Your Partner is Not Your Parent

To relate successfully as an adult, you need to move away from the needs of childhood and beyond consciously or unconsciously expecting the levels of self-sacrifice and devotion that you received or longed for from your parents.

Psychoanalysis and psychotherapy have paid close attention to how imperfect parental love can be. Many people sincerely believe that their adult lives are defined by their parents' failures and imperfections. And it's true that for some there are scars that last a lifetime. For the great majority of people, however, the story is different. We may find it difficult to acknowledge what our parents gave us. Certainly we may find it hard to thank our parents for what they have done. But ironically it's often the intensity, devotion, admiration and acceptance that we received from our parents that we also want as adults from a partner.

And when that's not forthcoming? We may howl and feel betrayed. We may overlook what we do have. We may feel as though nothing we have is enough – without questioning whether as adults we *need* that same level of care, or are capable of giving back the self-sacrifice and intensity of attention we are seeking.

If your partner fails to put you first, overlooks something you've done or sees something differently from the way you do, you may tell yourself that they are failing to love you. You may feel outrage as well as rage. But this is not helpful or appropriate.

To give up the unconscious dream that your adult partner should love you as a parent would love a child is truly liberating. Love between equals is different but no less precious. It offers unstinting love but also demands self-discipline; it is stimulating as well as reliable; it eagerly encompasses difference; it is respectful and sexy as well as romantic; it is not possessive; it doesn't seek to control or limit; it gives strength; it develops the highest levels of companionship.

- See your partner as a friend, lover, confidante, companion; not as a parent.
- Think about what you expect a partner to provide. And a parent? Scrap the latter list.
- When your partner expresses their individuality, enjoy and encourage that.
- Monitor and limit your demands scrupulously.
- Don't dump your tension or insecurities on your partner. Talk them through – but also share what interests you and lights you up.
- Talk openly about your relationship; what you value; what you want more of; where you want it to be heading. *And listen carefully to what your partner also has to say.*
- Establish your own goals and shared goals. *But also offer interest and encouragement as an investment in your partner's goals.*
- Find ways to express care for each other that are supportive not infantilising.
- Question roles based on age or gender. Do they serve you well?
- Respect and value difference – even when it's inconvenient.
- Negotiate and resolve difficulties on a win–win basis (conflict resolution teaches you how to do this – see, for example, Helena Cornelius and Shoshana Faire, *Everyone Can Win: How to Resolve Conflict*).
- Move through times of difficulty as *friends*, not opponents.
- Experience how your relationship deepens when you can work through difficulties openly and with trust.

- Don't boast about your relationship to other people or flaunt it. That sets up a dynamic that can become oppressive.
- Express gratitude for what you have through the way you treat your partner and the generosity you have available for other people.
- Create and enjoy small rituals to express your love: flowers, music, poetry, tiny gifts, notes, tasks done unobtrusively.
- Curb your possessiveness. Then grow out of it.
- Value sexual fidelity *as well as* your partner's freedom to enjoy intense friendships, independent interests and intellectual and social adventures. They keep the relationship fresh and alive. And increase your partner's pleasure in living.
- Be loyal always. Talk *about* your partner respectfully.
- Respect your partner's beliefs, values, friends, family.
- Welcome your partner's friends, family, colleagues into your home.
- Make it a high priority to have fun together, relax, make love, laugh, play and treat each other with tenderness and delight.
- Remain aware of the separateness and integrity of the other person. Respect that even when it cuts across your interests.
- Never play power games. Be frank about asking for what you want. And grown up enough to survive not getting it.
- Feel free to say no to each other without being punished.
- If you hear yourself speaking rudely or critically to your partner, stop. Apologise. Move on.
- Never manipulate. It is disrespectful of the integrity of your partner – and your own.
- Don't assume you know everything about your partner. That will close your mind, and it won't be true.
- Don't ask your partner to do something 'for the sake of love' that they don't want to do. That's manipulative and offensive.
- When your partner shares something you don't want to hear,

don't punish them for it. Take time to think about what you have heard. Then respond.

- Be prepared occasionally to give up something willingly for the sake of your partner. Both people need to do this. If one only is a sacrificer, this needs to be openly discussed.
- Remain genuinely interested in the other person's feelings, perspective, point of view, vision of the world.
- Think beyond your sitting room. Make a place in your lives for interests that express your concern with the wider community (environmental, neighbourhood, global issues). This adds a sense of spaciousness and interest to the relationship.
- Find something to believe in that is larger than yourselves.
- Practise forgiveness, gratitude, courtesy, delight – and live happily ever after.

HOW TO

Free Yourself from Resentment

Release your relationships from the burdens of resentment. Resentment inhibits love. But it can be transformed.

Many people grow into adulthood as virtual slaves to their own feeling states, doing things only when they 'feel like it', or feeling aggrieved when they are asked to do almost anything that they don't 'feel like' doing.

Maybe this worship of feelings came about as a reaction to earlier generations' denial of emotions. But there has been something of an over-correction! Respecting your emotions does not mean you must be ruled by them. There are times when it's good to pay attention to your feelings. But there are also times when it's more helpful to ask, 'What's needed here?', so that you can do it.

- Observe how freeing it is not to be dependent on 'feeling like it' to do something that's useful or essential.
- Experience how in doing what needs to be done your own mood changes.
- Keep a mood chart for a day. Notice the influences on your emotional state. Many will be quite trivial.
- Observe which feeling states catch your attention. This may be a matter of habit. You may be more used to noticing resentment rather than willingness; boredom rather than interest.
- It's not healthy either to be remote from your emotions.

Recognise feelings. Respect them. But don't be ruled
by them.

- Use your mind, experience and common sense as well as your
feelings to assess your responses to ambiguous situations.

- Know how to say no to something you really don't want to
do. When you are able to say yes easily, the times to say no
will stand out.

- Notice how a familiar task changes when you pay it close
attention. The more absorbed you allow yourself to be, the
more soothing it becomes.

- Notice how distracting resentment is. Give yourself a break.

- Move at half-pace sometimes. Let the task itself calm you.

- Do one task only. Then the next. Stress arises from half
doing several things while thinking about something else.

- When things are done routinely you can consider more
interesting matters, so free up routine matters ('Do I feel like
getting up? . . . going to the bank? . . . washing my hair?').

- Avoid blighting routine tasks with grievances ('Why should
I be the one to . . . ?').

- Avoid creating a hierarchy of tasks: try to value everything you
do equally.

- See your life in its entirety. View each 'section' with interest
and respect.

- Know what's causing you grief: the task itself or your inner
commentary.

- Move into a neutral description and reduce self-pity ('The car
needs cleaning', not 'I suppose it's up to me to clean the car
again').

- Balance complaint with gratitude ('I'm glad I have a car').

- Balance tasks with pleasure. No time? Check your priorities.

- Check if you're stuck with a lingering dose of the automatic
refusals.

- If there is *no one else* to do an essential task, fighting it will increase your sense of isolation. Better to get on with it.

- Be creative. Wipe the inside of the car with a scented oil. Clean out the garage and put up lively posters. Post tax receipts to your accountant in a bright pink folder. You will be least resentful when you are creative and playful.
- Many tasks feel better done in company. Can yours be shared?
- Bring your heart to everything you do.

HOW TO

Find Your Place in the World

It is a marvellous thing to discover your place in the world: to experience what you share with other people; how like them you are, while still being the unique individual that you also are. Your experience of the world and of yourself changes when you let yourself recognise the universality of what you most long for and feel most deeply.

You want to be loved. *And so do I.*

You want to give love. *And so do I.*

You want to believe that your life has value. *I do too.*

You want to make a positive difference to the lives of other people. *Yes. I also want that.*

You want to feel safe, trusted, accepted. *And so do I.*

You want to experience delight, tenderness, companionship, laughter. *That's what I want.*

You want to live in peace. And feel peace, harmony and joy within your own heart. *Yes. I want that.*

And you wish peace and happiness for others also. *In that too we are together.*

The greatest truth is love.

Every Day,

a New Beginning

The world is new to us every morning.

This is God's gift, and every person

should believe that they are reborn each day.

BA'AL SHEM TOV

*I*n the end, not much matters except love.

You are right to care about work, health, community. How good it is to know, then, that love is not something to be kept tucked away in our homes or bedrooms. Those other areas of our lives are also transformed when we bring to them a lively sense of spaciousness and tolerance. And allow them to bring to us the richness of interest, connectedness, enthusiasm and energy that speak of love.

You are right too to think of the needs of the starving and dis-possessed. Or of those who suffer from massive injustice they have not caused. But couldn't their lives also be different and less anguished if we individually and collectively believed in love and dared to live that belief openly and flamboyantly?

Live believing in the value of all that lives.

As it is, we squander time on what we hope will take us for-ward. In reality, it is often what holds us back. We talk about love, but live differently. We look for love, and forget that it's something that we could offer at any time.

We also live believing in our own immortality, assuring ourselves that there's time ahead to make things right; to be the person we want to become; to make up to other people for what we are not willing to offer them now; to give our attention to what connects us with others and our own deepest selves; to discover what life is for.

Postponing perfection, we live restlessly. Death and loss are everywhere but still we believe in that wonderful tomorrow when the love we want to feel will finally rise above every other pressing concern and change our lives forever.

How different life would be if we could keep things simple.

By that I don't mean that we should ignore or diminish complex issues. Complexity, paradox, the sifting of dross to find wisdom, the search for the big picture, a willingness to tolerate uncertainty or to change one's mind: that's all essential to a life worth living.

The most simple rules, though, are also too crucial to ignore. *Do what makes your heart sing. Encourage others. Be a true friend to all. Forgive readily. Stay away from situations that harm you. Allow yourself to feel joy. Create harmony. Treasure the moment. Delight in difference. Be kind without asking who deserves it. Express love.*

One more rule: do those things now, in real time. You can't afford to keep those practices locked up in your mind only. Nor should you save them for a future happy day.

Do I really believe that such benign attitudes have any chance of flourishing in these cynical times? In fact, I do. Speaking in public recently, I was asked whether the books I have written over the last two decades have been cathartic for me. 'No,' I replied at once. 'They have been instructive.'

As spontaneous as that response was, I can stand by it. I have learned a great deal from each of the books that I have written. But nothing is more crucial than my realisation of how universal our dreams and hopes of love are.

People everywhere long for love. They know their happiness depends on it. So do their physical health and wellbeing. Their sense of safety, connection and value depends on it. *People everywhere long to feel loving and lovable.* They long for trust and safety. They long to feel at peace.

Most people are much closer than they may guess to experiencing the quality of connection they yearn for. Nothing more solid than familiar habits of mind stand between them and the life they could be living: a life built on love, a life that freely expresses love, interest, respect. The changes they may need to make are a matter of degree only; a shift in attitude or attention; a lessening of self-pity or arrogance; a persistence with what's worth caring about; a waking up to the effect they have on other people; and an *understanding of how profoundly they themselves influence their own relationships.*

Every day offers us a new beginning, a fresh chance to see and understand how directly we create our own happiness through our attitudes, thoughts and actions, and the quality of presence we bring to our encounters with other people.

We might believe that our happiness is in other people's hands. But that belief gives our power away; it is also untrue.

We know how others affect us. We know that just a smile, a moment of patience or consideration, a shared joke or warm remark, a look of sympathy or tenderness can lift our day. We also know how an ugly remark or lack of thought can distress us. And how being treated badly can devastate us.

That distress – every bit as much as the warmth we feel in response to someone's kindness – reminds us of something vital. It gives us our best chance to recognise not just how interdependent we are. That's an exceptionally useful insight. More useful still, though, is the realisation that we affect other people every bit as much as they affect us. Understanding that, we claim for ourselves the vast, inclusive image of the Universal Heart. And step with confidence into the centre of our lives.

The quality of our presence surpasses all our other gifts. It reflects our values and intentions. It tells other people where we stand in relation to them. It eases the way towards a loving life. Or it obstructs it.

In the final weeks of writing this book I was told a quite exceptional story about two people I have observed together on several occasions. The younger man, Geoff, is profoundly intellectually and physically disabled. He has no speech. His movements are limited and out of his control. He is also deaf and blind. The older man, Bill, is the volunteer who comes unfailingly each day to see Geoff, to talk with him, hold his hand, share news with him and let him know that he is loved.

Nothing too remarkable in that, you may think. But what about this? When Bill enters the large building where Geoff lives, Geoff starts moving, smiling, making the noises that are for him the nearest approximation to speech. He cannot hear Bill coming. He certainly cannot see Bill coming. But through his senses he knows that Bill is in the building even when Bill is still several rooms away.

Geoff is someone whose powers of comprehension would seem to be minimal. Yet the sense that he has of Bill's presence, and the comfort and delight he draws from that, is unfailingly acute.

Your quality of presence is no less important or tangible to the people you care for, meet, work or live with than Bill's presence is for Geoff. (And Geoff's for Bill.) Your presence is that palpable. It can also be that uplifting.

This simple awareness – so obvious it seems almost laughable to spell it out – is at the heart of human consciousness. Be aware of what your presence brings to other people. Stand in their shoes. Look at what you are doing and how you are behaving *from their perspective*. Check it out. Reflect on it. Make changes when you need to. Choose to do whatever expresses concern and respect for other people. Experiment with how that increases your own happiness and wellbeing. Recognise how like others you are in the fundamental things – however different your outward self may be. Let yourself remember how a brief kindness 'makes your day'. Free yourself to be kind to other people.

Recognise your power to do that. *And don't leave yourself out either.* 'Make your own day' by removing yourself from harm; allowing time for what warms your heart; finding out what lifts your spirits and doing that.

The transformative energy of love is always available. To live lovingly, and to create the relationships and the life we dream of, we need only roll away the illusions of our own helplessness. We need only set aside those misguided beliefs that other people have what it takes to be really loving, but we do not. Other people are not the issue here. *The issue is what we can do.* What attitudes we can cultivate. How we can liberate ourselves from unhelpful patterns of behaviour or limiting thoughts.

Simultaneously we can cultivate self-love, love for others and love for life itself. Energy and vision arise from this great trinity of experience. It then becomes much less important who has done what; whether this person is 'worthy' of your kind attention or that person deserves another chance. The clear guidance of love itself supports us: *Does this express the best of who I am?*

Moving through your own challenging, contradictory life, there may be many days when you feel too tired to care. Or when you feel overwhelmed by thoughts of what you don't have and fears about what you may never have. There may be days when the pain of that fills your entire awareness. And you rage not against individuals only, but against life itself for how it has let you down and for what it has failed to give you.

There may be months or even years when you slump back into the old delusions that other people should make your life all right. That other people should bring meaning to it. Or that what you do doesn't matter anyway because no one cares.

There is no trinity of experience that is more powerful than self-love, love for others and love for life itself. Like any trinity, though, it loses more than its power when any one aspect of it is missing: it loses its balance.

Asking why we don't have the love we long for, forgetting what we ourselves could be offering, ignoring what we could be receiving, hiding from ourselves, refusing to see how directly our own attitudes influence us and how our lives influence other people, we may need to pause.

We may need to recall who we are and what our strengths are. We may need to recognise all that we are capable of. We may need to look with greater attention at how we are affecting other people. We may need to renew our knowledge of what love is. And find out, as if for the first time, what it is that we depend upon for our happiness.

At any moment of waking, love will be there for us. We have only to remember.

Waking up this morning, I smile, writes Thich Nhat Hanh.
Twenty-four brand new hours are before me.
I vow to live fully in each moment
and to look at all beings with the eye of compassion.

NOTES

All references to pages in this book are given in **bold**.

Page 7 'What is well planted . . .': *Tao Teh Ching* (by Lao Tzu), trans. John C. H. Wu, St John's University Press, New York, 1961, Shambhala, Boston, 1989, verse 54, p. 111. **23** 'Love by the way you walk . . .': Thich Nhat Hanh, *Teachings on Love*, Parallax Press, Berkeley, 1997, p. 141. **26** 'I am knowledge . . .': quoted in *The Nag Hammadi Library in English*, ed. James M. Robinson, Brill, Leiden, 1977, p. 271. **43** 'You are the future . . .': *Selected Poems of Rainer Maria Rilke*, trans. and ed. Robert Bly, HarperCollins, New York, 1981, p. 105. **65–6** 'Even our thoughts . . .': Rupert Sheldrake and Matthew Fox, *Natural Grace: Dialogues on Science and Spirituality*, Bloomsbury, London, 1996, pp. 81–2. **72** 'Do not believe in . . .': *Kalamas Sutra*, quoted in *Paths Beyond Ego: The Transpersonal Vision*, eds Roger Walsh and Frances Vaughan, Tarcher/Putnam, New York, 1993, p. 165. **81** 'Love is a way . . .': Andrew Harvey and Mark Matousek, *Dialogues with a Modern Mystic*, Quest, Wheaton, Ill., 1994, p. 196. **85** 'Read Thich Nhat Hanh . . .': Thich Nhat Hanh, *Peace is Every Step: The Path of Mindfulness in Everyday Life*, Bantam, New York, 1991. **96** 'I have thoughts . . .': for further insight see Piero Ferrucci, *What We May Be: The Visions and Techniques of Psychosynthesis*, Turnstone, Wellingborough, UK, 1982, pp. 61–2. **101** 'The effectiveness of your . . .': Howard Adams, *The Search for Wholeness: A Gestalt Approach to the Unitary Understanding of the Human Process*, Gestalt Institute of Australia, Springwood, NSW, 1993, p. 77. **106** 'You might be shouting . . .': for further insight see Stephanie Dowrick, *Intimacy and Solitude*, Heinemann, Melbourne, 1991, The Women's Press, London, 1992, W. W. Norton, New York, 1994, pp. 229–31. **111** 'When something goes wrong . . .': Jelaluddin Rumi, in *The Essential Rumi*, trans. Coleman Barks, with John Moyne, HarperCollins, New York, 1995, p. 191. **115** 'A good person . . .': Sheldrake and Fox, pp. 55, 56. **116** 'I also am mortal . . .': Wisdom of Solomon, 7:1–7. **122** 'Man often becomes . . .': Mahatma Gandhi, quoted in *The Words of Gandhi*, Richard Attenborough, Newmarket Press, New York, 1996. **161** 'If the partners are really . . .': Alfred Adler, *What Life Could Mean to You*, trans. Colin Brett, Oneworld Publications, Oxford, 1992, p. 232. **162** 'A loss of sexual attraction . . .': ibid. **163** 'How many times . . .': Swami Chidvilasananda (Gurumayi), *My Lord Loves a Pure Heart: The Yoga of Divine Virtues*, Syda Foundation, South Fallsburg, New York, 1994, p. 19. **178** 'My soul is . . .': Antonio Machado, in *The Soul is Here for Its Own Joy: Sacred Poems from Many Cultures*, ed. Robert Bly, Ecco Press, New York, 1995, p. 29. **187** 'In the middle of the night . . .': Anne Deveson, *Tell Me I'm Here*, Penguin, Ringwood, 1993, pp. 101–2. **193–4** 'Arguing with others . . .': Hanh, *Teachings*, p. 41. **209** 'The simplest actions . . .': Meinrad Craighead, 'Immanent Mother', in *The Feminist Mystic and Other Essays on Women and Spirituality*, ed. Mary E. Giles, Crossroad, New York, 1982, p. 80. **210** 'To begin with I thought . . .': Lionel Blue, interview with, in *Insights*, Naim Attallah, Quartet Books, London, 1999, p. 31. **228** 'Between the conception . . .': T. S. Eliot, *Collected Poems 1909–1962*, Faber and Faber, London, 1974, p. 92. **231** 'An inability to notice . . .': Daniel Goleman, *Emotional Intelligence*, Bantam, New York, 1996, p. 43. **232** 'The sum total . . .': Robert Musil, *A Man*

Without Qualities, reissue, Knopf, New York, 1995.   **238** 'When we adapt ourselves . . . ':
David Reynolds, *Playing Ball on Running Water*, William Morrow, New York, 1984, p. 68.
264 'In a year there are . . . ': Sri Sathya Sai Baba, www.saipages.com, 25 May 1999.
264 'Four unique human endowments . . . ': Stephen R. Covey, 'The Guiding Conscience',
in *Handbook for the Soul*, eds Richard Carlson and Benjamin Shield, Doubleday, New York,
1996, pp. 145–6.   **265** 'We are putting on plays . . . ': Aase Pryor, in Seekers Open
Letter, eds S. and R. Brindle, November 1999, p. 2.   **274–5** 'The thing a person . . . ':
Carl Gustav Jung, *Collected Works*, vol. 15, para. 470, quoted in *A Critical Dictionary of Jungian
Analysis*, eds Andrew Samuels et al., Routledge and Kegan Paul, London, 1986, p. 138.
275 'An unconscious snag . . . ': ibid., vol. II, para. 13.   **286** 'I had a patient . . . ':
Theodore Isaac Rubin, *Compassion and Self-Hate: An Alternative to Despair*, Macmillan, New
York, 1975, pp. 99–100.   **288–9** 'When one "projects" . . . ': Robert Bly, *A Little Book
on the Human Shadow*, ed. William Booth, Harper and Row, New York, 1988, p. 29.   **289**
'One of the marks . . . ': Katherine Anne Porter, interviewed in *Writers at Work: The Paris Review
Interviews*, ed. George Plimpton, Penguin, Harmondsworth, 1977, p. 149.   **312** 'The
people in our life . . . ': Piero Ferrucci, *The Gifts of Parenting: Learning and Growing with Our
Children*, Pan Macmillan, Sydney, 1999, pp. 56–7.   **329** 'It is the individual . . . ': Adler,
p. 12.   **331** 'Hate is not conquered . . . ': *The Dhammapada*, trans. Juan Mascaro, Penguin,
Harmondsworth, 1973, p. 35.   **335** 'They pay selective attention . . . ': Carol Tavris,
Anger: The Misunderstood Emotion, Touchstone, New York, 1982, 1989, p. 94.   **336** 'The
ultimate purpose . . . ': ibid., p. 319.   **350** 'The mandate to . . . ': James J. Lynch, *The
Broken Heart: The Medical Consequences of Loneliness*, Basic Books, New York, 1977, Bancroft
Press, Baltimore, 1998.   **353** 'In reality, it is anger . . . ': Chidvilasananda, p. 78.   **358**
'To create the circumstances . . . ': *A Course in Miracles*, 3 vols, Foundation for Inner Peace,
Farmingdale, 1975.   **361** 'The student asks . . . ': Anthony de Mello, *One Minute Wisdom*,
Doubleday, New York, 1985, p. 203.   **376** 'Friend, it's time . . . ': Ansari, trans. Robert
Bly, in Bly, *The Soul*, p. 13.   **378** 'This is my commandment . . . ': Gospel of John
15:12–13.   **378** 'Just as a mother . . . ': *Sutta Nipata*, 149–150.   **383** 'All the joy . . . ':
Shantideva, *The Way of the Bodhisattva*, 8: 25.   **392–3** 'As the tension rose . . . ': Dean
Ornish, *Love and Survival: The Scientific Basis for the Healing Power of Intimacy*, Random House,
Sydney, 1999, pp. 161–2.   **399** 'First, love yourself . . . ': Laurence Freeman, interviewed
by Dominique Side, in 'With the Eye of the Heart', *View*, 3, 1995, p. 8.   **403** 'We are
not there . . . ': *Reflections on the Art of Living: A Joseph Campbell Companion*, ed. Diane K. Osbon,
HarperCollins, New York, 1991, p. 20.   **405** 'Association with the evil minded . . . ': Sri
Sathya Sai Baba, 12 May 1999.   **405** 'No one has . . . ': ibid., 19 October 1999.
417 'Hate authority . . . ': *Pirke Avot*, a collection of rabbinic sayings, quoted in *Essential
Mystics: The Soul's Journey into Truth*, ed. Andrew Harvey, HarperCollins, New York, 1996,
pp. 100, 223.   **423** 'See, for example . . . ': Helena Cornelius and Shoshana Faire,
Everyone Can Win: How to Resolve Conflict, Simon and Schuster, Sydney, 1989.   **438** 'Waking
up this morning . . . ': Thich Nhat Hanh, *Present Moment Wonderful Moment: Mindfulness Verses for
Daily Living*, Parallax Press, Berkeley, 1990, p. 3. For further thoughts on courage, restraint,
generosity and forgiveness see Stephanie Dowrick, *Forgiveness and Other Acts of Love*, Viking,
Ringwood, 1997, The Women's Press, London, 1997, W. W. Norton, New York, 1997.